For Rose Mary, my anchor,
and Jim, my mentor,

for their steadfast love and support despite both my inability and
my reluctance to clearly explain any of this as it was actually happening.

All my love to you.

HARD *to* HANDLE

The Life and Death of
THE BLACK CROWES
A Memoir

STEVE GORMAN

with STEVEN HYDEN

NEW YORK

Hachette Books
Hachette Book Group
1290 Avenue of the Americas
New York, NY 10104
HachetteBooks.com
Twitter.com/HachetteBooks
Instagram.com/HachetteBooks

First Trade Paperback Edition: May 2020

Published by Hachette Books, an imprint of Perseus Books, LLC, a subsidiary of Hachette Book Group, Inc. The Hachette Books name and logo is a trademark of the Hachette Book Group.

The Hachette Speakers Bureau provides a wide range of authors for speaking events. To find out more, go to www.hachettespeakersbureau.com or call (866) 376-6591.

The publisher is not responsible for websites (or their content) that are not owned by the publisher.

Library of Congress Cataloging-in-Publication Data has been applied for.

ISBNs: 9780306922008 (hardcover), 9780306922022 (trade paperback), 9780306922015 (ebook)

Printed in the United States of America

CW

10 9 8 7 6 5 4 3 2

CONTENTS

PREFACE

A Good Day in The Black Crowes Was Just a Day That Wasn't Bad

My band The Black Crowes had a hell of a run. But, man, it was weird. Our first album, released in 1990, was huge. Our second album was also a success, and it solidified our place among the world's best and biggest rock bands. And then . . . things went sideways. Over the next twenty-plus years, we lost about 90 percent of our original audience. A lot of that was by choice. We purposely avoided doing things that would've helped to grow, or at least maintain, our fan base. We did what we did, and we didn't do what we wouldn't, for better or worse.

But here's one good thing about The Black Crowes' self-destructive streak: it weeded out our casual followers and tested the resolve of our staunchest fans. In the end, the people who stuck with us really, *really,* fucking loved us. And it's those people to whom we owe our career. Because of their support, The Black Crowes were able to maintain a healthy touring business for decades. Years after "Hard to Handle," "She Talks to Angels," and "Remedy" came and went from MTV, we could sell out theaters from coast to coast in the 2000s and 2010s, even as we continued to test the patience of our fans with a series of frustrating decisions and inevitable flameouts.

When the band called it a day for the first time in 2002, the primary cause of our internal misery was the constant battling between Chris and Rich Robinson. From the day I met them, they fought. It's not like they got famous and suddenly couldn't get along. They were never on the same page. But they had the same last name, so they figured, *Well, we have to do this together,* I guess.

The sibling rivalry between the Robinsons was omnipresent, and it had simply run its course. We weren't young, hungry kids anymore. When we were first starting out, we were all more tolerant of each other's bullshit. At the very least, we could ignore each other's bullshit, pretend it wasn't as bad as it actually was, and then get on with our day.

By the time everyone was in their midthirties, it had gotten much harder to do that. The prevailing sentiment was, *Guys, fucking enough already. Why are you always fighting over the same shit?* The brothers would always say, "This is our business. Don't worry about it." But that was impossible. Their nonsensical sibling rivalry infiltrated every aspect of the band's existence. Everybody else in the band and crew were pulled onto one side or the other, despite our best intentions to stay neutral and do whatever it took to keep the whole thing moving forward. It was exhausting.

The Black Crowes broke up in 2002, although at the time it was classified as a "hiatus," which is a great word to use when you think it's over but can't quite be sure if that's the case.

By 2005, there was a prevailing sense of, *Well, shit . . . let's do it right this time around.* Everybody had (allegedly) grown up, and after experiencing reality outside The Black Crowes, we realized that it probably wasn't as cool as life *in* The Black Crowes.

There was, initially, a very real and urgent desire to not repeat mistakes. Within eighteen months, though, it was apparent that we were back on the same hamster wheel: fight, tour, record, fight, tour, record. People don't change unless they truly want to change. And The Black Crowes didn't truly want to change. It felt very much like it always had. *We're a really good band, but it's a total pain in the ass to be here.*

There will forever be one overriding truth about The Black Crowes—we were, at our best, a great fucking band. Many people loved the music we made. But enjoying that love was simply never allowed in The Black Crowes. It's frustrating that the band could never evolve to a place where there was genuine appreciation for all we had done, and for the fact that we'd found and maintained an audience. I can point a finger, and people can point fingers at me. Everyone has their own perspective. But the whole thing was tense, angry, and difficult.

To be clear—there were a million laughs along the way, and there was at times a true esprit de corps in The Black Crowes. But many of those laughs and much of the bonding was fueled by denial and a desperate, gnawing fear of facing the toxic reality of our interpersonal relationships and admitting the consequences of our self-destructive decisions and lifestyles.

Between 2005 and 2010, we made three albums and toured constantly. We found ourselves living through the same grind as before. And, just as before, it became impossible to agree upon, much less maintain, a discernible set of goals.

By December of 2010, the band had completely run its course. Chris had checked out entirely. He no longer wanted any part of a band in which he didn't call every shot. He needed to be completely in control, despite a lengthy track record of calamitous decisions and misguided efforts with very painful consequences.

He put together a band called The Chris Robinson Brotherhood and then, for the second time in nine years, initiated a hiatus from The Black Crowes, intent on forging a new path that no longer required working with his brother.

I went to see that band in 2012 in Nashville. He was actually smiling. He rarely smiled that way, so genuinely, when he was onstage with The Black Crowes. I thought, *Well, good for him. I hope he's actually happy.*

So I was surprised when, after the gig, he asked me about doing a Black Crowes tour in 2013.

"Why do you want to go back to something that makes you so miserable?" I said, laughing.

But shortly thereafter plans were in full swing to tour in 2013 as a "test run" for an anniversary tour in 2015, to mark twenty-five years since the release of our multiplatinum 1990 debut album, *Shake Your Money Maker.* The tour in 2015 would also most likely be a proper farewell to our loyal fans.

We still had a few hurdles to clear. The Robinson brothers hadn't spoken in a year and a half. As our manager was putting the tour together, Chris and Rich were threatening each other in emails on a daily basis. "I'll kill you if you do this . . . I'll quit the tour if you do that," and all that standard bullshit.

At our first rehearsal in Brooklyn, the rest of the band was wagering on how long it would be before they actually came to blows. The over/under was three hours. During our first break, the two of them paired off and had a quiet conversation in the corner. To everyone's utter amazement, that one brief chat was all it took to bury the hatchet. We finished that rehearsal without incident. And then the next, and the next.

We played 120 shows that year, almost all of them sellouts. Promoters loved it. The reaction from the fans was consistently positive. The brothers got along very well, at least initially. We were set up perfectly for the tour in 2015. We talked, at length, about putting out new music in 2015. Maybe not an entire album, but certainly an EP of four or five new songs. If 2015 was going to be our last tour, it was important that we not kill ourselves. Shorter legs, longer breaks. Let's do it right. Do it smart. Go out on a high.

We made it about two-thirds of the way through the tour in 2013 before everything turned sour. No one saw it coming, either, as shortly before things started to unravel, the brothers had grown closer than they'd ever been. Their father, Stan, died, and Chris and Rich shared their pain in a way that seemed to pave a newfound acceptance and appreciation for each other.

The bond didn't last long. Three weeks later, we had a ten-day break in the tour. When we reconvened in Portland, Maine, it was immediately apparent that whatever closeness they had developed had just as quickly disappeared. That break was all it took for Chris to decide he no longer needed his brother, much less The Black Crowes.

We finished the tour as we had so many tours before, running on empty with all the screws coming loose. A year that had started with such promise, and so much positivity, finished on a note of relief, at best, as well as profound sorrow at another lost opportunity.

In early 2014, we played four corporate gigs: Las Vegas, New Orleans, New York, and Boston. Those were ultimately the last shows The Black Crowes ever played—private gigs for a select few instead of the grand anniversary tour we originally envisioned.

After our last show in Boston, I shared a car to the airport with the Robinson brothers: the three founding members of The Black Crowes taking what turned out to be our final ride together.

We were on different airlines. I got dropped off first. "All right, fellas, see you later," I said.

"Okay, see you, man," Rich said.

I looked at Chris, but he didn't say anything. He was staring at me, a million miles away, staring *through* me actually, with an uncomfortable look on his face.

I stared back at him, blankly. Again I said, "Later, man." And again, nothing.

After a few seconds, I laughed and said, "Well, all righty then!" I climbed out of the car and walked into the airport.

I texted Rich, who was still in the car with Chris. "He's about to blow this whole fucking thing up, isn't he?" I wrote.

"What do you mean?" Rich texted back.

"Look at him. He couldn't even speak to me. He's up to something."

By that point, we all knew each other so fucking well. We couldn't hide a thing from each other.

"Yeah, you're probably right. He's just staring out of his window," Rich wrote back, still sitting right next to his brother, wondering whether or not something dramatic was cooking in that drug-addled brain.

A few days later, we got our answer. Chris's wife sent an email to Pete Angelus, our manager of twenty-four years, stating his demands for his continued involvement in The Black Crowes. Moving forward, Chris wanted 75 percent of all the band's income. That was quite an upgrade from the 33⅓ percent share he had been receiving.

It was apparent that our existing partnership agreement no longer meant anything to him.

The terms were nonnegotiable. There would be no discussion. Give him what he wanted, or he wasn't coming back.

Pete and Rich then called me together, and Pete read the email over the phone. The email from Chris's wife was long and rambling, whereas Pete's response was simple and direct: "They both reject your new terms." And that was the end of The Black Crowes.

Twenty-seven years. One email.

As far as I know, Chris and Rich haven't spoken since. Chris and I haven't spoken, either. I can't imagine we ever will. I saw him once at the Nashville airport and he hightailed it away from me.

I'm not bitter about how things shook out. In fact, I'm genuinely amazed at how well we did, for as long as we did it, all things considered.

I think The Black Crowes overachieved for fucking ever. There's no reason on earth that *those* people should've had *that* run. We simply weren't made of the stuff of long-term success. We were too self-destructive, especially together.

There were tremendous strengths and there were crippling weaknesses within The Black Crowes. The band could never consistently ignore the weaknesses and focus on the strengths. The rare times we were focused, the results always spoke for themselves. The rest of the time it was a real battle.

In the grand scheme of things, I'm forever grateful for the experience.

As for me and Chris, we'd had huge ups and downs for years. He and I had conversations that lasted hours upon hours, leading me to feel connected to him as a brother. And the next day, or ten minutes later, we'd be telling each other to fuck off. For almost thirty years, we'd played very different roles at very different times in each other's lives. We'd been roommates, bandmates, friends, and enemies.

But no more.

I don't miss being in The Black Crowes. We had countless great moments, real highs, real dream-come-true kind of stuff, and within minutes the mood would always turn dark again. It was the inherent nature of the band when it was together. The highest of highs cut short by the lowest of lows.

A good day in The Black Crowes was just a day that wasn't bad. That's ultimately how it felt.

The idea of going back on the road again, or of simply being in a room together, is unimaginable. The Black Crowes are finished, and they should be finished.

I do have one eternal regret, though, and it's that we didn't pull off that last tour. The ultimate purpose of that tour was to say thank you: to our fans, the people most responsible for our existence, as well as each other.

I wish we had done that. I *really* wish we had. But we didn't.

I feel like there's some unfinished business. Neither Chris nor Rich have shown any interest in preserving The Black Crowes in any significant way. Chris seems to think singing Black Crowes songs on occasion with a pickup band is in some way meaningful, but it's dubious to suggest those shows are about anything beyond financial desperation.

So I felt compelled to tell this story. If I don't, who will?

At the very least, I can tell you what happened from my point of view.

HARD *to* HANDLE

1

The Jump

On **February 20, 1987,** I moved via Greyhound bus from my hometown of Hopkinsville, Kentucky, to Atlanta, Georgia, to start a band.

I was twenty-one years old and had dropped out of college midway through my senior year at Western Kentucky University, in Bowling Green, two months earlier.

My buddy Clint Steele had called me out of the blue back in September—it turned out he was playing guitar and wanted to know what I was doing.

"I'm dropping out of college and I'm going to start a band," he said. "You're drumming all the time now, right?"

Nope. Not at all. Well, at least not in reality. But in my head? Yeah. Always. Nonstop.

The only thing I ever truly wanted was to be a drummer in a rock band. For as long as I could remember, I had listened to music and imagined myself playing the drums. When I played records, I would focus on how the drums would play off the other instruments. And I would air-drum for hours, years after most people stopped doing that kind of thing. When I went to see bands, I would focus on the drummer, judging his playing with a critical ear as if I really knew anything about it.

While in college, I actually played on borrowed drum kits a handful of times, and had just enough irrational confidence to convince myself that with a real commitment, I could be a pretty good drummer.

But playing all the time? No way. Not by a long shot.

"Yeah, man, every day," I said, lying without hesitation.

"You any good?"

"Yeah, of course."

"Do you want to start a band with me?"

"Absolutely!"

"Okay, cool! Let's do it in January. We'll go to Boston, it'll be great."

I had never been to Boston. Hell, he could have said Bangladesh. It didn't matter. I was in. From the moment I hung up that phone, I was a changed man. I was in a band.

I never went to another class, but I did stay on campus for the rest of the semester enjoying what I viewed as a three-month college farewell tour which was, in every way imaginable, fantastic.

A month later, Clint called me and said, "Hey, man, I don't want to go to Boston. I'm going to move back home to Atlanta. It's cheaper there. It's a cool scene."

"Okay," I said. I mean, I really didn't care. It was all the same to me. It wasn't Kentucky.

In November, Clint called to say he was on his way to Bowling Green for a night to hang out. He was bringing his friend Sven Pipien.

"Sven was the singer in my first band a couple years ago," Clint explained, "but now he just started playing bass and he's really good. He's German, you'll dig him."

I'm already in a multinational band. This is gonna be great!

We had a summit meeting in my dorm. We immediately decided the three of us were going to make rock history. As Clint and Sven had already played a handful of club gigs in their former band, I took everything they said as gospel.

One thing our new band didn't have was a singer. I introduced Clint and Sven to a freshman on my dorm floor named James Hall. He sang and played guitar in a cover band that did songs by The Smiths and The Cure, which for Bowling Green in 1986 was mind-boggling. I suggested James come down and jam once we were in Atlanta. You know, just to vibe it out.

James insisted he had to finish the entire school year, but said that maybe he would come down for a week at spring break and then, if we all clicked, he would move for good the following May.

Just like that, we had a band.

About a week before I was supposed to leave for Atlanta, Clint called and asked if I could meet him and Sven in Tuscaloosa instead. He said their roommate Chris was playing a gig there that Friday night with his band, Mr. Crowe's Garden.

"We're going to drive over with them. It'll be a fun gig!" Clint promised. "They're opening up for some local band at a club, and we'll just party there, and then Saturday we'll all get up and drive back to Atlanta."

"Okay, cool," I said. Tuscaloosa was yet another place I had never been. I was gonna get on a bus and go *somewhere*, by God.

Then, the day before I was supposed to head out to Tuscaloosa, Clint called again.

"Fuck it, just go to Atlanta. The gig was canceled."

"Okay," I said. "Who is this Chris guy, anyway?"

"He's our roommate," Clint replied. "You, me, Sven, and Chris are gonna live together. He's totally insane but he's really funny. His band is about to get signed by A&M Records. They're doing demos for some guy from LA." I didn't really understand what that meant, but it sounded pretty damned impressive.

That Friday morning, February 20, my brother Doug took me to the bus station to catch a six o'clock bus. Atlanta is a big city, I remember thinking, *I've got to look tough.* I was wearing a flannel shirt, faded blue jeans, and a full-length black-leather trench coat, plus purple Chuck Taylors. That was a twenty-one-year-old Kentuckian's idea of looking tough. I had a lot to learn.

The ride took forever. I had a two-hour stopover in Nashville, and then we stopped in just about every damned town between Nashville and Atlanta. I had a giant WKU duffel bag stuffed with everything I needed for my new life: clothes, shoes, books, some CDs, and a dark-brown beer bottle with twelve $100 bills shoved inside.

It's happening! My real life is beginning. I was so excited. We pulled into Atlanta at five thirty in the evening. It was already dark outside. I stepped off the bus into the black, cold murk of an uncertain future.

As I looked around for a familiar face, I heard a voice I didn't recognize.

"Are you Steve?"

"Yeah."

"Hey, man, I'm Chris."

Short hair, big nose, really big eyes, skinny as a rail. *Holy shit, this guy looks just like fucking Emo Philips*. He wore a faded denim jacket, a white button-down, and jeans. It was the first time I saw my future bandmate, Chris Robinson.

"Where's Clint?" I asked.

"They went out to have a smoke or whatever. We've been waiting for a while."

Just then Clint and Sven walked out. We exchanged awkward guy-hugs. Clint asked, "You got all your stuff?"

"Yeah, I just have this one bag . . . and TWELVE HUNDRED-DOLLAR BILLS!" I yelled.

I just blurted it out. There was a beat, a pregnant pause, and then we all fell out laughing. There was something about the absurdity of loudly announcing to the world I was packing what might as well have been a million dollars. It struck us all as funny. We were off to a good start.

A couple of minutes later, we all piled into Chris's VW Rabbit. This was the first, and last, time I ever got into a car Chris was driving. I was fucking terrified. He was frantically sharing the story he'd seen on CNN that day about Hosea Williams, the famed civil rights leader. Williams had been marching in Cumming, Georgia, when the Ku Klux Klan showed up to throw rocks at him and his fellow protestors. Chris was acting out all the parts; he did an admittedly fantastic Hosea Williams impression, as well as all the various Klan spokesmen, the CNN reporter, and the hippie counterprotestors. He acted out the whole thing while driving through downtown Atlanta, all while looking at me and Sven in the backseat. To say he was animated would be a tremendous understatement.

"Dude! Look at the road!" we all yelled.

Chris was hilarious and completely frenzied. It was true mania with him right away, like a live wire. But he made me laugh.

We drove to Peachtree Battle, and pulled up to a Mexican restaurant called Jalisco. The four of us got a booth and all ordered Miller Genuine Draft, which was new on the market and therefore somewhat exotic to our minds.

We told stories and we all laughed a ton. I had never been so happy to be anywhere in my life.

"Don't worry, guys," I said drunkenly, "if we get into any shit tonight, I've got twelve hundred-dollar bills on me!"

We screamed with laughter. When the dinner check arrived, I grabbed it. "First night in town, boys, let me pick this up. I've got TWELVE HUNDRED-DOLLAR BILLS!"

Over the next few weeks, this was a constant running joke. Of course, that was my money to buy a drum kit, and soon enough I had burned through almost half of it and still hadn't gotten a job.

In the meantime, we moved into a two-bedroom house in Candler Park, at 292 Oakdale Road. The rent was $450 a month, which broke down to $112.50 per man. I remember thinking I could probably panhandle for rent, or do odd jobs in the neighborhood, if push came to shove.

Sven had originally signed the lease, and one time the landlord came by to check on the place. He was an old Georgia cracker. When he knocked, I opened the front door and he looked me up and down suspiciously before finally mumbling, "Sevens Pippi . . . where is he?"

Of course, we called Sven "Sevens Pippi" for years after that.

Anyway, Chris and I ended up as roommates. We didn't have beds, just mattresses on the floor, courtesy of his parents. Clint and Sven, the two smokers, took the other room.

Both bands, Mr. Crowe's Garden and our unnamed new band, would be able to rehearse at the house. As I had still only played drums a handful of times, I didn't have any sort of realistic idea of what I really needed to get started. I borrowed a car from Clint's mom and drove to a store called Rhythm City, where I proceeded to get royally ripped off.

"I need everything," I told the sales guy. "I need a seat, I need sticks, I need cymbals, whatever else I'm gonna need for my gig next week." I didn't actually have a gig next week, but I thought saying I did would make me seem legit.

"What's your budget?" the sales clerk asked.

"Seven hundred bucks."

I might as well have stamped "sucker" on my forehead. I bought a Pearl Export starter-level drum kit and these Zildjian Scimitar cymbals that sounded like trash-can lids, some pedals, some stands, some sticks, and some drum keys. I walked out with a receipt that read "$699.99." I literally had one penny to my name, but I didn't care. I was a real drummer now.

Back at the house, I stared at my new drums with a mix of excitement and apprehension.

What the fuck have I gotten myself into?

I didn't know much about the Atlanta music scene before I moved there. The Georgia Satellites had just blown up. Their big single "Keep Your Hands to Yourself" went to number two on the charts the very week that I moved there, but they were in their thirties. They might as well have been a hundred years old.

Athens was a different story. I was into a lot of bands from Athens, especially R.E.M. I had seen them on every tour since the *Chronic Town* EP came out in 1982, and they were far and away my favorite band. Like a million other college kids in the south at that time, Athens was my mecca. I figured, well, Atlanta is *close* to Athens, at least.

Upon arrival, the Atlanta band of the moment was Drivin N Cryin, who had just signed to Island Records. Clint and his friends were obsessed with them. It was pretty clear from the jump that they were the kingpins in the scene we were about to join.

Clint, Sven, and I named our band Mary My Hope. The first day we set up to rehearse, I was terrified. I couldn't hide the fact that, in actuality, I didn't know what I was doing. All those years of air-drumming, watching other drummers, imagining this very moment—it was all useless. I just played a straight beat for hours. No fills, not ever a cymbal crash. I hammered away on the same simple beat and either sped up or slowed down depending on what Clint wanted. He had written some songs, and he had already been in a band and rehearsed before, so he led the way. Little did I know that what most songwriters want is exactly what I was providing: a simple beat without any nonsense for them to work around.

It was late March, only a month after I came to town, and we already had a proper rock 'n' roll flophouse for two bands to rehearse and operate out of. As planned, James came down for spring break from WKU to jam. We played him the songs we had been working on, and he quickly learned them. By the second day, he announced, "That's it, I am finishing school in May and moving here full time."

I felt like I had just won the lottery.

Mary My Hope booked our first gig at a bar near Emory University called The Dugout, where I had found a job as a doorman. It was the end of May, and we were opening for Mr. Crowe's Garden.

I barely slept the night before. We loaded into The Dugout for sound check late in the afternoon. I set up the kit, and the house soundman came onstage to place mics around the drums. I sat down at the kit and a minute later he said, over the PA, "Okay, Steve, let's get some sounds. Start with the kick drum."

One, two, three, *four!* On the fourth strike, the mic was turned on and the drum blasted through the PA. I had never heard myself on an amplified kit. It sounded like thunder. It sounded like *The Guns of Navarone*. It sounded like John fucking Bonham.

It was the greatest thing I'd ever heard in my entire life.

I floated through the rest of sound check. We only had a couple of hours before our set: forty-five minutes, nine songs. We were ready. It was gonna be epic.

Boom. Showtime. Nine P.M. Mary My Hope stepped onstage to play our first gig, and I remember realizing, quite clearly, that I had no saliva in my mouth. I literally could not *make* saliva. I'd never felt that nervous in my life. My heart was racing. I looked out from behind the kit and the place was packed. Mr. Crowe's Garden already had a really big following, and this was an all-ages gig. The guitarist was Chris's younger brother, Rich. He was still a senior in high school, and it looked like his entire school was packed into the club.

I counted in the first song, and the entire set went by in a blur. The songs were all a little faster than rehearsed, but we got through the gig without any major train wrecks. I had played an actual gig in a club! I don't really remember a single moment from the show itself, but I remember walking off the stage and feeling euphoric. I watched Mr. Crowe's Garden from the back of the bar and felt very much like a new man. After the baptism of my first gig, I was an entirely different person from the one who had moved to Atlanta three months earlier.

Afterward, we went back to the house on Oakdale for a party. We all had such a huge feeling of triumph. The two bands who lived in this house played a packed club together and now we're having a party with a ton of people! It felt like the center of the known universe. Sounds ridiculous, but it did. Hell, a couple of guys from Drivin N Cryin even showed up, which lent even more prestige and relevance to the proceedings.

Music was blaring, dozens of people continually showed up with more and more alcohol, everybody was having a fucking blast—except for Chris, who without warning fell into a full-on manic episode.

He and I were in the front yard, and he started talking about how nothing adds up and it's all fucking bullshit and fuck this and fuck that. He just couldn't let himself enjoy the moment. He was drinking wine directly out of a bottle, chugging it down in huge gulps. He was referencing Baudelaire, James Joyce, John Coltrane, The Dream Syndicate, obscure poets, some friend of his who fried his brain on acid and now just made go-karts, his therapist, his failed attempt to get into Bennington College in Vermont—it was fucking all over the place. Ranting lunacy. Gibberish. Little did I know at the time that I would witness countless episodes like this over the course of the next few decades of my life.

I had never been around anyone so neurotic. It struck me as self-absorption to the highest degree. I was completely put off by him, but I also couldn't walk away.

"What's your fucking problem, man?" I yelled.

"Blah blah blah blah!"

"Fucking jump off a bridge and kill yourself if it's all so awful."

"Blah blah blah blah!"

"What kind of asshole freaks out when everything is so fucking great?"

"Blah blah blah blah!"

I thought for sure I could get through to him. But nothing I said made a dent. I don't think he even recognized that I was speaking.

Chris and I had already grown pretty close. When I first got to Atlanta, he just glommed onto me. We liked a lot of the same bands and, just as important, we liked the same comedy, especially Monty Python and SCTV.

He turned me on to a ton of music I'd never heard before. While I was still very much a fan of R.E.M., Chris had already decided they weren't cool anymore, though he acknowledged they gave him the kick in the ass to start his own band. Our friend David Macias gave us a Nick Drake box set, and we got into that together. That kind of thing matters. We had many lengthy conversations about art, religion, sports, comedy, whatever. The kind of conversations that stretch over days, cementing a newly forming friendship.

We would argue passionately about all kinds of things. My Christianity, his atheism, my liberal politics, his complete disregard for the entire political system, my belief that we should throw the trash away instead of leaving it in piles around the house, and his utter disinterest in cleanliness.

After a few weeks, it got to be a little much. Chris was just so intense. It never stopped with him. Nevertheless, I felt compelled to protect him. Over the next few years, I would get him out of a million jams, when he would get drunk and start shit. And then I would step in to end it, or at least get him out of there before he got beat up. After a while, I just accepted that this was my life now. I've got this guy who is always with me, and he drinks a shit ton, and I have to save him from himself.

I just wanted him to enjoy the moment. We had just played a sold-out show, and now some of the most popular musicians in Atlanta were hanging out at *our* house. But that night I saw for the first time that Chris is never able to appreciate the good things in his life. He's always felt the compulsion to blow it up right when things should be at their best. He was like that from the very beginning.

"Dude, all this shit you're talking about, you're choosing to view it like this," I told him. "You just played a show and there were eight hundred fucking people there. You have four hundred dollars in your pocket. What's the problem?"

Chris and I moved our little chat over to the vacant lot next door, where the grass was knee high. After twenty minutes, I noticed we had carved a figure-eight into the grass with our footsteps. We were literally walking around in circles and feeling angsty when we should've been partying and having fun. A tidy metaphor for the career of The Black Crowes if ever there was one.

After a while, Chris went back to the party. He put down another bottle or two of red wine and eventually passed out on his mattress, still grumbling and dissatisfied. I, too, went back to the party. I put down a dozen beers and a few shots of cheap whiskey before passing out on the mattress next to his, floating on a cloud of contentment with my newfound perfectly fantastic fucking life. The most miserable drunk in Atlanta sleeping it off next to the happiest drunk in Atlanta.

The next morning, we didn't talk about what had happened the night before. We just got up, made coffee, put on a record, and eventually walked to Little Five Points to get a slice of pizza and look at used records, like any other day.

The die had been cast.

2

Do Not Join This Band, They're Fucking Crazy

The first time I saw Mr. Crowe's Garden play a gig was my second night in Atlanta. I'd only known Chris for twenty-four hours, but there was one thing I was already sure of. *There's no fucking way this guy can be the singer in a band.*

He walked onstage at the Metroplex in downtown Atlanta wearing black jeans, a white oxford shirt, a black blazer, and black Beatles boots. The Peter Buck look. Clint pointed at the guitar player and said, "That's Chris's brother."

Rich was wearing blue jeans and a white oxford shirt, no jacket, and penny loafers. My first thought upon seeing Rich Robinson was that he looked like a prototypical character out of a John Hughes movie. Not a lovable, dorky misfit struggling to figure out who he was, but rather a preppy, handsome, cocky, big man on campus. The star quarterback douchebag dude. The contrast between the brothers was incredible. At first glance there was absolutely nothing about the Robinsons that would suggest they were related.

Chris said into the mic, "We're Mr. Crowe's Garden, but you already knew that!" And then he turned to Rich and flashed an impatient look that said, *Start the fucking song already!*

I was skeptical, to say the least. Then Rich started the first song, the rhythm section joined in after a few bars, and they were off and rolling. They were really tight. Totally locked in.

Finally, Chris opened his mouth . . . and he *wailed*. His intensity was immediate. He was in a zone. That sucker *really* meant it. I was shocked. He had a much higher voice back then, and he was quite neurotic onstage, constantly messing with his hair and working very hard to look comfortable holding the mic stand. But, holy hell, he was delivering that shit for real.

Throughout the set, he didn't move much, just some random gesturing with his hands and some half-hearted head banging in time to the tunes. He spent most of the set somewhat stuck in place, quaking like a pot about to boil over.

When Mr. Crowe's Garden played, there was an unmistakable buzz. A very real vibe. Between songs, however, was a different thing entirely. Moments after each song finished, Rich would tune his guitar. It could go on for up to a minute or even longer, which in rock-club time felt like an hour.

To fill the silence, Chris would talk. A lot. His stage banter was some truly incredible Richard Lewis–esque stream of consciousness shit. "This next song further advances the concept that within a looking glass filled with sand comes a moment of impeachable certainty that this ain't no Stanley Kubrick rap about the man trying to box you in, but anyway . . ." and on and on. It made absolutely no sense. I loved it.

Chris was weird, inventive, and completely authentic. Very different from the Chris Robinson the world would come to know in a few short years.

Eventually, Rich would finish tuning and the band would then be stuck waiting for Chris to shut up. Rich showed his contempt for Chris's nonstop verbiage by starting the next song, interrupting Chris midsentence, center stage, leaving him fuming. If they played twelve songs that night, this cycle happened at least six times.

But I couldn't take my eyes off Chris. All of the manic energy that was already starting to wear on me offstage turned into undeniable charisma onstage. He had "that thing." Chris Robinson was born to front a band.

Meanwhile, Rich's energy couldn't have been more different: he sulked, barely moved, and never once acknowledged the audience on any level. He just . . . sucked on stage. As a player he seemed to be proficient enough, but there were no guitar solos. He struck me as the kind of guy who could only play the songs he had written. For a while anyway, that was indeed the case.

I met Rich for the first time that night, about an hour after the set, in a Burger King parking lot. I have no idea why we went to a Burger King parking lot on a Saturday night, but whatever. Chris introduced us, telling Rich I was a drummer who had moved from Kentucky to play with Clint and Sven.

"Hey," he mumbled, skeptically sizing me up. I would soon learn that Rich looked at everybody that way.

I don't remember exactly what I said back, but I made fun of his obvious lack of communication skills.

Chris laughed and, actually, Rich smiled, too. He liked me taking the piss out of him.

When I looked away, he punched me in the arm, hard. I couldn't believe it. *I'm twenty-one years old, and some fucking high school senior just lays into me like that? What a fucking asshole!*

"I wouldn't do that again if I were you," I said.

"Shit, man, he's from Kentucky, he's a redneck," Chris warned Rich. "He'll kill you."

Rich turned away, carried on with some of his friends, and that was the full extent of our first meeting.

"Man, he likes you," Chris told me later. "That's his way of saying, *We're cool.*"

I couldn't believe it. One guy wouldn't shut up and the other guy was monosyllabic at best.

Over the next few months, I learned all I would ever need to know about the dynamic between the Robinson brothers. They were constantly sniping at each other. It was *always* something. There was no grievance too small, no argument too trite.

We'd been living in the Oakdale house for a few weeks when Chris woke up one morning and said, "Hey, let's go to my parents' house this afternoon. They'll buy us dinner, we can hang for a few days, and take real showers." I leapt at the chance. The shower at Oakdale had become virtually unusable. Black mold had formed in the corners and was starting to grow up the walls, and there was an omnipresent smell one might associate with an EPA contamination site.

A few hours later, Chris and I drove up to Cobb County. We pulled into the driveway outside of a nice house in one of those entirely non-descript Atlanta suburbs. Chris's mom, Nancy, was home and offered us something to eat. She was very welcoming, super friendly. Chris gave me the tour of the house. We walked into Rich's bedroom. There was a stack of four or five quarters on his chest of drawers. Chris turned it upside down.

"Rich is so OCD, he'll notice this as soon as he gets here," Chris said. On cue, Rich walked into the house, and we heard him coming up the stairs. He walked into his room to find me and Chris standing there, and was not at all pleased.

"What the fuck are you doing in here?"

Chris laughed and said he was just showing me around.

Rich noticed the quarters. He immediately flipped them back over. "Leave my shit alone!"

When their dad, Stan, got home from work that evening, he took us all out for Chinese food in his Mercedes. I was impressed. I don't think I'd ever been in a Mercedes before. Hell, I was still thinking about what life would have been like to grow up in my own bedroom. As the youngest of eight kids in a middle-class family, I didn't get a bedroom to myself until I was in ninth grade.

We were seated at a round table, me and the four Robinsons. They'd clearly been to this place a million times; all the waiters warmly greeted them as they walked by. There was no getting-to-know-you segment of the conversation. I guess I had expected to be the focal point, initially, as the new guy at the table. Nope. They were all off to the races as soon as we sat down; the four of them fighting for the floor, wildly telling stories, questioning each other's recall of events, bitching about teachers, coworkers, politics, arguing over who ordered what the last time they'd been at the restaurant. It was like a scene from a Woody Allen film but with southern accents.

Even Rich was loud. Compared to Chris, as he would invariably be for life, Rich seemed like a quiet and thoughtful guy. Hell, compared to Chris, anyone would come across as such. But at that table, he was as animated as anyone else.

At one point, Rich mocked my opinion on something—it could have been anything from R.E.M. versus The Replacements to Iran-Contra—and I said, "Well, things look a certain way when you're still in high school living at home with your parents."

That established, for the most part, how we would talk to each other for years. I treated him like a spoiled punk who knew nothing about the real world, and he saw me as some sort of interloper, a wedge between him and his brother.

When I would side with Chris during one of their arguments, he said many times, "You just want Chris to yourself."

And I'd always respond, "I think you have that backwards, dude."

"Fuck that shit! I don't care."

But Rich did care. A lot.

Throughout that spring and summer, when Mr. Crowe's Garden rehearsed at the Oakdale house, Rich would sit in his car and wait until everybody else was inside. Then he'd walk in, plug in, play until the end of rehearsal, and leave. He would *never* hang out. There were a dozen dudes in other local bands who would come by and stay until we forced them to leave, but not Rich.

I never understood it. If I were still in high school out in the suburbs and had the chance to hang out in town with my older brother and his friends, I'd have been all in.

But in Rich's mind, being in town meant he was on Chris's turf, and he wasn't having it.

Meanwhile, Chris and I were out every night, hanging with all kinds of different people. We were two barflies, good cop and bad cop wherever we went. In 1987, we were inseparable.

As Mary My Hope was quickly becoming a powerhouse band, a divide was developing in the Oakdale house. Clint, Sven, and I got along well enough, but usually I felt like the odd man out with the two of them. They were very tight, and I spent most of my free time hanging with Chris.

Also, Clint and Sven were doing acid regularly, and it was freaking me out. Clint said once, "I'm only excited about the band when I'm tripping. If I'm totally straight, I don't get excited about much of anything." I knew next to nothing about drugs at the time, but that didn't sound good. We had played one gig, and my guitarist was already struggling to find inspiration? Not cool.

Just after that first gig at The Dugout, our friend Randy Blazak took off to Europe for the summer and asked me to house-sit. Thank God! I needed some space to myself, and Randy's apartment was pretty deluxe: he had two bedrooms, a balcony, functional plumbing, and an awesome record collection.

Chris turned up at Randy's apartment just about every day. He'd crash on the couch there as often as he'd make it back to Oakdale. I couldn't get away from him. One night, sitting out on the balcony drinking beer, Chris casually suggested that I join Mr. Crowe's Garden. Their drummer had just quit to join Drivin N Cryin. I wasn't surprised that he asked, but I was adamant that I was staying in Mary My Hope. I had moved to Atlanta to play with Clint. Hell, I convinced James, a kid I barely knew, to move down with me to be our singer. No way was I gonna walk out on them.

Chris backed off from the offer to join the band, and instead said simply, "Okay fine, but you gotta play on this next demo with us."

"I've played two gigs in my life," I said. "I can't go make a demo for A&M Records."

"Just fucking do it!" Chris insisted. "It's a straight song. You're as good as anybody else in town."

I would have never admitted to anyone I thought I was already really good. I couldn't play many fills, but I always knew instinctively what *not* to do. Young drummers tend to overplay, but that was never an issue with me. I played simple, straight, and strong.

"All right, what the fuck, I'll do it."

When I told the Mary My Hope guys that I had agreed to be the drummer for the next Mr. Crowe's Garden session, they weren't happy.

"Dude, don't quit and join that band," Clint said.

"No fucking way," I insisted. I truly had no intention of joining Mr. Crowe's Garden at that point.

A few days later, we drove to Chapel Hill, North Carolina, and loaded into a studio to record a new tune the brothers had written called "Gravedigger Blues." After we got the sounds dialed in, Steve Gronback, the producer, came over to me and said, "You've got a good feel, man."

I looked at him and blurted, "Man, I've only been playing for three months. I'm in way over my head here."

"You're fine, man," Gronback assured me. "I just want you to find the pocket. You don't have to play any fills."

We played through the song for a few hours and finally had a drum take that was good enough. Like that, I had played an actual recording session.

We had some extra time to kill, so Gronback suggested we record a few more tunes straight to tape, no overdubs. The brothers had a few new songs in progress, so Ted, the bassist, and I tried to think of parts to play as Chris and Rich finished writing them.

By then, Chris and Rich had already figured out their writing process. Rich would play a few chords and Chris would say, "Do that again, just stay there, that's a verse." Then Chris would start singing, and tell Rich, "Go up somewhere so I can go down." Then Rich would play one of the twelve chords he knew and wait for Chris to give him the yea or nay.

Rich would play parts and Chris would put them together. That was their process. Years later, Rich would describe himself as the architect of The Black Crowes sound and I'd think, *No, dude, you're the lumber and parts supplier. Chris is the architect.*

Just before we hit the road back home, Chris started in with me again. "Dude, just join this band."

"No, man, I have my own band," I said. "I'm not going to join a band with two brothers. It'll never be mine."

"You'll be an equal! We've never had a real third guy," Chris promised.

"Rich fucking hates me," I countered.

"So what? He doesn't like anybody."

"I don't know, man."

"Well, let's figure it out. You need to be in Mr. Crowe's Garden," he insisted.

A few nights later, Mary My Hope played our third gig, at Margaritaville. The night before, Chris had come over to the apartment. We sat on the balcony, this time drinking wine. He had bought two bottles, figuring that if he couldn't convince me to join his band, at least we'd catch a good buzz.

I had to admit it was making more sense. He just kept on saying, "Come on, man, we have fun together. Those other guys are acid heads, let's just get drunk and rock. Rich actually likes you, he hates everyone else. It'll be the three of us. Come on, just do it."

"Well, Mr. Crowe's Garden would be more fun . . ." I said.

"Come on, man," Chris pressed. "A&M is going to sign us."

Chris opened the second bottle of wine.

"We're going to drink this bottle of wine and you're going to join the band. Come on, let's do it."

I was going back and forth in my head. I didn't want to let him down, but I also knew he was nuts. I was debating with myself for what felt like hours. I sincerely felt this decision would change the course of my life. Obviously, it did. But, just as obviously, it's ridiculous that I was actually thinking it at the time.

I walked into the bathroom and stared into the mirror. I said out loud, "Just do what your gut tells you."

My gut immediately told me, very clearly, "Do NOT join this band, they're fucking crazy."

That's it. It's settled. I'm staying in Mary My Hope. Phew.

I walked out of the bathroom, sat down in my chair on the balcony, threw down a big gulp of wine, looked Chris directly in the eye and said, "All right. I'm in."

I was fully aware of the fact that I had completely disregarded my internal compass. I couldn't make sense of it. It was just what it was.

Chris and I high-fived, knocked back the rest of the wine, and then I ran across the street to the market for some beer. We spent the next couple of hours drinking and plotting our next steps.

3

"He is Rotting from the Inside Out"

The next night, I played my third and final show with Mary My Hope. We killed it. Truly the best we had ever played. It did not make what was gonna happen next any easier on me.

In the parking lot after the show, once we had loaded out, I said, "Hey, guys, I gotta tell you something: I'm joining Mr. Crowe's Garden."

Clint, Sven, and James all stared at me for a few seconds. Then they got fucking mad.

"Are you serious?!?"

"What the fuck?"

"This is bullshit!"

I felt awful. "Mr. Crowe's Garden are gonna have a record deal soon," I said, sighing. "How can I turn that down?"

I saw the disgust on their faces. The worst part was that it wasn't even true. I didn't give a shit about the potential record deal. I just thought it might sound good as an excuse. The real reason was I didn't think they had what it took to make it.

When I looked at Chris, I saw desperation. I *shared* that desperation. He wasn't going to let anything stop him. I didn't get that when I looked at Clint. It was just that simple.

Sven was clearly pissed off but got past it pretty quickly, at least to my face. Always a gentleman, he offered support in a way that made me feel even worse.

"Dude, you can't go with Chris," Clint warned. "He is rotting from the inside out. There's nothing inside of him. He is just a black hole."

"Maybe," I replied, "but he's my friend."

Clint kept going on about Chris. "He fucking hates himself," he said. "He's self-destructive, and he'll ruin whatever you do. And you know it, too."

Not long after, I told Chris what Clint had said that night, and we laughed about it. Chris would always joke about how he was "rotting from the inside out," though by a certain point Clint's words had more than just a ring of truth. But I honestly don't think the guy I met when I got off the bus in 1987 was "just a black hole," like Clint said.

I really liked that guy. He was, like all of us at that age, just trying to figure out who he was. Chris had tried college, but it hadn't worked for him. He'd been in therapy, but that didn't work for him either, and right before I moved to town his therapist had killed himself, for fuck's sake.

He went cold turkey on his prescribed antidepressants and consequently was drinking a ton. It's funny in retrospect that he hated pot back then. He mocked Clint and Sven for being stoners. He was all about drinking. I drank a lot at that time, and more and more as the years went on, but never like Chris. I'd buy a case of beer and he'd have sixteen to my eight over the course of a few hours.

Chris was obsessed with books and music and movies and conversation. He was exhausting and hilarious. He took everything to the nth degree. We'd watch a French film and he would *have* to drink red wine afterward. He went so far and hard into everything, but it was real. That authenticity eventually gave way to something else entirely, but in 1987 it was worth believing in.

So did I really know, at that particular moment, that things truly would play out pretty much exactly as Clint predicted? Maybe. But I thought I could rescue Chris from his self-destructive impulses, just like I had already bailed him out of a bunch of bar fights. At times it felt like I had become the older brother Chris never had. His default reaction to just about any situation had become "get Steve here." He needed me around. And, obviously, there was something in me that needed to be that guy for him.

Chris needed me in a way that Clint and Sven didn't. So I chose Mr. Crowe's Garden. That's really what it was all about to me.

Within twelve months of my departure, Mary My Hope had a record deal and were booking flights to England to make an album with a dude who had just produced a Jesus and Mary Chain album.

Meanwhile, it felt like Mr. Crowe's Garden couldn't get arrested.

My first gig with my new band was in August at a club called the Einstein a Go-Go in Jacksonville Beach, Florida, opening up for Gordon Gano of The Violent Femmes. It was also the first and only gig for a new bassist named Gary who stepped in at the very last minute.

It was about a six-hour drive from Atlanta, and we weren't making more than a hundred bucks at best. But a gig was a gig. David Macias, who booked the gig, had a blue 1975 Gremlin that was somewhat reliable. David, Chris, and I, along with my drum kit, piled into the Gremlin. (Google "AMC Gremlin" sometime. Feel free to imagine cramming three adults and a full drum kit into that sucker.) Rich and Gary rode in Rich's Honda Accord, which was similarly crammed with guitars, basses, and amps.

David was the band's manager at the time. Now, by "manager" I mean he called clubs and booked gigs and was generally on hand to help out wherever he could. Macias also happened to work in the mailroom of the A&M Records Atlanta branch. In late 1986, Mr. Crowe's Garden recorded a four-song demo at a local studio. David mailed a cassette of those tunes to A&M Records in Los Angeles, from the A&M office in Atlanta, explaining that he was working with a young band and hoped someone would take the time to listen. As the package came from an envelope with actual A&M letterhead, it somehow found its way to a guy in the A&R department named Aaron Jacoves. He listened to the songs, liked what he heard, and called David to set up the band's recording session. From setting up demos with a record label to providing transportation to out-of-town gigs, David's early impact was quite significant.

We drove down the day of the gig, loaded in, were given a proper sound check, and then had a few hours to kill. The owners of the club were fantastic, and they put out a great spread for us. There were a couple of really sweet, dreadlocked, patchouli-soaked college hippie girls in the club, too. Chris and I were hanging with them after sound check. One of them was dating a guy in a local band called Beggar Weeds; he turned up later and was a great dude. They offered to take us to a used-record store, showed us around the neighborhood, and told us which bars not to go to because they'd be full of drunk Marines.

I had only played three club gigs before, and they had all been in Atlanta. This was a new experience and it was amazing to me—exactly the life I was hoping to live.

A few hours later, we played our set. Within twenty seconds, you could tell all of us felt . . . weird. It was going to take a while to feel like a real unit. But there weren't any train wrecks, so by my standards it was a success.

We finished the gig, cleared our gear from the stage, and within ten minutes Rich said, "Help me pack up the Honda, I'm taking off." He was going to drive the six hours back home, right then.

"Dude, stay over!" we begged. "We'll drive back in the morning!" The club had two rooms for us to crash. Chris and I were gearing up for a big night in a foreign land full of strangers and free booze. We couldn't believe Rich wouldn't hang with us.

"No, I'm driving home, I don't wanna sleep on a shitty couch," Rich said. He and Gary split, and Chris, David, and I had such a blast that we decided to stay an extra day to see The Long Ryders, who were playing at the Einstein the next night.

The Long Ryders were one of Chris's favorite bands, and in fact he had met them a year earlier when they played in Atlanta. The next afternoon, we approached them as they loaded in. They all remembered meeting Chris and, as he had assured me and David, they were really nice guys.

I thought it was so cool that The Long Ryders had an English tour manager. That really struck me as a sure sign they were the real deal. His name was Mark Botting, and three years later to the month he became the tour manager for The Black Crowes.

After the gig, we had to drive home so David could get to work the next morning. He hopped into the driver's seat as Chris and I stumbled across the parking lot with a case of beer courtesy of The Long Ryders. Chris and I started working over the beer while David drove steadily along, precisely at the speed limit.

David's car was full of trash. Empty cans, burger wrappers, receipts, unopened mail—he never threw anything away. It reminded me of an anti-littering TV commercial I'd seen a million times as a kid. The "Tennessee Trash" ad showed an unshaven slob driving down the interstate throwing garbage out of a convertible. I started singing the jingle, Chris jumped in with me, and soon the two of us were singing the words to "Tennessee Trash" at the top of our lungs. Then we started slinging trash, as much as we could, right out the windows. David was horrified. He *hated* litter.

"Stop that! What are you doing?"

David was screaming at us. Chris and I were laughing hysterically, still singing the jingle, and mercilessly enjoying David's obvious displeasure. In other words, we were a couple of real assholes.

David pulled over on the side of I-75. "You have to stop littering! You can't do that! You got it? It's not funny! I'll stop managing you! I'll quit, I swear!"

We were dying. The louder he yelled, the harder we laughed.

Eventually, we settled down, apologized, and David turned back onto the road. As Chris and I steadily pounded through the beer, the three of us talked about all things Mr. Crowe's Garden: upcoming gigs, A&M Records, our quest to find a permanent bass player.

Without warning, the muffler on the Gremlin came undone. In an instant, the volume of the car's engine increased a hundredfold. It was truly ear splitting. Painful. And, to me and Chris, hilarious.

"I've got to fix it," David yelled. "We can't drive like this!"

He pulled over to the shoulder. The muffler was under the car, disconnected yet somehow dangling in place. Chris and I got out while David dug through the car, looking for something he might use for an ad-hoc repair. He was as focused as a NASA engineer on launch day.

David finally emerged with a flashlight, a three-foot length of twine, and a Michael Jordan beach towel.

"I think this is gonna work."

The sight of David holding the beach towel and twine was too much to take. Chris and I, yet again, were laughing hysterically.

David ignored us and crawled under the car. "I just need something else, like a T-shirt," he said. Then he popped up, dropped his pants, and slid off his briefs.

"Okay, this will do it."

A Michael Jordan beach towel, a three-foot piece of twine, and some Fruit of the Looms—that was David's managerial solution to our car problem. By this point, Chris and I were literally rolling in the grass. I've never laughed so hard.

"Come on, guys, this is gonna work," David promised.

I crawled to the side of the car and held the flashlight for him. I checked out David's handiwork. Sure enough, everything looked like it was back in place.

We all hopped back in, Chris and I toasted David's ingenuity, and we regaled ourselves by immediately retelling the story we had just lived through. Even David was laughing now.

Ten minutes passed. We were settling down again.

David calmly asked, "Do you guys smell something burning?"

Why, yes, we DO smell something burning.

"Maybe someone started a fire in the woods?" David asked.

We looked in all directions, but it was pitch black out there. We were in the middle of nowhere.

Chris finally yelled, *"It's us! It's the car!"*

David whipped over to the shoulder, killed the engine, and hopped out of the car. He frantically jumped down onto his back, threw his feet under the car, and began kicking at the muffler, which was indeed very much on fire.

He kicked the muffler free of the car, completely demolishing it in the process. The towel and his underwear were almost entirely burnt up. It all lay in a smoldering pile on the shoulder of the highway.

David was furious. He couldn't even speak. For the first time, Chris and I didn't laugh. We really wanted to, but David was sincerely upset.

We piled back into the car without a word. He turned the engine over. It roared again like a jet engine. He pulled back onto I-75, leaving behind a much larger mound of trash than Chris and I could have ever, in our wildest dreams, conjured.

After driving for a few minutes, Chris and I couldn't hold out. We started laughing. Roaring, in fact. But this time David joined in. He couldn't deny it. That shit was funny.

There we were, driving through the pitch-black nothing of rural Georgia, an hour before sunrise, in a car louder than a freight train—all three of us crying, screaming, convulsing with laughter.

As the sun came up, we rode along quietly staring out the windows, having grown accustomed to the obscene volume of the engine.

It was only six in the morning, and it was already the greatest day of my life.

In the spring of 1988, we somehow got an offer to open for the Wild Seeds, a band from Austin, at a club in New York City, for $500. It was a sixteen-hour drive from Atlanta. We would have done it for free.

New York City was awesome. Even with the long drive on either side of the gig, we had two full days to hang out at St. Mark's and the West Village and all the other places we had read about or seen in movies. The actual gig almost felt like an imposition. *Shit, we gotta focus on something now?*

We played a club called Drums, near the Fifty-Ninth Street Bridge. I don't remember a single thing about sound check or the gig. The significance of that night began after we cleared the stage. We were sitting in our dressing room, having a drink and making plans to find a bar for the night, when the door swung open and our lives changed forever.

A giant, manic, whirling dervish loudly walked in. He was about six feet tall, 250 pounds, had long dark hair, was oddly unshaven, and crazily gregarious. We'd never seen anyone like him.

"Hey, Mr. Crowes's Garden, what's up?" he said. "I'm George Drakoulias. I'm with A&M Records."

We could tell immediately that George was different from every other A&R rep we'd met. He was the first label guy we clicked with, because right away we saw him as an actual creative person. George had been Rick Rubin's roommate and partner back when Rick was running his first label, Def Jam, out of his dorm room at New York University in the early 1980s. When Rick moved to LA to start Def American Recordings, George stayed behind in New York, having been hired to do A&R for A&M Records. He had heard the tapes we did for the label the year before, and when he saw our name listed on the bill for the gig, he decided to come by and check us out for himself. In every way, George struck us all as the exact opposite of every other record exec we'd come across. He was only a year older than me, he was funny, and he immediately made us feel good. Above all, he was brutally honest, and we actually appreciated that.

"What did you think?" Rich asked.

"Well," George said, "the truth is, you guys aren't very good. I mean, I kinda get what you're going for, but your songs are terrible and you can't really play yet. But those two covers you chose were pretty cool."

We had played "Down in the Street" by the Stooges and "No More No More" by Aerosmith. George was clearly struck by that juxtaposition: gritty punk and arena-rock swagger.

"I mean, who the hell covers the Stooges *and* Aerosmith?" he wondered.

Chris laughed. "We do, man!"

"Yeah, well, that worked at least," George concluded. "You guys kinda suck now, but you definitely got something."

Chris, Rich, and I all looked at each other with the same thought. *This guy is fucking awesome.*

4

"No, No, No . . . Try Open G, Like Keith"

The next day, all we could talk about was making a record with George. We were all buzzing.

Well, everyone but our on again/off again bassist, Ted.

"I don't get why you're so excited about this guy," Ted said. It was hardly a surprise. Ted was out of step with the rest of us about a lot of things.

A week or two later, we played a frat party at Auburn University in Alabama. It was a $1,200 gig, but we had to play three sets. We played inside a gazebo in the backyard, about thirty yards away from the actual party, on the back deck of the house. No one came anywhere near the band while we played. It was essentially a glorified rehearsal.

Chris could never stand to play for an inattentive audience, much less a *nonexistent* audience. This caused problems for us later on when The Black Crowes became a big-time band. But it was already an issue in the Mr. Crowe's Garden days.

After the second set, Chris got in the van and said, "Fuck it, I'm done."

Rich and I argued back, "No, man, we gotta play one more set or we don't get paid!"

"Fuck them! I'm not going back!" Chris insisted as he took his boots off.

We went back and forth for a minute or two and then I snapped. That was three hundred bucks of mine that he was jeopardizing. I

27

needed that damned money. I grabbed Chris in a semi-headlock to drag him back out of the van. Rich pulled me off, screaming at me, but Chris swung at Rich and they ended up clenched together. Then it was my turn to break *them* up.

Chris finally said, "Well, I can't sing now, you fucking choked me!"

"Fuck it, I'll sing," Rich countered. It was so unexpected, and so out of character, that I burst out laughing.

"Cool, let's do it!"

We stumbled through a couple of our originals that we'd already played and then butchered a few covers. Rich sort of knew Led Zeppelin's "Misty Mountain Hop," and at one point he simply repeated the verse riff over and over while Ted and I drunkenly played along. We could have done literally anything, as long as we made noise until midnight.

At one point, I looked over to see Chris standing next to the van and watching, with a big asshole smile on his face. He thought it was hilarious.

We finished, packed up the van, got paid, and hit the road back to Atlanta. We were still angry at Chris.

Ted broke the silence. "I gotta say, I am embarrassed to be in this band right now."

For a few minutes there, Chris had been the man on the outside, and Rich, Ted, and I were rightfully furious at him. The second Ted opened his mouth, the dynamic shifted entirely.

All three of us turned. "Oh yeah? You're *embarrassed? To be in this band?* Well fuck you, then! Quit, you asshole!"

It was some real *Lord of the Flies* shit. And it showed the three of us what we hadn't wanted to admit: we needed a new bassist.

That spring, Stan Robinson bought a two-bedroom condo in Buckhead and, shockingly, the brothers both moved in. I couldn't believe it. *They're going to live together?*

They had nothing but time to work on new tunes. Like Chris and me, Rich had become obsessed with Nick Drake's music. Unlike Chris and me, Rich put that obsession to good use. He began experimenting with open tunings like Drake played, and almost immediately he wrote the parts that would become "She Talks to Angels."

He played it for me when I stopped by the condo one day. I was blown away. He hadn't written anything like that before. Granted, I pretty much always thought our songs were great. But this was different. That intro alone was all it took, really.

At our next rehearsal, we started to put the song together. Chris had written some lyrics, and the two of them had hammered out an arrangement.

I was all in. Only Ted didn't like it. "This is terrible! Those lyrics are so cliché! We can't play this live!"

We had a gig downtown at the Royal Peacock that weekend. After sound check, Ted took a stand. "I'm not playing that song tonight. We can't play a ballad like that."

We didn't play "She Talks to Angels," arguably the most popular song The Black Crowes ever recorded, that night. But afterward, back at the condo, we decided definitively to move on from Ted after our next gig.

That gig was a few days later in Birmingham, at The Nick. About an hour before we were supposed to leave, Chris complained to me and Rich. "I can't do this, man. I can't go play the gig with Ted." Rich and I actually agreed. It would suck to drive all the way over there and back pretending everything was cool.

We needed to let Ted know. We all liked Ted, but there was no denying he wasn't the right guy. It wasn't gonna be easy—hell, he and I lived in the same damned house at that point—but we needed to man up and just tell him the truth.

We agreed one of us should tell him. It'd be easier on Ted if it weren't all three of us. We all stared at each other. A real Mexican stand-off.

Rich and I told Chris that since he'd known Ted the longest, it should be him.

Chris and I told Rich that since he wasn't really very close with Ted, it should be him.

Chris and Rich told me that since I lived with him, it should be me.

No one stepped up.

Instead, we decided to prioritize: let's make up a bullshit story to get out of the gig in Birmingham, and leave that whole "firing Ted" part for later.

I called Ted at Clark's Music, where he worked. "Hey, man, have you seen Chris? I think he's on a bender somewhere. I don't think we can do the gig." As I lied, Chris sat right next to me.

"But we can't cancel tonight," Ted said. "They'll never have us back."

"I know, man, he's really fucking us over here," I said. "Let me know if you hear from him—me and Rich are at the condo."

Then I called the club.

"Hey, man, our transmission just fell out of our van near the state line and we're fucked."

"Where are you?" said the guy from the club. "I have a huge van. I'll come pick you up."

"No, man, that's okay," I stammered. "We're gonna get someone from Atlanta to come get us and take us home."

The guy from the club knew it was bullshit. "Yeah, right," he said, hanging up on me. Bridge burnt.

I called Ted back a few hours later. "Chris just showed up. He's wasted. No way we can play the gig."

"Man, that's bullshit!" said Ted.

"Yeah, I know. He's an asshole."

I crashed on their couch that night, the first of many nights on that couch. I woke up early the next morning, got on my Vespa, and rode home. I assumed Ted would be at work. Instead, he was sitting in his bedroom.

I had to be the one to fire him. Shit.

"Ted, you're out of the band," I said. "Sorry, man."

Ted started to cry a little bit.

"Dude, it's not personal, you're a great guy and a great bass player," I said. I meant all of it, too.

It was hard to fire Ted, but we didn't have a choice. Things were starting to get serious for Mr. Crowe's Garden. George Drakoulias, our crazy benefactor from A&M, was on his way.

The condo became the new headquarters for Mr. Crowe's Garden. We couldn't rehearse there, but at least we had a centralized location where we could listen to records, work on new songs, and hang out together. I was on the couch most of the summer. Ted and I got along after I fired him, but it still felt really awkward at the house, plus the condo had air conditioning.

Chris or Rich called George once a week or so, and it was pretty clear he was serious about us. In May, George finally agreed to come to Atlanta to hang out for a few days. We were fucking thrilled—but we needed a bass player.

I was working at this local pizza joint called Fellini's, a hub for the local music community, and one of the guys there, Scott Shamel, was a free agent. He wore his bass down by his knees, like Paul Simonon from The Clash. I didn't really know what kind of musician he was, but he looked cool onstage and was a great dude.

"Hey, man, you wanna play with Mr. Crowe's Garden?" I asked him one night at work.

"No, man," he demurred. "You guys ain't punk at all. And Chris's brother doesn't like me."

"He's fine, you just gotta get to know him," I promised. "We're making demos again for A&M. Just join our band, it'll be cool."

"I'll think about it, man."

We had that same conversation for about two weeks.

During that time, George came to town. We took him to see a bunch of bands, including Mary My Hope, who were killing it at that point. They were *the* buzz band in town. He stayed three or four days, bought us a ton of meals and drinks, and booked a studio for early July to record some demos.

We finally got Scott into a rehearsal room, played a few times, and he jumped in. He seemed a little standoffish at first. He wanted to play loud and hard and that was that. But he had fun with us.

George booked three days of studio time at the Protestant Radio and Television studios for the first week of July. We tracked five songs, though George actually ended up replaying all the bass parts himself, as Scott was pretty sloppy. We also brought in a friend named Johnny Dee from a local band called Right as Rain to play the guitar solos. George called him "Johnny Lightning" and suggested we get him in the band, but Johnny Dee was pushing thirty, which was, of course, ancient to us.

None of those songs ended up being keepers. We were still a long way away from the band that made *Shake Your Money Maker*. But during those sessions, George started steering us in that direction. Crucially, he told Rich he should start playing in open tunings. Rich told him he'd already written something in open E, "She Talks to Angels," but George waved him off.

"No, no, no, try open G, like Keith. You gotta rock it out. Go get some Stones records, check out *Beggars Banquet* and *Let It Bleed* and *Exile*. You already play like that, but you don't know it."

George was adamant. *Study The Stones.* We had all heard those records before, of course. But now it was different. Digging into The Rolling Stones suddenly took on a very different meaning.

There were two versions of Mr. Crowe's Garden: before George Drakoulias and after George Drakoulias.

We spent months on end going back through Stones, Faces, Humble Pie, even Allman Brothers records—things we'd heard our whole lives, only now we were listening with a newfound purpose. We were trying to find a way in, trying to figure out the path to that level of playing.

I changed my approach entirely. Instead of driving the band forward, I began consciously trying to pull the band back, to get just behind the beat. It usually felt clunky and dragging, but every now and then we'd catch a real groove. We'd feel it right away, and then we'd lose it just as quickly. But at least now we had a sense of what we were looking for.

For the first time, our rehearsals actually mattered. Rich and I would continue to play together when the others took a break. He'd work through endless chord changes and I simply would play along, trying to follow wherever he went.

We were nothing like the band we would eventually become in terms of individual and group playing, but the summer and fall of 1988 are significant because that's when we finally allowed ourselves to really work hard. No more ironic detachment. No more waiting around for something to happen.

Rich exploded as a guitarist. The open tunings were more than just a boost to him. It was as if he was handed an entirely different instrument, one he'd been waiting to find for years. He was always solid rhythmically; his right hand was always great. But suddenly he had all kinds of new ideas—dozens of riffs, tons of progressions—just pouring out of him. He and Chris were writing new songs at a frantic pace. Anyone who came to two gigs six weeks apart would have heard two very different sets. We were adding new songs, and dismissing old ones, constantly.

The brothers finally finished an arrangement for "She Talks to Angels" and we put it into rotation. The first time we played it live was at a club in Jackson, Mississippi, called W.C. Don's, that was really just a double-wide trailer.

From the very first notes of the intro, "She Talks to Angels" got a noticeable response. A drunken, rowdy, Saturday night crowd fell into a hush. By the time the chorus hit, they were dancing. I don't mean a club of people swaying in time to the music. I mean couples paired off and slow dancing like it was a high school prom. We didn't know what to make of it. Chris fucked up the lyrics a few times because he was trying not to laugh. It was weird, but it spoke to the power of the song, even at an early stage.

By October we had worked up another song, "Jealous Again," that ultimately became the first single from *Shake Your Money Maker.* We had the verse, the chorus, and the groove, but we didn't yet have that signature breakdown—the "stop, understand me" part. (That would come later on a prompt from George in preproduction.)

We played the Exit/In, in Nashville, opening for Drivin N Cryin, who were still very much the kings of the Atlanta scene. When Kevn Kinney, DNC's frontman, heard "Jealous Again" at sound check, he stopped dead in his tracks.

"Where did THAT come from?" he asked, excitedly.

"We just wrote it," Chris said, proudly.

"Wow. That's a whole 'nother thing."

"Jealous Again" wasn't quite finished, but Kevn picked up on it anyway. The open tuning, the groove—we were getting somewhere.

In hindsight, things with George fell into place very quickly. His first trip to Atlanta was in May of 1988, and we were making our album thirteen months later. But at the time, it felt like an eternity.

George kept putting us off. One time he explained that A&M had just signed Soundgarden, from Seattle. "They don't want another 'Garden' band just yet," he said.

One day on the phone, he was impatient with Chris's badgering, and he cut to the chase: "You guys just aren't ready. We *have* to take our time. You're getting better and better but once we commit, we gotta deliver for real or there's no second chance."

In the meantime, we kept seeking out road gigs in the south and up and down the East Coast. We lined up a four-night run scheduled for early November: Washington, DC, Boston, Albany, and New York City at CBGB.

We called George. "We're playing CBGB!" He said we could crash at his place, a townhouse in the West Village owned by Peter Mensch, who managed Metallica, Def Leppard, Tesla, and a few dozen other giant acts. George had the place to himself that week, with plenty of floor space for all of us.

We drove to DC on a Monday. This was gonna be our longest trip ever, a full week. We found the club, which was actually across the river in Virginia. Rich and Scott stayed in the van, and Chris and I walked in to figure out the load-in/sound-check schedule.

"Mr. Crowe's what?" the club manager said quizzically. "I've never heard of you. Who said you had a show here tonight?"

Not a great start.

We got right back in the van and headed to NYC, hitting it in plenty of time to go out. George was buying the drinks, and we were all ecstatic to have three nights in NYC before the gig on Thursday.

Those three nights just about killed us. By the time Thursday rolled around, Chris, Scott, and I were a mess.

Plus, it was nerve-wracking to be at CBGB. We'd never played such a historic room, and we were dumb enough to let that get to us. George introduced us to a number of industry people before our set started, and the entire vibe went from exciting to off the rails in no time.

We played for thirty minutes and it was, by a mile, the worst gig we played that fall. False starts, missed changes, dropped sticks, bad tunings—every little thing that can go wrong went wrong. We knew it after two songs. We shrunk a little more with each passing minute. It was truly awful.

The next day at Mensch's townhouse, George laid some pretty significant news on us. He was leaving A&M Records and moving to Los Angeles to work for Rick Rubin's new rock label, Def American.

"I'm heading out there first of the year. Gimme a few months to get settled and then I'll sign you," George promised. "We'll make an album for Def American."

His word was his bond. As far as we were concerned, we were made men.

Earlier that summer, we had played at Elliston Square in Nashville opening for a local band called Rumble Circus. Their singer was a kid named Jeffrey Williams, who had actually gone to high school with me and Clint Steele back in Hopkinsville. Small world, man. I hadn't seen him in a few years and, like all of us, Jeffrey had transformed pretty remarkably. The preppiest kid from school had become a Michael Stipe clone.

Rumble Circus were all good dudes. We hit it off right away, and the night ended around the corner at The Gold Rush, drinking beer, shooting pool, and making plans to have them open for us in Atlanta sometime.

After our week in the Northeast, we finally had a chance to pay Rumble Circus back. We had a gig scheduled in Atlanta with Mary My Hope, and asked them to come down and open the night. Three bands, each one including a kid from a tiny school in Hopkinsville. Weird.

We met with Clint, Sven, and their new manager to discuss the gig. Mary My Hope made one thing clear: they were headlining. With a label deal now signed, they had the upper hand. There was also the undeniable yet painful fact that they were far more popular than we were locally. We gave in and agreed to take the middle slot on the bill, but weren't happy about it. All three bands had great sets that night, and whatever competition we felt gave way to long-standing friendships by the time it was all said and done.

After the show, Clint had all three bands over to his place for a party. His girlfriend was a stripper at The Gold Club, which afforded them a really nice apartment up in Buckhead.

Chris and I were sitting with the guitarist from Rumble Circus, Jeff Cease. We were just shooting the shit, telling stories, when Clint's girlfriend walked across the room to hand Jeff an ashtray. She said, "Here you go—don't want any ashes on the rug!" No attitude whatsoever; she was very sweet about it. Jeff took the ashtray, said, "Oh, great, thanks!" with a big smile, and simultaneously flicked his cigarette, sending ash right onto the rug. She didn't notice, but Chris and I did. We fell out laughing.

Chris was catching Jeff up on our recent developments. "We're gonna make a record with George Drakoulias. But we gotta find another guitar player," he said.

"What about me? I'll do it!" Jeff said.

Chris and I looked at each other. "You would?"

"Yeah, man! I fucking love your band. Can I try out?"

"What about your band?"

"We're not going anywhere. My singer can't even sing." Jeff was right. Jeffrey Williams was a good frontman, but not such a great vocalist.

"You'd be cool with moving to Atlanta?"

"Fuck yeah!"

I don't think we even had an audition.

The next day, we told Rich we wanted to hire Jeff. "That guy from Rumble Circus?" Rich asked. "Can he even play solos?"

"Yeah, man. He's great."

George set up shop at Def American in Los Angeles in January of 1989. By March, he was ready to focus on Mr. Crowe's Garden again. He came to Atlanta to work on songs with Chris and Rich. It was time for preproduction, which is when you get your songs in good enough shape to record.

They spent a few days at the condo, just the three of them. I stopped by the first day, but it was obvious I was in the way. I distracted Chris, so Rich and George finally told me to take off. It was cool, though.

They'd already turned a few loose ideas into songs, so it was clear that great progress was being made.

We all met at our rehearsal space one night so they could show the new songs to me, Scott, and Jeff. "Jealous Again," "Thick n' Thin," and "Could I've Been So Blind" had all existed for a while in various forms, but now they were finished and fully arranged. We were all jacked up. We played through them for a couple of hours.

The next day, I stopped by the condo and they took a break. "Look, I don't think Scott is going to work," George told us. "I love the guy, I'm not saying he shouldn't be in the band, he just can't play on the album."

George braced himself for us to argue for Scott, but we surprised him. As far as we were concerned, if Scott wasn't good enough to play on the record, he didn't belong in the band.

Scott hadn't ever fully bought into the band, anyway. We were never quite hard enough, or punk enough, for his taste. That didn't make us feel better, though. We genuinely loved him.

Chris mentioned he'd just seen a guy playing at Magruder's who was fantastic. *Magruder's?* As far as I knew, Magruder's was where cover bands played. The kind of place where makeup-wearing Poison-looking wannabes hung out. What the fuck had Chris been doing there in the first place?

"His name is Johnny Colt," Chris said.

Rich and I couldn't believe our ears. *Johnny Colt?* That's someone's name?

"He's a rock dude and he's a badass bass player," Chris said. "You gotta check him out."

Chris had already started wearing scarves, leather pants, and eyeliner onstage. He surprised me one day by putting on *Appetite for Destruction*. He was really into the album. Guns N' Roses had become the biggest band in the world, but I didn't expect Chris to go with the flow on that one. He wasn't necessarily a die-hard fan of the songs—the attitude was the thing.

Before GNR, the hair bands were soft posers. We mocked them all the time. But with Guns N' Roses, we couldn't deny they were real. You could tell they dug The Stones and Aerosmith, and even punk bands. Rich and I were slower to embrace this mind-set, and we didn't necessarily see any connection between GNR and Mr. Crowe's Garden. But Chris could see it.

"We have got to be harder," Chris declared. "We have to be a little more rock."

Rich and I went to see Johnny's band, The Law. They had a light show and a fog machine, and the whole "big rock" vibe. We kept exchanging dirty looks. It was slick and super polished. We couldn't deny they played great, but at the same time it sounded to our ears like Bon Jovi. Worse, it *looked* like Bon Jovi.

We hopped in Rich's car afterward and he immediately put on R.E.M.'s *Chronic Town*. "I just have to hear some real fucking music after that bullshit," he said.

"I can't be in a band with this guy," I insisted. "No fucking way."

But Chris wasn't having it. He had his mind set. Johnny was the guy.

A week later, all three of us went to see The Law. This time around, we met Johnny and hung out a bit. He was wearing leather pants, multiple chains, necklaces, and he had a few tattoos. He looked nothing like anyone we'd ever played with. But I really liked him. Right away a few things were obvious: he was a solid fucking dude, he was solid as hell on the bass, and he really, really loved Mr. Crowe's Garden. He had seen us a few times, and was as intrigued by our band as we were initially repelled by his.

We set up a time for him to come to our rehearsal room to jam. From the jump, he and I locked in. Mr. Crowe's Garden had never sounded so good. In the course of three meetings with the guy, I went from "no fucking way" to "hell fucking yes!" Rich felt it, too. It was a no-brainer.

5

The KKK

We rehearsed with Johnny a few times in May 1989 and played a gig in the parking lot at Frijoleros, a local burrito joint. Robin Zander from Cheap Trick, of all people, turned up and seemed to enjoy himself. We had to cut the gig short because I broke my snare head and didn't have a replacement. We were days away from loading into Soundscape Studios in Atlanta to record our debut album, and a backup snare drum was still beyond our means.

George hired a local producer named Brendan O'Brien to engineer the album. In the wake of *Shake Your Money Maker*'s success, Brendan became one of the world's most successful rock producers, working with Pearl Jam, Stone Temple Pilots, Bruce Springsteen, AC/DC, and pretty much anyone else he wanted. But in the spring of 1989, he was just a guy I recommended when George asked if I knew any local engineers.

"Is he good?" George asked.

"Hell, I don't know. He's hilarious, though."

While I did my small part to help Brendan get the gig that would ultimately transform his career, my own place in the band was in temporary jeopardy. As it turned out, I was really nervous in the studio.

I was playing on borrowed drums, as my kit was the same starter-level Pearl set I'd bought two years earlier. Johnny's drummer from The Law, Billy Pitts, loaned me his Sonor kit for the album. It was a great kit, but it was a real adjustment. If it had been a single gig, I wouldn't have cared, but I was hyperaware of every little thing now that the pressure was on.

This was only my third time in a recording studio, and my first time playing along to a click track. I really hated the click. Just the sound itself was so unnatural to me. I was accustomed to listening to the whole band, and being guided by the vibe in a club. Pushing faster, pulling back, following Rich or Chris on a whim regarding the intensity of a moment. I was totally unprepared to play the steady, monotonous tracks needed for the album.

We spent four days in the studio, after which we had exactly zero drum tracks suitable for use. I was completely stressed out. Rich went to George after the first day and suggested we bring in a "real drummer" who could knock it out quickly. I didn't know about it at the time, but I could certainly feel the vibe growing darker with each day, and I assumed all the responsibility. George stressed to Rich that we were all equally bad, and that it wasn't as simple as just me not being able to play well enough. We weren't a real rhythm section yet. Johnny had just gotten there, and we hadn't done enough demos to get used to the studio.

George was very patient, and Brendan was encouraging, but we were about to come apart at the seams. We'd try a song a few times, hit a wall, take a break, and then try a different song. We were getting closer, but we just couldn't break through.

On the fourth day of recording, George warned me about falling off the click. I couldn't believe it! How could I be falling off the click? I felt like I was pushing everything as it was.

"Stay focused," he said.

I tried again.

"Nope, you fell off, start over."

It happened over and over and over. I was beyond frustrated.

Finally, I put the sticks down and walked outside. We were burning through money we didn't have. I felt like I was having an anxiety attack.

George followed me out and suggested we drive to Steak 'n Shake. We ordered some food and George told me about Rich's demand to find another drummer. "Look, no one wants to replace you, they just think we should call in a studio drummer to get the tracks done. I don't want to do that. You can do this, you're really good. You just *have* to figure out a way to stop falling off the click, man. Just chill out, stop rushing so much."

"Wait, I'm pushing because you keep telling me I'm falling off," I said defensively.

"Well, that's why you're falling off."

"How can I be falling off the click if I'm pushing?"

"You keep speeding up because you're pushing, that's what I'm saying."

"*'Falling off' means slowing down! That's what that means! If you mean speeding up, then say 'speeding up'!*"

This was our one shot, and I was blowing it all over a stupid miscommunication? I was relieved, though. I knew I hadn't been slowing down, so at least I wasn't crazy.

We went back that night and over the next twenty-four hours we had four tracks done. As it turned out, I was pretty good playing to a click track. All it had taken was a nervous breakdown at Steak 'n Shake and I was good to go.

On our subsequent records, we rarely used the click track. We would just set up and play live. But the truth is, in 1989 we weren't nearly good enough to do that. We needed the regimentation. The dreaded click even came up the first time I met Rick Rubin, who came to Atlanta to meet the band several months after we finished the record. Rick scheduled his trip to coincide with some big wrestling match in town, which illustrated to us how much of a priority we were to him at the time.

Rubin has since become one of the most respected figures in the music industry, a Buddha-like figure who has guided the careers of icons like Johnny Cash, Tom Petty, and Neil Diamond. But in 1989, Rick was still an upstart best known for producing Run-DMC and the Beastie Boys.

Rubin came to see us backstage after a local gig. His first words to me were "do you ever play to a click?"

"In the studio," I said.

"Do you ever rehearse with one?"

"No."

"I'm gonna get you one."

This was Rick's way of saying I was a shitty drummer who couldn't keep proper time. *Nice to meet you too, dude.*

One day, George asked Rich about "that slow blues thing" he had been messing around with. Rich played through a series of chord changes he'd strung together, but there wasn't any real structure, much less a full arrangement yet. Chris was suddenly inspired and George guided the two of them through a few suggestions. An entire new song came together very quickly. Chris went to the lounge to write lyrics, and Rich showed the rest of us the parts. In just a matter of minutes, Chris came back to say he was ready. We had a brand new song called "Seeing Things" ready to record. Three takes later, it was done.

We were turning into something, right then and there. It was undeniable.

We had most of the basic tracks recorded when George told me and Johnny to disappear for a couple of days. He wanted to work on guitar parts and knew it'd be easier, and more focused, with fewer people hanging around.

I had gone back to work at Wax n' Facts, a used-record store in Little Five Points where my responsibilities were twofold: stocking albums alphabetically and shooting nerf hoops with Danny Beard, the owner. George called the store to find me and asked if I could come back to record a track. I asked Danny if I could take off, and he told me it was cool only if I made it back before the evening rush.

I left the store at three and drove to the studio. It was just Rich, me, and the click track. In fact, I think Rich had already played an acoustic-guitar part to a click track, so I just played along to that. I did one pass and George said, "That's great, see you later." In and out in thirty minutes. I went back to work, surprised that George had dusted off such an old song. We hadn't played it in months, and I hadn't even thought about it once during the sessions. It was "She Talks to Angels."

After I closed up Wax n' Facts, I went back to the studio and listened to the track with some of the other instrumentation added. It was sparse, but it was a good take. The more I listened, the more impressive it sounded. But it wasn't as if the clouds magically parted and destiny shone upon us. The track still felt like an afterthought. I certainly didn't think that "She Talks to Angels" was destined to become one of the band's signature songs.

If "She Talks to Angels" felt like an afterthought, another big song for us, "Hard to Handle," felt like even less. For months, we had been listening to the new Otis Redding box set. One day at rehearsal, George suggested doing an Otis cover for the record. "You know, Georgia band covers Georgia singer—whaddya think?"

We were dubious. Chris was particularly not interested, with good reason. How insane do you have to be to cover the greatest soul singer of all time on your first album? But George pressed us. "Come on, let's just see if we can make something sound good." Chris finally gave in, suggesting we do "Hard to Handle," and away we went.

We figured out the tune easily enough, but we couldn't possibly swing like the Otis version. We just weren't close to that level of musicianship. We had to play it straighter, whiter, more rock. Then George had an idea. He took "Hard to Handle" and added a whole lot of "Walk This Way" by Aerosmith. After that, it all fell together pretty quickly, and we thought it was pretty great.

We recorded "Hard to Handle" late in the sessions. We didn't want a cover song on our album, but George pointed out that we would need B-sides for singles and for foreign markets, where there are often extra tracks added to albums.

A little under three weeks after we started, we wrapped the basic tracks for *Shake Your Money Maker.* I was elated. Soon enough, that album would change all our lives.

Shake Your Money Maker was finished in LA, without most of the band. Chris, George, and Brendan flew out west to record the vocals. For George, it was like pulling teeth—he and Chris both reported a lot of arguments.

When a singer is recording vocals, it can take a while to warm up. Once you're ready, you gotta really lay it out. When your voice is closing down and fatigue is settling in, you can still find some interesting tones. It's a whole process that's easier observed than explained. Chris didn't want to hear it. He wanted to do a few passes and then move on. He didn't understand the level of commitment required to sing in the studio. He'd always relied on pure talent and drive. George wanted him to focus on the melodies—sing them the exact same way every single time—and Chris couldn't stand to be so regimented.

When Chris got home, he had a finished copy of the record. For some reason, we all went to the Robinson family home in Cobb County to listen. Right away, Chris's vocals stood out. George had pulled it out of him. He stuck to the melodies, he hit the notes, and he really delivered across the board.

We listened to the whole thing straight through twice. "Seeing Things" blew me away. I'd never heard backing vocals like that on one of our songs, and I'd never heard Chris sing like that. I couldn't believe how fucking good it was. None of us could. We were thrilled.

I was shocked, however, to hear "Hard to Handle." I never thought it would be on the album. None of us did. I had to admit it was pretty great, though.

"This is fucking amazing!" we all said repeatedly. "Let's go home and get drunk right now because this is fucking awesome." We all floated out of the house to head back to town.

Our initial experience with Rick Rubin was flat-out horrible. After our in-auspicious greeting, when he gave me shit for my inability to keep time, the relationship went downhill quickly.

A full month after the album was finished, we finally had a hang with the guy writing the checks. He wasted no time letting us know he didn't quite get us.

"I just don't see it. I don't know what to make of you guys," he told us. "You're a southern band and you don't look southern."

"What does that mean?" we asked him.

"Overalls and flannel shirts and work boots," he said. "You know, like Skynyrd and Molly Hatchet!"

I thought, *We're sitting at a bar in a city of four million people, and this guy thinks we should dress for the farm? What the fuck is he talking about?*

His biggest problem was our band name. Rick liked the "Crowe" part, but thought we should change it to something more memorable. He suggested naming ourselves after Cobb County, the northern suburb where the Robinsons had grown up. One thing though—he wanted us to spell it with *K*'s instead of *C*'s: Kobb Kounty Krows, or KKK. We laughed politely, assuming it was a joke.

"I'm not joking," he said.

That was just too much. We were genuinely pissed off. *You want us to call ourselves the KKK? Well, fuck you! How about that?*

Rick told us we were overreacting and that he was just trying to think of something that would get attention.

Chris told him, quite seriously, "How about we kick your ass right here in this bar tonight? That'll get some attention!" Looking back, it's easy to see he was just amusing himself. He'd done the early Beastie Boys records, and he loved pro wrestling. He was always looking for gimmicks.

Rick Rubin was right about one thing. We really needed a new name.

I thought Mr. Crowe's Garden was a cool name until I actually joined the band. Then it became a pain in the ass. No one ever got it right. People often misheard it as "Mr. Coast Guard." I remember thinking that even Mr. Coast Guard was better than Mr. Crowe's Garden.

Chris originally found the name in the children's book *The Tale of Old Mr. Crow.* One of the chapters was called "Mr. Crow's Garden," and Chris added the *e* for the fuck of it.

I found a legal pad and a Sharpie and wrote out a list with all suggestions. We started with this: let's just be The Crowes. That's how people referred to us in Atlanta anyway. Then we thought it should be The *something* Crowes. The Stone Cold Crowes? The Flying Crowes? The Heartless Crowes? Someone suggested The Black Crowes. No one ever took credit later for it, but I remember writing it down and immediately dismissing it. For starters, it was redundant. Have you ever seen a crow that wasn't black?

The only guy who dug in and was passionate about keeping Mr. Crowe's Garden, surprisingly, was Johnny.

"I used to see that name and think, *Who the fuck would name their band Mr. Crowe's Garden?* It's just cool, and different."

It was Johnny's first real stand on anything—and it worked. He fired us up. *Yeah, fuck the label, man! We're Mr. Crowe's Garden, motherfucker!*

Not long after we decided to dig in our heels on keeping our shitty band name, we got a message to call the label. Rich was designated to make the call, and we told him to make it clear that we were Mr. Crowe's Garden and if they didn't like it, they could fuck off. Now, we still hadn't signed a record contract at that point. We literally had no power here. Rick Rubin could've just deleted us from his Rolodex and hired five other guys to be the band that made *Shake Your Money Maker*. But we didn't care—the esprit de corps was strong among us. We wanted to make a stand. The Replacements wouldn't have put up with this bullshit, and neither would we.

After Rich took the call, he promptly put our delusions of grandeur in perspective. Apparently, the label's international distributor hated our band name so much that they weren't going to release the record outside of America. If we stuck with Mr. Crowe's Garden, *Shake Your Money Maker* wouldn't be released in England, or Canada, or anywhere else. Oh, and radio programmers also hated Mr. Crowe's Garden. And so did EVERYBODY else who would have any measure of control over our destiny.

"I'm supposed to call back in ten minutes," Rich said. "What do I say?"

Fuck!

I'm fairly certain now that none of those threats were real, of course. The label just assumed, quite correctly, that we wouldn't know any better. As much as we all wanted to take a principled stand for our lame-ass band name, we were *not* prepared to have the record not come out.

"Rubin likes the name The Black Crowes," Rich said. We figured that somewhere along the line, somebody must've mentioned that name to George, who subsequently told Rick. "That's what he wants us to be."

We all looked at each other, waiting for someone to pick up the flag and lead the charge.

Nope. Not gonna happen. We folded.

"Okay, fuck it, we're The Black Crowes," Chris finally said.

6

Michael Corleone Will See You Now

George Drakoulias took care of us in the studio, but we needed someone with a clear vision to watch over every other aspect of our career. A real manager. Someone who mattered.

Our debut album was scheduled for a February release, and we were coming down to the fucking wire. Def American was sending out promo copies to radio stations, and we didn't have a promotional plan. We didn't have a touring plan. We didn't have any plan.

Finally, George heard from someone who loved the record. He called to say he'd come to Atlanta to meet with us as soon as possible. His name was Pete Angelus. We'd never heard of him.

"He was with Van Halen from the beginning and now he manages David Lee Roth," George told us. "It's a bit of a circus with Dave, but Pete seems to really dig the record. I think you should meet him."

Great, a Sunset Strip guy. That was not our scene at all. We told George to forget it. But he didn't let it go. "Guys! It's fucking December! The record is coming out in eight weeks! You need a real manager!"

We reluctantly agreed. Fine, we'll meet him. But Angelus had an immediate stipulation: he wanted to see a gig and we had nothing booked. We called everywhere in town looking for an open night to showcase for him. The Cotton Club said we could have a Sunday night. They went one step further. Not only did they give us the gig, but there would be no cover charge, and the first draft beer for anyone in the house would be free as well. That would help to get a good crowd.

We talked ourselves into believing it would be a big night. This Van Halen dude would be impressed by our local stardom, if nothing else.

We didn't have quite the turnout we had hoped for. I did a quick head count before the set. I counted to twelve. Twelve! And one of those people was my mom, who just happened to be driving through town on the way to my brother's house for Christmas.

Jesus.

After the set, Pete came back to see us. He was like George—he didn't bullshit at all.

After quick introductions, he laid it right out on the table.

"We've got *a lot* of work to do," he said.

Unlike every other manager we had met, Pete had an immediate vision of what we needed to do to get our career in gear. "We coordinate with Geffen," he said, referring to Def American's distributors and the biggest rock label in the world at that time. "There are two things that have to happen immediately: one, I have to get Geffen's radio staff and PR people to love you. Two, I have to get you on the road . . . and keep you on the road. You need the experience."

Pete already knew we hated Rick Rubin. I guess George had told him as much. "I'll deal with Rick," he promised.

"The manager's job, ultimately, is to protect you, to create opportunity, and to bring your vision to fruition in as many ways as possible," Pete said. "We are going to build a brand and your future. You're going to take care of the music. I'm going to handle everything else."

We hadn't hired this guy yet, and five minutes in, he was giving us an education in the music business. He knew how to get songs on the radio and how to book a national tour. He was on a first-name basis with all the concert promoters, booking agents, program directors, label PR journalists, and MTV executives—all the people who would either make or break our debut album.

He turned to Chris. "Prepare yourself, you're going to be talking to every rock station in America," Pete promised.

More than anything, Pete made it clear to us that we were woefully behind on setting the table for *Shake Your Money Maker*. "If I had been managing you from day one, we would have been starting on all of this last summer," he said. "There would have been showcases, photo shoots, video shoots, meetings with key journalists and MTV. But we don't have time for any of that. We have to come from the rear fast."

The next day, we called Pete and hired him.

Right after Christmas, Pete came back to town to solidify our deal. We met again at his hotel suite at the Ritz-Carlton, and he immediately informed us just how bad our financial situation was. "There's two things that have become clear to me," he said. "First of all, you guys have made an incredible album and you are to be congratulated. Second, you signed an incredibly shitty record deal."

Pete explained that, under our contract affording us only a $10,000 advance, we had a very low royalty rate and had given Rick a large percentage of the band's publishing and merchandising. We would never make any real money from *Shake Your Money Maker*, no matter how many copies we sold. So, in addition to getting our music on the radio and the band on the road as much as possible, he had a new underlying goal: renegotiate, or get us out of our shitty deal.

For now, we had to learn a new skill: play nice.

"If you see Rick, it's a handshake and a smile and a thank-you, and that's it," Pete said. "You have to have Rick Rubin as your friend. That's what you have to do so I can do what I have to do."

"But he's an asshole," we argued back.

"This is business, and if you want a renegotiation of the deal," Pete maintained, "you don't want Rick feeling like an enemy or an outsider."

It was very clear to all of us that Pete was a very driven and brilliant guy, and it seemed like a no-brainer to take everything he said to heart. Unfortunately, Chris and Rich were never very good at listening to anybody. That seemed especially true when the person was in a position to help us.

"Everything we ever talk about—every decision we make, every plan we make, every idea we float—this is a closed society," Pete maintained. "There's five guys in the band and there's me. Band business is for our six pairs of ears, and that's it. You don't tell anybody outside this room any band business, unless I deem it necessary or beneficial."

In my mind, honest to God, I was sitting at a table with Michael Corleone. I was all in.

"Yeah, man, of course," Johnny agreed.

"No problem," Jeff concurred.

I looked over at Chris and Rich and thought, *There's no fucking way they'll keep this shit to themselves.* Sure enough, that very night, Chris and I were sitting with Stan and Nancy and he told them every single thing we had discussed that afternoon.

I pulled Chris aside and confronted him. "We don't tell anybody anything outside the band," I said.

"It's my parents!" Chris said. "Who are they gonna tell?"

Chris was going to do what he was going to do. Before long, his inability to control himself or his behavior would have far more devastating consequences for all of us.

7

Are We Gonna Win or
Are We Gonna Lose?

With the release of *Shake Your Money Maker* fast approaching, Pete got to work on cramming all the promotional setup that would have normally taken six months into just a few weeks. In early January, he set up a whirlwind trip to Los Angeles that included scores of interviews, photo shoots, a showcase gig at Riki Rachtman's infamous hairmetal club The Cathouse, and a video shoot for our first single, "Jealous Again." Pete, who had several iconic Van Halen and David Lee Roth videos on his résumé, including "Hot for Teacher," "Panama," and "California Girls," rejected Def American's attempt at our first video and was going to direct it himself.

Shake Your Money Maker was released on February 13, 1990. Right out of the gate, rock radio liked our first single, "Jealous Again." It went to number one on rock radio, and then our next single, "Twice as Hard," went to number two. By the summer, when "Hard to Handle" came out, we were flat-out rolling. MTV loved us, too. Our first three videos, all directed by Pete, were played constantly.

One year earlier, while recording *Shake Your Money Maker*, we thought selling fifty thousand records would be amazing. We had no thoughts whatsoever that the album would be hugely successful. It didn't sound like the indie bands that inspired us. It didn't sound like anything on the radio. It was always kind of in its own corner. And yet we wound up selling over five million copies.

The one thing we did understand was that *Shake Your Money Maker* was the best album we could have possibly made. That couldn't have been clearer as we hit the road for the first time. As much as we wanted to play as many gigs as possible, the truth was we needed to play as many gigs as possible in order to become a band worthy of that album.

In the end, we played 350 shows in support of *Shake Your Money Maker*. It was an exciting, hilarious, confusing, and ultimately grueling tour and we all went a little insane. One of us actually dropped out of the band by the end, signaling the demise of the original lineup and an omen of things to come. But when it was all said and done, we were no longer in over our heads. We'd become a great fucking band.

As The Black Crowes were first getting noticed, the music press lumped us in with a band called The London Quireboys. Everybody heard them and said, "They sound just like the Faces!" just like everybody heard us and said, "They sound just like The Stones!"

For context, you gotta remember that this was 1990. Grunge was still a few years away, and mainstream rock was all about hair bands. Some were more clownish than others, but we lumped them all in together. We opened for Aerosmith that summer, replacing the band Skid Row. We played a bizarre conference for some distribution company and shared a bill with Slaughter. We were in magazines next to Cinderella and Winger.

We just couldn't find a place that fit comfortably for us. We thought the guys in Slaughter were douchebags, and we knew Paul Westerberg probably thought we were douchebags.

Our first national tour started about a month after the album came out. We opened for Junkyard, who were from LA and had just released their second album. They were a harder rock band than we were, taking cues from Guns N' Roses.

The first gig of the tour was in Anaheim. Our tour manager was a buddy of mine from Atlanta named Kenny Gordon. He quit a sales job to hit the road with us. Junkyard paid us $250 a night, flat fee, so Kenny pretty much just needed to make sure we got paid and then get us safely to the hotel in the next town. Stan Robinson, always doing what he could to support us, gave us his Dodge Ram van for the tour. There were two seats up front, two captain's chairs in the middle, and two captain's chairs in the back. Room for six. We had one crew guy, but without space for him in the van, he ended up riding in Junkyard's bus.

As we were about to head south to Anaheim, Pete sat us down and issued a grave warning. "Don't ever leave the venue with a stranger. You meet a girl, she's got a car, you don't get in that car," he said. "You never know what pissed-off boyfriend, husband, or father could be on the other end of that ride. You stay together."

And then he told us some completely bat-shit crazy road stories about Van Halen, like the time a frenzied father showed up at their hotel with a roaring chainsaw looking for his daughter and David Lee Roth.

Now, we had all been playing bars and clubs for a few years. I never thought twice about what kind of trouble we could find. Hell, we were usually looking for it. But this felt different. Now, suddenly, we had to be . . . responsible? What the hell?

To a bunch of guys from the south, California might as well have been the moon. Nothing about the day felt normal or comfortable. It's so funny looking back, but Pete really freaked us out. We figured disaster was looming around every corner.

After the gig that night, as we loaded our gear into Junkyard's trailer, things started to feel normal again. There we were, hanging in a parking lot drinking beer, talking to some locals, and suddenly Anaheim felt an awful lot like Raleigh, or Athens, or any other town we'd already played a few times. Play a gig, drink beer, talk to folks—it's the same wherever you go.

Eventually, Kenny said it was time to head out. We started to pile in the van when Chris noticed Rich walking across the parking lot with a girl. We all watched in disbelief as he nonchalantly hopped into her Jeep and drove away.

This was exactly what Pete had told us not to do! And the one sober guy is the one who takes off with a stranger?

We started chasing after the Jeep and tried to wave Rich down. "Yo! What the fuck, dude?" But Rich and the girl were long gone.

We assumed the worst. She was gonna take him to a cult out in the desert and we'd never see him again. We were gonna be the band who played ONE FUCKING GIG and then our career ended because Rich wound up in some sort of Manson family situation.

Rich was gone for a half hour at most. They just drove around for a bit. When he got back we all let him have it. Chris was the most vocal, of course, but the rest of us weighed in as well. "Fuck you guys," Rich screamed. "I'm not going to sit around here just to watch you drink." Now, to be fair, Rich was angry because the rest of us were generally drunken idiots. But this time we had every right to be angry back at him. The argument devolved quickly into a series of insults, but it didn't take long to blow over. One tour day down, a few thousand more to go.

We went everywhere with Junkyard over those six weeks. Anaheim to Savannah, then up to Portland, Maine, and then back to Oakland. When Junkyard had a night off, we would play our own gig at an even smaller club. We did fifteen nights in a row at one point.

After the tour finished in Oakland, we went back to LA for a week of promotion. We shot the video for "Twice as Hard" and did countless interviews and photo shoots. After six weeks on the road, we were already a very different band. All we had ever really needed was steady work. Once we played night after night, the pieces fell into place very quickly.

We were still coming from a place of *this might not last long,* so we were playing every gig like it was our last. We were having a great time on the road, but the gigs themselves were all business. We wanted to be a great band right away. To our credit, we didn't fuck that part of it up. We'd been waiting three years for the chance to be a full-time touring band and we weren't going to squander it.

We then did another four-week national tour opening for McAuley-Schenker Group. A mismatched bill to be sure, but we would have toured with anybody. MSG was a very slick hair-metal band with poppy hooks over sampled vocals—in a word, it sucked. Their audience couldn't have cared less about us, and we couldn't have cared less about impressing them.

Robin McAuley, the singer, told us one day that they were about to confirm the summer leg of the Aerosmith tour. He was pretty excited about it, and said they'd lock it down when we played Boston. He was right about that, except he had one key element wrong. Aerosmith's management sent an emissary to offer the summer tour to The Black Crowes, not MSG. Holy shit! Open for Aerosmith? In arenas? We had done six weeks in clubs with Junkyard, a month in clubs with MSG, and now we were getting the summer leg of the Pump tour.

As excited as we were for Aerosmith, nothing compared to what was going to immediately precede those dates. In June, we went to England for the first time. As a lifelong Anglophile I couldn't have been more excited.

Chris and I were literally jumping for joy as we boarded the plane at LAX. Everyone was excited, but he and I were over the top with it. In a misguided gesture of solidarity, Pete flew in coach with us. He regretted it instantly.

As we entered the plane and turned right to find our seats, Pete turned left and walked into first class. "I've made a terrible mistake. I've booked myself in coach. If anyone wants to trade seats with me, I'll give you three thousand dollars in cash right now." Nobody moved.

He came back to his seat, directly in front of Chris and me, and conceded defeat. "What the fuck was I thinking riding coach with you animals to England?" We were dying. Pete was having a laugh, too, of course, but I had no doubt he would have paid out if someone had offered to switch with him.

Pete hated English cuisine. At LAX, he picked up personal pan pizzas from Pizza Hut for each of us. "I'm advising everyone to eat one of these," he said, "because it might be the last thing resembling food that you're going to see for two weeks."

On the plane, Chris and I were already running our schtick, cracking each other up, acting like idiots.

"I bet I'm going to meet some of The Beatles and Eric Idle will probably be there," I babbled excitedly.

As if we weren't already jacked up, we were drinking screwdrivers throughout the flight. In no time at all we were hammered.

"Guys, you really are gonna want to get some water in you," Pete warned. "It's a long flight. You're going to be dehydrated."

"Pete is jealous! He's afraid to drink a screwdriver! Pete is jealous!" we taunted. "Come on, Pete—if we were Van Halen, you'd get drunk with us!"

We were delirious with anticipation, acting loud and obnoxious for the whole flight. We were just going and going and going . . . and then we both passed out.

When we woke up, the plane was nearing London. Chris and I were covered in spitballs—Pete, sitting with Rich, had entertained himself on the flight by wadding up bits of napkins and shooting them through a straw at our heads. But we were both so hung over that we didn't give a fuck.

Once we got off the plane, we piled into a van for the one-hour drive to the hotel. Even though my head was pounding, I was euphoric. I never imagined I'd get to Europe, much less England, home of everything I thought was cool in the world.

Our hotel was in Knightsbridge, a very ritzy part of town, right around the corner from the famous luxury department store Harrods. We had always stayed at shitty motels because we were still broke. But the label in England already had a great buzz going for *Shake Your Money Maker*, so they put us up at a really nice place. A Holiday Inn would have been a real upgrade and this was like a fucking Four Seasons.

Pete took out a wad of cash and handed us each $500. "We're going to Kensington Market," he said. "They've got a lot of great rock 'n' roll shit over there. Whenever you're in London, you just load up on clothes, guys." He was like Willy Wonka, handing out candy to street kids.

Pete was right—the stuff they had at Kensington Market was way cooler than anything you'd find in the States. There was a huge international influence you just didn't get at home. We were all buying shirts and jackets, and everything was super cheap.

After a couple of days in London doing press, we flew to Amsterdam. Our first-ever show in Europe was at the Pinkpop Festival. We opened the first day of the festival with a 10:30 A.M. set to a tiny crowd. The next day we played the Paradiso. Apparently, the Dutch were also ahead of the Americans. Fans in the crowd were singing along. Not just "Jealous Again," but all of our songs. We couldn't believe it.

After the gig, we sat at the Bulldog Cafe smoking weed and hash for hours, like all the other stupid American tourists over there. I'd never been much of a stoner, but it was a blast. We stumbled back to our hotel very late that night and put on MTV Europe. The video for "Jealous Again" came on. A few minutes into the song, I said, "Is this like an extended dance mix or something? This video is twenty minutes long." I was so stoned I could barely get the words out.

Back to London for a quick UK tour. Our first gig was the Marquee Club, legendary for launching bands like The Rolling Stones, The Who, and The Yardbirds. Before the gig Pete said, "Fellas, the show sold out in minutes. Everybody in the English press that matters is here. The fans are ready, the stage is set, and you are going to kill it tonight, which will go a long way toward setting us up here for the next few years." We walked out onto the tiny stage and the place erupted. We'd never, ever played in front of an audience like that. We opened with "Thick n' Thin" and the roof blew off the joint. We walked into the dressing room afterward like conquering heroes. I don't know that any show, ever, felt quite like that again.

We played three or four more shows in the UK on our own, then went out and did a few nights opening for a band called The Dogs D'Amour. They were, in every way imaginable, hilarious to us, and not in a good way. All four of them dressed like Johnny Depp in the *Pirates of the Caribbean* movies. They could headline clubs around the UK and apparently that meant they were big time. Their attitude toward us was basically, *We'll show you Americans what it's all about.*

Our first show with them was at the Barrowlands in Glasgow. It's an old ballroom, with a sprung dance floor and great acoustics. It's ideal for rowdy rock 'n' roll crowds, and few cities are more rowdy than Glasgow.

The bass player for the Dogs walked into our dressing room before our set holding a bottle of Jack Daniels, just staring us down. He didn't say a word. After a few seconds, he took a long slug of Jack, glared at us some more, and walked out. We fell out laughing. If he was trying to impress or intimidate us, he picked the wrong band. We yelled at him down the hall, "Hey, little man! Walk into our dressing room again uninvited and you will NOT walk out! Come back and get your ass kicked anytime!"

We hit the stage that night ready to destroy anything in front of us. And that Glaswegian crowd? Holy shit, they went crazy. Not many bands would have wanted to follow us in a club at that moment in time, and the Dogs were most definitely not up to the task.

It was 1990, a new decade, and by God they still loved rock 'n' roll music in the UK.

We loved Aerosmith. Well, we loved *early* Aerosmith, the 1970s bad-boys Aerosmith. Unfortunately, *that* Aerosmith wasn't the band we toured with.

The Aerosmith tour simply sucked. For a million reasons, it was awful. Now, Steven Tyler was great to us. So were Tom Hamilton and Brad Whitford. But Joe Perry was a surly prick and Joey Kramer was just kinda weird. Beyond that, though, the whole setup was ridiculous. They were headlining arenas, sold out every night, and they paid us $500 a gig. We had to upgrade to a bus (no complaints about that), but we needed a full crew, too. You can't do arenas in a van and hump your own gear. But taking thousands of dollars each week in label support meant we were going into massive debt.

We went in there thinking, *This is going to be a fucking great time with a real rock 'n' roll rock band.* It was the exact opposite. The Aerosmith guys were newly, and quite aggressively, sober. The entire tour, therefore, was sober. Their whole crew, dozens of them, had signed agreements stating they wouldn't drink. Not even on days off! As for us, our alcohol had to stay on the bus.

It was just as bad onstage. Aerosmith used triggered backing vocals, so they were basically lip-syncing to their own record. Steven sang, but most of the backing vocals were not real. Like all those weird harmonies at the end of "Love in an Elevator," the guys would stand in a circle around Steven's mic and pretend to do it.

We were horrified. It was like we were in eighth grade and found out our favorite athlete did steroids. We were like, "Fuck them! They're the fucking biggest phonies!" Maybe it seems like a silly overreaction in hindsight, but we were obsessed with '70s Aerosmith and that entire vibe.

In 1990, Aerosmith was living out a media-friendly redemption story. They were the comeback kids, and nothing was going to make them slide back to their old, druggy, rock 'n' roll existence. They were all about living large, but in a straitlaced kind of way. Each of those guys had a security guard with him everywhere he went.

We would have been less hostile if Aerosmith had actually supported us in any way. But they undermined us, not just with the shitty pay, but also at the shows. The first night of the tour was our first-ever arena show. I don't remember if we even got a sound check. We just walked out cold, with no idea about how to play to that size of a crowd. We were terrible. We knew it, too.

That very night, Aerosmith's manager called Pete and said, "Hey, I gotta take your band off the tour. The crowd hated them. They can't even play." Apparently, Joe Perry was the one who pushed hardest to get us kicked off the tour. We had been told he was a fan of our album, and now he wanted to fire us after one day? He wanted to bring back Skid Row, a "real" band who knew how to put on a show.

"That's not going to happen," Pete said. "They've never played in an arena before. I'm coming out there tomorrow. I'm going to work with them. It's going to be fine."

Pete flew out for the next gig. He told us we had to get our shit together, and fast. We told him we would be fine to leave—fuck it, let's go back to clubs. Pete said, "No fucking way are we letting this band and their fucking manager kick us around. We're gonna get up to speed and blow their asses off the stage!

"Someone will videotape the show every day, and we'll watch it together," he instructed. "And then we'll fix the mistakes. You need to learn that it's a different way to work a crowd when you play the big rooms."

Pete wasn't even with us that long. It was only three days. But the change was like night and day, and most of it had to do with Chris. He took Pete's performance direction to heart.

"Make that stage yours," Pete told Chris. "You mark your fucking territory."

He impressed upon Chris the need in an arena to do everything big.

One thing Chris always had trouble with was when people didn't stand up or appear to be into what we were doing. It would get in his head and throw him off.

"Stop looking at the people that you think don't like you," Pete said. "Find the people that do like you and perform to them, point them out, even if they're in the last row. Make people remember what they saw and heard when The Black Crowes leave the stage."

Chris took to it like a fish in water. It started at the Spectrum in Philly.

"I'll tell you one thing about Philly, man—all you people in the back are cool, it's too bad you can't switch places with these contest winners in the front row," he screamed.

The people upstairs, the proletariat, fucking loved it. And the people up front were pissed! They were flipping us off and screaming, "You suck!" But finally there was some energy onstage. We could all feel it. From then on, every show was a challenge. Are we gonna win or are we gonna lose? We were determined to fucking win.

With our newfound sense of purpose, we weren't about to let Aerosmith psyche us out. I started walking around backstage every day with a Jack and coke. The crew guys could smell the whiskey but they wouldn't say anything. That little act of defiance felt like victory.

One night in Omaha, I decided to give the Aerosmith guys a pep talk in their dressing room. Actually, it was the dressing room for everybody but Steven, who had his own apart from the rest of the band.

I walked in and they were all getting ready for the gig, putting on their scarves and all that crap. Then, in unison, they turned to look at me like, *What the fuck is this guy doing in here?*

"Listen," I announced with mock seriousness. "This is a big one tonight. It's Omaha, and I know you guys are probably a little nervous. Think of it as a boxing match. We just jabbed the audience out there. And we jabbed, and jabbed, and jabbed. We set them up." I started shadowboxing, stepping up my trolling game. "They're on their back heel now. They're wobbly. All you have to do is land that big fucking Aerosmith uppercut and finish them off!"

They stared at me for a moment in bewildered silence.

"Get the fuck outta here!" Joe Perry finally snarled.

"No problem!" I replied, and walked out laughing, drink in hand. Fuck 'em if they can't take a joke.

8

Uncle Bob

Every month, we improved by leaps and bounds. Bands who play five nights a week in shitty clubs for years do all that when no one's looking. We had to do it in arenas.

But we did it.

Our next big tour was opening for another rock icon, Robert Plant. We all loved Led Zeppelin. Robert Plant was like a god to us. But after Aerosmith, we had no idea what to expect. When we flew out to Red Rocks Amphitheater outside of Denver to start the six-week run, we assumed he'd be a bit of a letdown.

We couldn't have been more wrong.

We met Robert for the first time moments before we walked on-stage. All of a sudden, our dressing room door flew open, and the "golden god" himself was before us.

"Good to see you guys made it!" he said. "Do you need anything? Just let us know! Can't wait to see you play! It'll be a great run! We're going to have some fun, eh?"

Whoa, is this really him?

"You made a really good record!" he continued. "I'm so excited to have you. I love real rock 'n' roll bands, but there's so few left anymore! I'm trying to get my guys to loosen up and be a real band, but they don't know how yet. But this is gonna be great!"

Two minutes in and Robert was treating us like long-lost friends. Hell, he'd already complained about his backing band to us!

None of us would have dared ask him to tell war stories from the Led Zeppelin days, even though we were all dying to hear them. I wasn't sure if Robert would even utter the words "Led Zeppelin" during our six-week tour. But, sure enough, almost immediately, Robert launched right in.

"Man, Red Rocks! This is fucking great!" he said. "We opened Zeppelin's first American tour in Denver in December of '68. Fuck, we didn't know what we were getting into, man! I was eighteen, and here I was flying to America! I just wanted to get to California, hear some music, see the Pacific, and chase some fucking birds!"

It was all too much. I almost couldn't take it. Robert Plant was just so . . . *cool.*

Every day of the tour was like that. Robert always came to check on us and hang out once we got to the venue. "What are you boys up to today?" he would ask. "There's a good Peruvian restaurant around the corner, if you like fish." He knew shit about every town we went to, a thrift store or a good used record shop worth checking out.

In Chicago, he took us to the Checkerboard Lounge, the historic blues club Buddy Guy originally ran. Sitting in a blues club in Chicago with Plant was mind-boggling. It was an older crowd in the house that night, and no one seemed to have any idea who he was. After a little while, the emcee for the night made an announcement: "Ladies and Gentlemen, we have a very special guest in the house tonight . . . a man you have all heard of . . . a man who came to America from England because he loved the blues . . . a man who brought the blues to the whole world . . . a living legend . . . ladies and gentlemen, put your hands together for Mr. Led Zeppelin! Where are you, Led? Stand up!"

We all fell out laughing, no one harder than Robert. He stood up and accepted the applause from the house. For the rest of the night, we called him "Led."

Robert was always up for a laugh. Like, you'd be in catering, eating dinner, and you'd notice your fork was gone. And you would look over at Robert and he would be holding two forks. The fact that this was *Robert Plant* taking your fork always added a layer of surrealism to the pranks. Why is Robert Plant, the guy who sang "Stairway to Heaven," fucking with me? What's funny is that Robert also appreciated that aspect of his persona. He exploited his larger-than-life stature all the time, usually in order to laugh at it.

Chris called him "Uncle Robert" once, and it stuck. By the end of the tour, it had been shortened to "Uncle Bob."

Robert often rented a car to drive to the next town by himself, stopping at every flea market or other notable spots along the way. Wherever he went, he wanted to see everything he could and learn. All of Plant's world-music, get-out-to-the-hinterlands, learn-as-much-as-you-can shit—it's not an act. It's a legitimate extension of the adventurous way he lives his life.

His band was a little synth-heavy—this was around the time Robert had a Top 40 pop hit with "Tall Cool One"—but at the same time we could see right away that when you've been in Led Zeppelin, you can't do anything like Led Zeppelin. His guitarist, Doug Boyle, was a great player, and he would talk about how he couldn't play a Les Paul onstage. "If you put on a Les Paul, you're just doing Jimmy," he said. It's like they were all always under *that* shadow.

About two weeks into the tour, we had a few days off, which struck me as odd. We were in Canada, and the Plant crew had decided to set up camp at this national park in Manitoba, so we followed them there. The park was mostly deserted, but there was still stuff to do, like horseback riding and golf. At night, we would grill out and drink around roaring bonfires. Robert's crew, most of whom had been with him for years at that point, were a great bunch of guys.

But still. Why were we camping on a mini-holiday when we should have been out working?

Later, I found out it was the tenth anniversary of John Bonham's death, and Robert wanted to be home for a few days to pay his respects.

As the tour progressed, we could see how we were starting to matter on the bill in ways we didn't matter with Aerosmith. People were coming to see *us*.

If the Aerosmith tour was a trial by fire, the Robert Plant tour was the party we always hoped these big-time rock shows could be. The only thought we'd ever had finishing a tour up to this point was, *Great, what's next?* But now I was genuinely sad. Hell, we all were. We were gonna miss Uncle Bob. We loved him.

By the time the Robert Plant tour ended, our onstage communication skills were sharp. Conversely, our communication skills offstage were getting trickier. Chris was quickly becoming famous. Really famous. The rest of the band could go anywhere, but Chris had lost that freedom within eight months of the album release. It was a classic case of a guy doing everything he could to get noticed, and then suddenly feeling boxed in by the notoriety. He was fraying around the edges. We saw his mood swings blowing back and forth, way beyond what they'd ever been before.

We all tried at various times to talk to him about it. There was genuine concern. And yet, with every passing week, he was blowing up more and more.

As the singer, Chris was also doing the lion's share of interviews. His anger was no longer something we just dealt with on the bus or in the dressing room. It was coming out, publicly, in all directions.

Around the end of the Plant tour, Chris did an interview where he called out Aerosmith for using backing tracks onstage for "Love in an Elevator." It got a lot of attention. We didn't mind, because we were all still very much in the camp of "fuck those guys."

But then Chris also ripped into a shitload of other bands, even Robert Plant.

Chris was always a walking contradiction. On a good day, he could give the most charming and funny interview you've ever heard. I mean, *really* funny. But then, without warning, Chris could turn into a flaming asshole. And, unfortunately, the times when Chris was a jerk during an interview got noticed a lot more than the times he was hilarious.

"Listen, you're a great interview," Pete told Chris in the dressing room one night. "But you've got to stop talking shit about other artists. You're not there to talk about other bands. You're there to talk about The Black Crowes. There's no purpose served by you alienating the fan bases of other bands. People like your music. You don't have the right to turn around and insult the rest of their fucking record collection."

Chris just shrugged. "Why is this on me? Everybody else in the band says this shit all the time, too!"

"I don't give a fuck what you guys say to each other. But if you spew some negative shit to a journalist or a DJ, it's gonna become a story."

We didn't need to tear someone else down to build ourselves up now. The game had changed. But Chris refused to change with it.

9

When the Student is Ready, the Teacher Will Appear

We did the MTV New Year's Eve show in 1990, with Vanilla Ice, Wilson Phillips, and Cinderella. The show wasn't live, though. We taped it December 10 and it aired three weeks later. When I walked onto the stage for sound check that day, Vanilla Ice was sitting on the drum riser. He was the single biggest thing in pop music right then. He was wearing those crazy-ass pants, he had the ridiculous hair, the whole getup.

As I approached, he looked up at me.

"Get away from those drums, dude! What the fuck are you doing up here?" I said, scowling.

"Oh, sorry, dude, it's cool!" he squealed, and ran off to the backstage area.

I started to say "man, I'm just fucking with you" but I stopped myself. It was funny to see him run off like that, actually. Plus, I couldn't stand that he had ripped off Queen for his big hit. So yeah, fuck off, dude.

On the show we played two songs, "Jealous Again" and "Hard to Handle," which hit a new peak on the pop charts that month, landing at number forty-five. Rock radio had embraced us from the start, and now the more rarified, mainstream pop world was kicking the tires on The Black Crowes. So, while we didn't fit with Wilson Phillips and Vanilla Ice either stylistically or musically, we actually, *weirdly*, did fit in as far as how popular we were becoming.

We played our two songs dutifully, but it was clear one of us hadn't pulled his weight: Jeff. He butchered the guitar solo on "Hard to Handle." Now, everyone hit bad notes or dropped a beat now and again. But this was really bad. And even though the show wasn't live, we didn't get a chance to redo the song.

When the show aired on New Year's Eve, we had all gathered to watch it together at our friend Mac Dorton's apartment. We were in a celebratory mood. It had been one hell of a year. When "Hard to Handle" came on, though, the mood evaporated. It was worse than we remembered.

"Fuck, man, I'm sorry, guys," Jeff said sheepishly.

Jeff was always a solid, working-man's rock 'n' roll guitarist. He was absolutely good enough for The Black Crowes in 1990, but heading into the new year we were evolving at a rapid pace. Some of the songs that would appear on our next record were already in the works, like "Thorn in My Pride" and a tune called "Words You Throw Away," which ultimately turned into "Remedy." The new stuff was way more involved and more musical than the songs on *Shake Your Money Maker*.

There was no conscious thought of replacing Jeff as we watched the show that night. But looking back, a seed had clearly been planted.

We always wanted a keyboard player on tour, but throughout 1990 we didn't have the means to pay another musician. The five of us were equal partners in the band, and understood we weren't gonna see much, if any, money for a while. Hiring someone to play keys was only going to further reduce our revenue. By the end of the year, though, with the record almost platinum and all signs pointing toward continued growth, we could finally bring someone on board.

The keyboard parts on *Shake Your Money Maker* were played by Chuck Leavell, an absolute god of southern rock, who had played with The Allman Brothers for a few years during the band's highly successful post–Duane Allman *Brothers and Sisters* period. In the early 1980s, he landed a gig with The Rolling Stones, playing alongside the band's longtime piano player Ian Stewart. When Ian died in 1985, Chuck became the sole keyboardist, and he's been an integral part of every Stones tour and album ever since. When he recorded his tracks for

Shake Your Money Maker in 1989, he was preparing for the Steel Wheels tour. Oh, and when Chuck wasn't touring with The Stones, he worked as Eric Clapton's musical director.

In other words, there was no fucking way Chuck Leavell was going to join our band.

He did, however, sit in with us for our final three gigs of 1990, at Center Stage in Atlanta, and it was amazing. We all knew after the first night that we HAD to get a regular keyboard player for the band.

Chris asked Chuck, "Who do you know out there that can make us forget about you?"

Chuck laughed and immediately suggested a Canadian dude who lived in Detroit named Eddie Harsch. Chuck didn't mention Eddie was a musical genius—we would soon figure that out ourselves—but anyone Chuck recommended was probably gonna be good enough for us.

I was, at twenty-five, the oldest member of The Black Crowes, and Eddie had me by ten years. In musical years, though, Eddie was already a senior citizen. While the rest of us were growing up in the '80s inspired by post-punk, new wave, and indie bands, Eddie was touring with blues legends Albert Collins and James Cotton.

We flew him down for the last night of the tour. He was six foot five and weighed 150 pounds, tops. He had a mullet haircut and was wearing a bright, multicolored blazer. And yet his voice resonated as deeply as James Earl Jones's. He was a complete freak. We loved him instantly.

Musically, Eddie was a fucking wizard who immediately raised the bar for musicianship in The Black Crowes. Every day with Eddie was an education. We had collectively become a formidable rock 'n' roll band, but now there was a realization that everyone needed to get much better. We instinctively focused more, and worked harder, on our individual abilities.

Ed raised the bar in other ways, too. At the beginning of 1991, we were still very much a drinking band. Everyone (excluding Rich) smoked pot casually, but only Chris had established pot as a part of his everyday life.

When Ed joined, well, he made doing drugs seem like a lot of fun. For starters, he could make a bong out of anything: a plastic cup, a power strip, a television set, *anything*. It was like a parlor trick. Just give him a block of hash, some kite string, and a Game Boy and before you knew it you were high as a fucking kite.

Up until this point, there were nightly blowups on the bus whenever the last man standing with Chris would decide to crash. He was always frustrated that no one could, or wanted to, keep up with him. With Ed around, Chris always had someone with whom to get high and keep the party rolling. There was a sudden uptick in drug usage for The Black Crowes, and once that ship sailed, it never really came back to shore.

That was not Ed's fault. He was never the kind of guy to pressure someone else. We all made our own choices. It was an inevitability that drugs would play a large part in the band's story. What Ed did, unintentionally, was open a door that would have eventually opened without him. Unfortunately, when everyone else ran through that door, they didn't bring Ed's charm, warmth, and empathy along with them. They just brought the darkness.

10

Welcome Home. You're Fired.

Our first tour with Ed, in January of 1991, was yet another high-pro-file arena tour, this time supporting ZZ Top. By the time the tour ended—or, I should say, by the time the tour ended for *us*, because ZZ Top fired The Black Crowes before the tour actually ended—we would be much bigger and Chris would be far more famous than ever.

The first gig was January 4 in New Orleans. We walked into the arena that afternoon and ZZ Top was onstage, sound checking, which as it turned out was the only one they did the whole tour. They were playing some straight-up blues, and Billy Gibbons was just killing it.

During the shows, Billy and Dusty Hill played those fuzzy white guitars from the ZZ Top music videos, and they stuck with their synth-oriented hits from the 1980s, all that "Sharp Dressed Man" and "Gimme All Your Lovin'" shit. They didn't do any blues or anything remotely like that. ZZ Top wasn't the powerful roadhouse band you hear on their classic '70s records. They were a big-time arena rock act: they had conveyor belts onstage and dancing girls everywhere. But people loved it. The tour was massive.

When sound check ended, Billy and Dusty walked out into the arena where we were still sitting.

"Hey, you guys must be The Black Crowes. Good to meet you," Billy said.

"Hey, man, fucking sounds great, good to see you!" we said back.

Dusty looked us up and down without shaking our hands. "Hey, you got a good little record there," he said. "Man, that's some good rock 'n' roll music."

"Thanks man!"

"Well, y'all have a good tour," Dusty said, kinda deadpan. With that, he turned and walked off.

Johnny said, "How funny would it be if we literally never saw him again?"

Well, as it turned out, we never *did* see him or Billy again. Not once. Frank Beard, the drummer, came by a few nights later to say hello, and then we never saw him again, either.

Early in the tour, Chris did an interview with a grocery store magazine—*People* or *Entertainment Weekly* or something like that—and he made an off-hand comment about beer. Something like, "On the road, as long as I got a twelve-pack of beer and this and that, I'm fine."

"You obviously drink light beer," the reporter replied, because Chris was so skinny.

"Man, light beer sucks. I don't drink that shit," Chris shot back.

When the article came out, the reporter spelled *light* beer as "L-i-t-e," referring to a specific brand of beer that happened to be a sponsor of the ZZ Top tour. If the writer had just spelled it "l-i-g-h-t," which was what Chris meant, nobody would've cared. But because it was *Lite* beer, ZZ Top's people freaked out.

At the next gig, their tour manager confronted Chris directly.

"Hey, man, you need to keep your mouth shut about our sponsor."

"Who the fuck do you think you're talking to?" Chris spat back.

"You don't go to the media and say, 'Lite beer sucks.'"

Chris honestly didn't know what he was talking about. "When the fuck did I ever say anything about Lite beer? It does suck but I didn't say it," he said, his voice rising with anger. "You want to get a message to me? Talk to my tour manager, motherfucker. I don't talk to you. Get the fuck out of here."

"Who do you think you're talking to, punk? I'll tell you this—"

"You're going to fucking limp out of this room, motherfucker," Chris exploded. "Take your sorry old ass out and go talk to my tour manager."

Chris was still funny, even when he was threatening someone twice his age who could probably choke him out in ten seconds.

So their tour manager talked to our tour manager, and then ZZ Top's manager called Pete. All of a sudden, "The Black Crowes don't like corporate sponsorship" became a storyline that would soon take over the tour.

That very night, before our last song, Chris grabbed the mic and poured some gasoline on our simmering feud with the ZZ Top camp. "I don't care what it says on your ticket stub—The Black Crowes are brought to you by The Black Crowes," he hollered. "Nobody sponsors us. Have a great night!"

As soon as we walked offstage, ZZ Top's guy came running over. "Don't you ever fucking do that again," he seethed.

"I'll say whatever the fuck I want," Chris sneered back.

"Not if you want to finish this tour, you won't," he yelled as Chris walked away.

That night, Pete got a heated call from ZZ Top's manager. The situation had escalated dramatically, which Pete saw as a possibly advantageous opportunity for the band. So he decided not to interfere with Chris's rants for the time being.

Chris went after ZZ Top and Miller Lite again the next night. "This is sponsor-free, commercial-free rock 'n' roll! We don't need a fucking beer company to tell us what to listen to!"

Now, the actual guys *in* ZZ Top—Billy, Dusty, and Frank—I don't think they knew what was happening. I truly believe they could not have cared less. Their production people and Miller Lite—that's who we were really shitting on. For them it was a big deal, because Miller Lite had put a ton of money into the tour.

But for us, Chris's nightly rants served a few purposes. In the moment, the crowds always ate it up. In our dressing room afterward, it became a rallying point as we were starting to wear down from our workload.

"I'm sick of fucking opening anyway," Chris started saying regularly. "I'm ready to headline. Fuck this shit. Tell them to fire us." Sounded good to us. Pete was on board, too. He had already considered that getting fired could be used to our advantage, but only if we *strategically engineered* getting fired.

"Guys, we can make this work but it's all about timing. So for now, let me put a few things in play and let's agree that you don't say anything else until the time is right."

The record was exploding. The first million copies sold in eleven months. The second million copies sold in one month. And the third million in the month after that. By the time we were plotting our evacuation from ZZ Top, we were the hottest young band in America.

Pete was handling another piece of band business that depended on proper timing: we suddenly had a possible way out of our record deal with Rick Rubin. Our contract gave Def American the option of putting out our second record, a no-brainer now that our debut was a hit. But because Def American employed a skeleton crew staff, they missed the deadline for enforcing the second-record option, which made us free agents and required Rubin to renegotiate if he wanted to keep working with The Black Crowes.

But, as of now, Pete was the only person who had noticed Rubin's fuckup.

"When I inform Rick that we are renegotiating, we want to be at our strongest," he said. "We want all the leverage we can get. So, for now, we don't get fired."

Chris kept his mouth shut and we finished the first leg of the tour without incident in early March. The second leg would soon bring us back home to Atlanta for a three-night stand at the Omni. Sixteen months after we first met Pete, after we played a free show and only twelve people showed up, we were playing our hometown arena for three nights on the biggest tour of the year. That felt pretty fucking good, I gotta say.

A week before Atlanta, Pete told Chris it was time to start ranting again. In Richmond, Virginia, Chris announced to the audience, "Hey, thanks for coming down early to see us! We hope you enjoyed your commercial-free music! We now return you to the commercially sponsored portion of your night!"

Then both ZZ's manager and the promoter immediately called Pete at home and told him in no uncertain terms that if Chris said one more word about Miller Lite, or any beer or corporate sponsorship, The Black Crowes were going to be thrown off the tour.

Pete called Chris and asked him to not say another word until the second show in Atlanta on Monday night, which was only days away. Not a word, and then let 'er rip.

Pete had arranged for Rolling Stone to send its star critic, David Fricke, to Atlanta to write a profile. Also on Monday night, Chris and Rich were scheduled to appear on Rockline, a syndicated radio show broadcast throughout the United States and Canada. Plus, MTV turned up to cover our big hometown shows, along with every local news affiliate. Oh, and two weeks prior, we had played Saturday Night Live for the first time. So, suffice to say, we had plenty of attention now.

The Sunday show went off without a hitch, as planned. Monday was D-day.

"To be home in Atlanta, it means the world to us. We've all dreamed about playing The Omni," Chris said at the end of our set. "I've never been prouder to be a part of a commercial-free enterprise. This music that we write is for us and it's for you, not a fucking beer company. They shouldn't tell you what to do. That's not freedom. That's oppression. Fuck these corporate motherfuckers!"

The crowd went apeshit as we walked off the stage. They loved seeing a young rock 'n' roll band actually rebel a little, instead of obediently going along with the status quo like everybody else.

"You're fucking fired," ZZ Top's tour manager announced as we walked off the stage.

"You're goddamned right we are," Chris replied.

With that, he and Rich were on their way to Rockline. Pete called to remind them to make damned sure the entire world knew what had happened.

The story blew up, unquestionably giving us the most press we would ever receive. Two months later, David Fricke's article had been upgraded considerably, from a one-page feature to the cover of Rolling Stone. The headline read "What's So Bad About The Black Crowes?"

Well, David, time would surely tell.

11

The Exhaustion of Success

Everything fell into place in the spring of 1991. A solid year of busting our asses turned into what looked to the general public a lot like an overnight success story. There were nights with ZZ Top where we outsold them at the merch stand. The opening act, playing for forty-five minutes, outselling the long-established headliners? That *never* happens.

Chris had become the opposition voice to corporate involvement in rock tours. Just as calling out Aerosmith and Robert Plant didn't come back to haunt us, amazingly neither did pissing on ZZ Top.

There was one very real problem with all of this, however. Chris Robinson would never again think twice about saying anything to anyone, at any time. He felt bulletproof.

As all of this was swirling, Pete went back to Rick Rubin to renegotiate our contract. Rick was not at all pleased to hear we were suddenly free agents. *Shake Your Money Maker* was Def American's first major success, and he was printing money off of us. And not just on album sales: he had a substantial share of Chris's and Rich's publishing as well as half of our merchandise.

We were his golden goose, as they say, and yet he still managed to leave the farm gate open.

Pete went to other labels and pitched us. What would you give for The Black Crowes *right now*? The offers were insane. Pete took the best offer back to Rick and said, "Either you match these terms, or we're gone." Rick had no choice but to agree.

Then Pete dropped a bomb on him. The new terms had to be retroactive to include *Shake Your Money Maker*, too. Rick wasn't about to be the guy who let the biggest new band since Guns N' Roses walk away scot-free, so he signed off on it.

The Robinsons got all their publishing back, the band got all its merchandise back, and the royalty rate per record sold jumped up considerably. It was a tremendous win for all of us.

Like I said, everything fell into place. And then, just as quickly, one piece of the puzzle fell out of place.

Geffen Records suddenly severed all ties to Rick Rubin and Def American. Rick had released albums by Andrew "Dice" Clay and the Geto Boys, both of whom were incredibly controversial. David Geffen wanted no part of either act, so suddenly Rick Rubin needed a new parent label to distribute his records.

By the time we released our follow-up to *Shake Your Money Maker* a year later, the dust had settled and we were working specifically with Reprise Records, a subsidiary of Warner Bros. founded in 1960 by Frank Sinatra. Despite our success, it was clear from the jump that things weren't quite copacetic at our new home. The top execs at Reprise never saw us as *their* band. Or maybe one of the execs at Reprise was just pissed off about the time Chris walked into his office, put his feet up on the guy's desk, and lit up a giant joint.

Whatever the reason, Reprise never seemed to be fully on board. *The Southern Harmony and Musical Companion* debuted at number one, and we still couldn't get top guys at the company to focus on us. We still did really well in the United States, where we had established a large core audience, great relationships with promoters, and a ridiculously successful track record at radio. Internationally, however, the story was quite different.

Pete spent the rest of the decade fighting all kinds of issues, from label disinterest to an overall lack of cohesion in promotion. Initially, we'd had great success in Europe in the fall of 1991, but over the next few years it seemed like every territory was devising their own marketing and promotion plans on the fly. The single played in Italy might not be the same as in France or Germany. And if they did agree on the single, the scheduled releases weren't coordinated. Who was making all these decisions? It sure wasn't us.

We started our first theater tour at the end of April. Six weeks of shows, and every one of them was sold out. The day before the tour opened in Macon, Georgia, we all got together in Atlanta to go over some pending details. We were going to be in Europe for the second half of the year, and there were a million opportunities and routing options to consider.

Pete started off the meeting with a laugh, saying, "Well, guys, good news! Bud Light has offered to sponsor our tour!"

We all laughed. But then Pete said he had actually received a phone call from someone at Bud Light. They had offered to back our tour for a million dollars.

Pete said, "Can you believe these fucking guys?"

After a moment or two, Chris said, "How much would that be per person?"

Pete laughed. "Oh, so we're gonna take some Budweiser money now?" He assumed it was a joke.

"No, seriously, how much?" Chris said. "I mean, that's a lot of money, right?"

We were all thinking the same thing. *Do you have any idea what it would do to us, credibility-wise, if we signed a deal like this? What the fuck are you smoking?!?*

"Chris," Pete began, "it's *inconceivable* to me that you would consider taking money from Budweiser. That would be EXACTLY what ZZ Top did with Miller Lite! You would be doing the exact same thing you just spent three months decrying and attacking!"

Chris immediately got defensive. "I was pissed off because some fucking corporate prick thought he could tell me what I could or couldn't say."

Pete said, exasperated, "That's it? All of that was just because someone thought they could tell you what you couldn't say?"

"Yeah, fuck those dudes," Chris said curtly.

The rest of us, even Rich, looked at each other and came to accept in that moment something that was no longer avoidable—we had a madman at the helm.

We killed it every night of that theater tour. At the Beale Street Music Festival in Memphis, we ran into Warren Haynes, the guitarist in The

Allman Brothers Band. We asked him if he wanted to sit in, and maybe we'd play "Dreams." Warren said sure, and asked if we wanted to have Gregg Allman sit in as well. *Holy shit.*

Two hours later, we played "Dreams" for the first time live, in front of forty thousand people with Gregg Allman playing organ and singing.

Only Rich wasn't that psyched about it.

"It just didn't feel all that amazing when it was happening," he complained. "I mean, I thought I was gonna be really excited but, I don't know . . . it was just another song."

There it was: our dark cloud of the day.

We were young, successful, and playing fucking great. To me, every day should have been a good day. What was the problem? Why couldn't we just allow ourselves to feel good about all we were accomplishing?

I figured Chris and Rich didn't know how to handle success because they'd never succeeded before. By their own accounts, they had been lousy students, subpar athletes, and generally thought of as trouble-makers throughout their school years. They were incapable of feeling truly satisfied. That kind of behavior was all on display from the min-ute I met them. It's not like they had been different before we were successful. But, as a local band, there were times we would go days without seeing each other and the tensions would have a chance to dissipate. Now we were rarely, if ever, apart, and the walls were clos-ing in on us all.

And, of course, they were still fighting with each other, too. Every day. *That* never slowed down.

Anything could turn into an argument, and whatever we were working on got thrown out the window while they raged. For the rest of us, it was bullshit. It's unimaginable that Johnny and I would have forced a sound check to end early because of an argument. A breach of professionalism was inexcusable coming from anybody else in the band. But the brothers were clearly and flagrantly operating under a different set of rules than the rest of us. And they were blind to the damage it was doing to the entire process.

One day in Omaha, after they had a blowup at sound check, I told Rich, "Take that folding chair and hit Chris in the fucking face as hard as you can. Send him to the hospital. I swear to God, he'll never touch you again."

I was dead serious.

Rich said, "I can't do that."

I got in his face. "You're going to just sit here and take his shit and then complain to the rest of us until you die, otherwise. You have to end this. He will NEVER back off unless you show him that you're not his little brother anymore."

"You never did that to your brothers," he said.

"I kicked my brother Dave in the nuts one time with everything I had. I dropped him right in the fucking hallway. And he was twice my size then. You have thirty fucking pounds on Chris. I'm not saying it will end this bullshit, but at least you'll give him something to think about."

But Rich had lived his entire life in Chris's shadow. He wasn't happy there, but he couldn't imagine anything else.

At the Aragon Ballroom in Chicago that spring, Marc Ford sat in with The Black Crowes for the first time. Marc's band, Burning Tree, had opened for us in December of 1990 on our first headlining tour in clubs. Burning Tree was a power trio in the mold of Cream or The Jimi Hendrix Experience, so the band was essentially built as a showcase for Marc's playing.

Marc was a great player. Hell, we all knew that the first time we heard the Burning Tree record a year earlier. But when he sat in with us I was surprised by how much it clicked. There was a definite "oh shit, that was amazing" buzz. We all felt it. Ed had already raised everyone's game, and Marc hopping onstage with us compounded the shift.

In Milwaukee, Marc took the solo on "Dreams" during the encore. It was jaw dropping. He was a fucking beast. Having Marc playing with us was like being on a high school football team and then seeing Tom Brady step into the huddle. But that's as far as it went with Marc at the time. For now, anyway, Jeff was still our guy. Soon, Marc flew home and we continued down the road.

The shows were all stomping, but there was no denying we were exhausted. For the first time in a year and a half, there were some nights where we'd walk offstage and I'd go straight to my bunk on the bus.

The US tour for *Shake Your Money Maker* officially ended a month later with two sold-out shows at the Greek Theatre in Los Angeles. The next night, we did a surprise gig at The Roxy on Sunset Boulevard. It was an incredible few nights to cap off a sixteen-month run.

We were off to London the next day. We were going to be on tour in Europe, Japan, and Australia from August 1 until Thanksgiving, and this quick trip in June was for promotion ahead of that tour. The plan was to be in London, Paris, and Amsterdam for about ten days, then head home for the entire month of July. All five of us had already booked vacations.

On our third night in town, we were at a dinner with about twenty people from the record label and a handful of journalists. In the middle of the meal, Chris collapsed. I saw it happen across the table—he stood up abruptly, turned gray, and fell over like a tree. He had completely worn down from exhaustion. I'd never seen anything like it. That boy was toast.

Our tour manager, Mark Botting, picked him up like a sack of potatoes to load him into a taxi back to the hotel. We all followed a short time later, and although we were all concerned about Chris, the rest of us continued on with a big drink-up at the hotel bar with the label folks.

The next morning, a knock at my door woke me up. I opened it to find Chris. "I'm going home, man," he said. "I'm fucking dead."

"Does anyone know you're leaving?" I sincerely thought he was going AWOL.

"Yeah, Rich is going with me, and I think the rest of you are flying out tomorrow. Botting is figuring it all out."

Chris looked shattered. He started crying.

"I'm really sorry, man," he said.

"Dude, it's okay. Go rest. Just take care of yourself."

By the summer of 1991, Jeff was having a pretty hard time with the band. The negativity and the constant tension really bummed him out.

As our European tour rolled on that summer and fall, Jeff kept to himself more and more. He started drinking more than normal, and a few times he turned into an angry drunk. It was hard to see—that just wasn't Jeff, at all. He is a great fucking guy, but he was very unhappy, and we were not a group you could be unhappy around. If you showed vulnerability, you'd get eaten alive.

Ultimately, Jeff had less tolerance for dysfunction than the rest of us. He had a better sense of himself, and was smart enough to ask himself, *What the fuck am I doing this for, anyway?*

The rest of us didn't know enough to simply say to Jeff, "Hey, dude, what's up?" We were in our early twenties. How would it have occurred to us to do that?

The biggest difference between Jeff and the rest of us was that the misery of being in The Black Crowes was still worth it to us. We didn't care about anything except the band. So now, at the precipice of worldwide glory, we're all miserable and it's not any fun?

Well, too bad. Buy the ticket, take the ride.

12

The End of
Shake Your Money Maker

We left Atlanta on August 1, 1991, for the longest leg of the Shake Your Money Maker tour. Seventeen months down, four more to go.

We had a whole lot of everything on that leg: festival dates, club dates, theater dates, and most notably we were the opening act on the Monsters of Rock tour with AC/DC, Metallica, Mötley Crüe, and Queensrÿche.

AC/DC was a band we all respected deeply. Every show on that tour, we hung out with them. They loved our record, and we found an immediate kinship with them. They were heroes to us and their friendship was validation. We loved every minute we spent with them.

Metallica? Not so much. Nothing against Metallica. They were totally cool to us, but we just weren't Metallica fans. None of us were into metal, really, on any level. So while we got on with them, it didn't mean much beyond that. The guys from Mötley Crüe were great, too—really friendly and super complimentary. So was Queensrÿche, as it turns out.

I was sitting backstage at one of the gigs with Pete and I said, "Man, these bands are all so cool."

"Do you think they're all saying that about The Black Crowes?" Pete asked.

We both burst out laughing. No, they most certainly were not.

It's not like we were starting fights with these other bands. We weren't calling them names, or throwing beer bottles at them. But we just had this *thing*, this air about us. A punk, indie, or whatever you wanna call it, *thing*. We'd never really felt like part of the local scene in Atlanta, and now that we were flying high in a much thinner atmosphere, nothing had changed. We just couldn't relax and take things as they came. By nature, we drew up battle lines, and there were far more of our peers on the other side of those lines than on ours.

Ross Halfin, for one, always called us out on it. The legendary rock photographer, a good friend to us throughout our entire career, was blunt: "You don't like Metallica because they have a plane! You don't like Mötley Crüe because they actually have fun! You all think you're better than these other bands, but you're not! You're just different. That's all you are. There's always one band that are assholes to the other bands. Don't be that band!"

The Monsters of Rock dates put us out in front of huge audiences, but we didn't love the experience. We felt out of place on the bill. Not that we actually tried to fit in. If a crowd didn't dig us, we played slower. We played "Dreams" one night for eighty thousand angry white-boy metalheads screaming, "Faster! Faster! Faster!"

After touring for so long, we would do just about anything to shake up the monotony.

In Frankfurt, Johnny befriended a motorcycle club called the Black Devils. They were the real, honest-to-God, Hells Angels of Germany. Just a bunch of badass motherfuckers. These guys were, among other things, drug dealers who carried bricks of cocaine with them wherever they went.

I walked over to Johnny's room, on my way up from the hotel bar, and two of these maniacs were crashing on his floor.

"What the fuck's going on, man?" I said.

"They're cool," Johnny replied.

Sure enough, I spoke with them and we did have a really fine conversation. I can't remember their names, but I do recall one of them having a really big-ass knife.

"Are you sure these guys aren't going to fucking stab you in your sleep and take your kidney or something?"

"No, man, they're great," Johnny said, laughing.

I walked into his bathroom and saw his electric clippers. He had very inventive facial hair, so he always kept it tight. My hair was really long by then, almost halfway down my back.

"Man, I shaved my head in 1986. It felt great," I said. "I think it's time for a fresh start."

Johnny laughed. "Don't shave your head, dude. Seriously."

But it was already too late. I took the clippers, removed the length guard, and shaved forward to back. A straight line, like a landing strip. A reverse mohawk.

"You've got to finish it, man," I said. We both burst out laughing.

"Well, okay, but let's leave it long in the back," Johnny said, taking the clippers.

He got right to work, shaving my head so I was bald on top and long in the back, like a character out of a *Mad Max* movie. To me, it felt like when The Replacements shaved their eyebrows.

It was essentially a reaction to the fact we were turning into rock stars. It's fine to be rock stars. I expected Chris to act like a rock star onstage, and even backstage if we were around fans. But when it's just us in a dressing room, dude, you're still that guy who used to sleep on my floor. Don't act like an insufferable rock 'n' roll dickhead around us, because we all knew you when.

I felt us all turning into actors playing a cliché. I didn't like it. Shaving my head, as stupid as it sounds, and as stupid as I looked, helped to keep me sane.

We were three weeks into the European tour when we called Pete and said, "We can't do this."

"Guys, it's simple. Maybe try a little less drinking, maybe slow down with the drugs, get some sleep, and fucking pace yourselves," he said, for the millionth time.

But we weren't having it. The European dates wrapped up in late October, and then we were scheduled to hit Japan, Australia, and New Zealand for a month. As much as we wanted to see those countries, we couldn't imagine doing another four weeks.

"*You cannot cancel*," Pete insisted. "We have to hit these territories on the first album cycle." It was a good, if ultimately losing, argument.

We were constantly at each other's throats by then, and I think more than anything, Pete recognized maintaining band unity meant more in the big picture than the lost touring opportunity. So he relented and killed the dates.

Knowing we would now go home after October should have made the rest of the tour easier. But that conversation really impacted the last month of the tour because we had all cried "uncle!" and then we hated ourselves for it. Naturally, we took it out on each other . . . and sometimes our own fans.

At a show in Oxford, Chris laid into the audience for being unresponsive. "Hey, wake up! We are HERE right NOW! Tomorrow you'll be back at work and you'll wonder why you just sat there instead of shaking your asses and having a good time!"

After the gig, Chris and I were in the dressing room with a couple of music journalists who had come up from London. Chris was jabbering on, occasionally interrupting himself to wail on a harmonica for a few seconds.

Then these two dudes walked in, punters from the crowd who had somehow eluded security. One of them walked right up to Chris and stuck a finger in his face. "Look, mate, next time you play a gig on a Sunday night in a venue where they don't serve alcohol, don't take it out on the fucking crowd!"

There was a pregnant pause as the room filled with tension.

Chris said, casually, "Oh yeah? Well look at this!" Then he tossed his harmonica into the air. As the dude's eyes tracked the harp's arc, Chris punched him square in the mouth with everything he had.

It was incredible.

The dude reeled back and Chris went after him, wrapping him up in a headlock and charging toward the hallway. I grabbed his buddy, who was frozen in shock, and ran him out to the hallway, too. The four of us were a whirling dervish of punches and kicks, all screaming at the top of our lungs. It was a full-on rumble.

Johnny heard the commotion and came flying in from another room. Now there were five of us in the scrum. We all maneuvered into the stairwell somehow, went down one landing, and found ourselves at a dead end. There was nothing to do but fight it out until someone dropped. The backstage security guys were suddenly alert and chased after us. They didn't know who was who—we always refused to wear our passes backstage. They just saw five guys having a donnybrook, and moved in to break it up. I noticed a giant red-haired dude who looked like a rugby player ball up his fist and throw a punch. It missed its target, one of those fans, and caught me right in the jaw.

"Motherfucker! I'M IN THE BAND!" I screamed. The other security guard pulled down a fire extinguisher and held it over his head, screaming, "That's enough! Stop it right now! I'll fucking kill someone with this thing!"

We all suddenly stopped.

"These two fucking assholes came in the dressing room," Chris screamed. "Where were you then, you stupid cocksuckers?"

Three more security guards showed up. They grabbed the two punters and took them away. We walked back to the dressing room. The writers from London were just staring at us. One of them said, "That was the most amazing thing I've ever seen!"

Turns out it was just a warm-up.

The next round was a couple of weeks later, in Edinburgh.

Early in the set, we noticed a local band in the third row. We could always spot those dudes. They would be decked out in their finest stage gear: scarves, hats, leather vests, the whole nine yards. It always cracked us up.

Chris came back to me at the kit between songs. He said, "I bet they can't play for shit but that one dude has a cool hat. I might take it from him." We both laughed and it was on to the next tune.

At one point, the dude with the cool hat threw a coin at Chris, hitting him in the chest. He didn't even try to hide what he was doing. Chris looked down at him and said into the mic, "Motherfucker, you throw something at me again and we're gonna get to know each other."

The crowd ate it up. They loved moments like this. A few songs later, another coin flew onstage. This one missed Chris, but still, the hat dude wasn't backing down.

During the last song of the set, I could see the hat dude lining up to throw another coin. Chris had his eyes closed, front of the stage, holding out a long, wailing note. Uh-oh.

The kid threw it and it drilled Chris dead center in his chest once again. And this time it was a pound coin. Those fucking things are thick and heavy.

Chris turned his back to the crowd and stormed over to the front of my drum kit. He was fucking furious. He looked at me, shaking his head, calculating what to do. There was a quick guitar break, so I wasn't actually playing. "Go ahead, man, I got your back," I said, smiling.

Chris didn't hesitate. As soon as the words were out of my mouth, he spun and started running.

Holy shit, he's going in!

I threw down my sticks and jumped up to chase after him. As I rounded the kit, Chris went airborne. He literally jumped over the first two rows of fans. His feet came down right on the hat dude's chest. The venue was a proper theater, with rows of permanently fixed seats, so no one could easily move out of the way. Everyone was pinned in where they stood.

Chris and the kid disappeared. They were down on the floor scrapping. The kid's friends all jumped in, and suddenly Chris was in a fight with four guys. I got down there just a couple of seconds after it started, but he was already getting the worst of it. One of the guys had him in a choke hold and the others were throwing haymakers at him. I waded down the aisle and went for the guy holding him. I punched him a few times and threw the other guys out of the way.

I looked up to see Johnny coming in hot. He grabbed one of the instigators, threw him down in the aisle, and started kicking his head in. I grabbed Chris's hand and pulled him to his feet. He had been choked, really hard, for about ten or fifteen seconds. He'd almost passed out. I helped him to the front of the stage and boosted him back up.

I looked up to see Rich, standing on the edge of the stage, taking it all in. He hadn't even taken his guitar off. *Thanks, dude. Way to have our backs.*

Other fans were involved now, too. I was yelling at them to get out of our way. They shoved me around a bit. I threw a few more random punches and then hopped back onto the stage. The entire theater was going berserk: screaming, cheering us on, booing us, whistling, every reaction possible.

House security ran down from the lobby to break up the melee. Clueless as ever, they grabbed Johnny. We watched from the stage as four of them carried him all the way up the aisle and out into the lobby.

We weren't sure what to do. Our crew were all onstage, checking to see if we were okay. T-shirts started raining down on us. Fans who had bought our merch were throwing it onstage. They had totally turned on us.

In the midst of all this chaos, Rich started the song up again. Chris and I looked at each other, shrugged, and went with it. I walked back to the kit, he grabbed his mic stand, and Jeff, Ed, and I all fell in. Within a few seconds, Johnny came screaming back down the aisle with security chasing him. As crazy as it was, we all laughed as he vaulted right back onto the stage and picked up his bass. Boom! We were back.

We finished the song, raging, and ran offstage immediately and got on the bus, where Mark was waiting with the driver. The bus was rolling less than thirty seconds after the final downbeat.

We didn't go back to Edinburgh after that. Ever.

The Shake Your Money Maker tour came to a close with a two-night stand at the Hammersmith Odeon in London.

We left the hotel for the final gig in a small convoy of cars. No need for a bus anymore. Chris and I climbed into the back seat together. As the car wound its way through London, we didn't say a word to each other.

We weren't even excited to finally be going home the next day. We had nothing left. We were toast.

At the venue, there was a raging party in a side room filled with dozens of label guys, journalists, and friends all there for the end of the tour. After a quick sound check, none of us could even fake an ounce of enthusiasm. We never went near the party.

Two days earlier, in Dublin, Chris and Rich had an actual fistfight. They went well beyond the normal threats, name-calling, and grappling. This time it seemed like they were trying to kill each other. In London, during those last two gigs, they barely looked at each other onstage.

There was a case of champagne waiting for us in the dressing room. What should have been a loud and celebratory blowout party, to commemorate a job well done, turned out instead to be a brief and muted acknowledgment that all of our dreams had come true.

The Black Crowes were unquestionably one of the biggest new rock bands in the world. But the album and tour that made us, and then nearly killed us, was behind us.

What now?

13

Round Two

I snapped awake at five thirty on the morning of October 21, 1991. I had been back in Atlanta for twelve hours and I felt lost. The only thing I'd wanted for the last two months was to get home. Now that I was home, nothing added up. Immediately, I felt out of sorts.

The phone rang around noon and I listened as Chris left a message on the answering machine.

"Hey, man, me and Rich are going to Turkey King in a bit for lunch."

Fucking hell! It's our first day back and you're already calling to get lunch! What the fuck?!? Give me some fucking space man! Get a life!

I walked right downstairs and drove to Turkey King. The three of us sat together outside at a little table, silently eating turkey burgers. Just three dudes with ringing ears and thousand-yard stares. They were as lost as I was. That's all it took. I felt much better. *I might be fucking crazy, but at least I'm not alone.*

That good feeling didn't last long, though. Within a few days, I was really struggling to reconcile my current life in Atlanta with my former life in Atlanta. Mr. Crowe's Garden had come from a mind-set of "fuck that, tear it down!" Suddenly, *we* were the band up there on that pedestal. I bought a Range Rover and almost immediately felt like an asshole driving it around. How do you make sense of becoming the very thing you were throwing rocks at two years ago?

It was the same dilemma bands like Nirvana, Soundgarden, and Pearl Jam were just starting to famously grapple with. The grunge and alt-rock band scene exploded as we were putting together our second album. Back in 1988, Mr. Crowe's Garden had been very much like all of those bands in both our mind-set and in how we presented our-selves. By 1992, we had become something else entirely while those bands, in large part because of their very public struggle to reconcile massive success with indie rock ethos, went on to define '90s rock. There was an immediate and permanent disconnect between The Black Crowes and the other successful rock bands of the '90s.

Without Pete coaching him to perform to the audience, Chris might have stayed closer to what he was originally, which was a singer in the early Michael Stipe mold. Which means he would've been more like Eddie Vedder and Kurt Cobain. Those guys weren't traditional rock stars. Eventually, they were thought of as rock stars when enough people decided they were cool, but they weren't great performers like Chris was.

For lack of a better term, we went pro. Little did we know that act-ing like an amateur was about to become the new trend.

You know who didn't have an ounce of guilt about our success? Rich. Good for him, because it was a waste of my energy.

Rich bought a BMW, and then he bought another one. Then he bought a house, and then he bought a Porsche, and then he bought like a hundred guitars. And he didn't give a flying fuck.

The other guys all fell somewhere between my guilt-wracked neu-roses and Rich's unabashed embrace of our new reality. Everyone had their own internal battles to wage, but within a few months we had found the cure for whatever was ailing us: our second album, which would prove once and for all that we deserved our success.

But before we could look forward, we had to address the Jeff Cease situation.

Ten days after returning home, we had a meeting at Rich's house to figure it out. We all showed up in new cars: me in my new Range Rover, Chris in a Jeep Cherokee, and Johnny of course in the coolest car of them all, a 1968 El Camino. Combined with Rich's two BMWs, that driveway looked pretty fucking impressive.

We sat outside on Rich's deck, drinking a few beers and bullshitting for a bit before Rich finally spoke up.

"I just don't think we can keep going with Jeff. He's miserable to be around and his playing can't keep up," he declared.

He wasn't angry. He said it very matter-of-factly, with a logic hard to dispute.

Chris immediately concurred. "Yeah, it's too bad, but fuck him. He's out."

I bristled. I already hated this whole process.

"Hold on a second," I interjected. "We're talking about someone's livelihood. A real livelihood now."

Johnny agreed. He and I were more conflicted about this than the brothers. We didn't want to hurt Jeff, and we were also thinking about the value of an "original lineup." As a fan, I hated when bands changed members.

To Chris and Rich, it was simple—if something isn't working, you change it. To my surprise and relief, they slowed down and considered the points Johnny and I were making.

Chris said at one point, "I know Jeff hasn't been happy for a long time. You can't play well when you're miserable. I feel bad for him. It must suck to get out there every night and feel like it's not the right thing."

As much as Johnny and I were conflicted, we weren't really arguing to keep Jeff. It just felt like talking it all through before making an official decision of this magnitude was the right thing to do. We all knew what we were going to decide ahead of time. Marc Ford was at home waiting for his phone to ring, and bringing him on board would be a real game changer.

Still, I was happy that we all spoke our minds and considered each other's points of view without animosity. It turned out to be one of the last times we ever had such a peaceful conversation about anything of importance. If nothing else, we chose a worthy subject upon which to respectfully come to an agreement. Finally, we decided to call Pete and tell him the news: Jeff Cease was out of The Black Crowes. It fell on Pete to get the word to Jeff. But Jeff had taken off to Hawaii for a vacation, so we couldn't reach him for a few days. When Jeff got back, he beat us to the punch and told Pete he was quitting.

Jeff said, "I don't want to be here anymore. No harm, no foul. I just don't want it to be ugly. I don't hate anybody and I don't want them to hate me."

That is classic Jeff Cease. He's just a good fucking dude.

It dawned on Johnny and me that the rest of us only had a verbal agreement between us as partners. There was a record contract, and the brothers had signed a publishing deal, but there was no legal documentation stating for the record that The Black Crowes were Chris, Rich, Johnny, and me.

So, for the first time, we drew up a partnership agreement. And now it was officially and legally the four of us, each with an equal stake.

Chris called Marc in early November and asked him to join the band. Soon Marc was on a plane to Atlanta, and he joined us at Chris's house, where we set up in the garage to make our next record, *The Southern Harmony and Musical Companion*.

George was back as our producer, but his role had changed. We didn't need any molding this time. We were already an undeniably great band, and we had just upgraded at lead guitar. Anywhere we wanted to go musically was within reach.

Marc's first day in the garage was spectacular. He stepped in like he'd always been there. We started with a few new ones we'd already been playing live, including "Thorn in My Pride" and "My Morning Song." And then Chris and Rich presented a brand new one, "Sting Me."

Marc later said in an interview that Chris and Rich fought during his first rehearsal with the band. As Marc tells it, the brothers were arguing about "Sting Me," which ended up as the lead track on *Southern Harmony*. The opening riff for "Sting Me" was plucked from a much older, never recorded tune called "You're Wrong" we had played off and on throughout the Shake Your Money Maker tour. But this new tune was better across the board. I loved the call and response verses, and there was a middle break that Marc destroyed with a guitar solo.

According to Marc, Chris and Rich apparently were arguing about how to play "Sting Me." Chris got so pissed at Rich that he picked up his microphone stand and swung it at his brother. And that pissed off

Rich so much that he charged Chris and supposedly threw him against the wall.

Now, you'll notice that I qualified my language while describing Marc's story, because Marc claims Johnny and I were there when this happened, and I don't remember any of it. Not because I was wasted or not paying attention. I'm sure I was just so used to stuff like that happening *all of the fucking time* that I didn't even make note of it. By this point, if I wasn't directly involved in one of their fights, it wouldn't have made much of an impression.

No matter how tense things could get between the brothers, we were still incredibly efficient. We could rework songs on the fly, quickly and easily. We were as sharp, collectively, as we would ever be.

The expected centerpiece of the album, "Words You Throw Away," was a song we had already played live several times. We'd even recorded a demo version in Los Angeles during a tour break. It was basically finished, but now that we were officially working on our new album, Chris wanted to change it up. He heard something very different in his head and wanted to chase it down. He liked the groove, but wanted it a little quicker. Chris also thought Rich should basically chop the riff in half, discarding the first part and starting in the middle.

No one, other than Ed, had a proper music education. We never used proper "music language." Chris was gesturing, humming, pointing, dancing. It was an immersive process for him when he was trying to get five other people to hear something in his head, without having the right words.

"What is this bullshit?" Rich said. "We have the song already. You're just rewriting it because you're bored."

I was on Rich's side. Chris was just in the midst of one of his manic episodes. But as we started playing around with the new arrangement, within a few minutes it was obvious to everyone that it was great. Really great. I stayed on the ride cymbal for the verses, and then went to the hi-hat for the choruses just to do something different. Everyone threw a few ideas of their own against the wall like that, and it all fell into place.

"Words You Throw Away" was now "Remedy," one of our all-time classics.

The mythology of *Southern Harmony* is that we were all drunk and high and surrounded by dangling Christmas lights and candles the entire time. We were actually (mostly) sober and razor focused. When we went back to the studio to shoot a video for "Thorn in My Pride," we made it look like a fucking stoner den from the '70s. Once people saw the video, they assumed that was how it looked when we made the record. And that's how Chris decided to remember it, too. But that's not the truth. Chris forgot the part about how when we actually worked on the album, the studio was bare boned and stark, with minimal distractions.

On our subsequent albums, Chris would become obsessed with "setting the mood" by decorating the studio. To me, you don't have to light a hundred fucking candles before you track. The mood is set by the music. You plug in and start jamming. It doesn't matter if there is incense burning, straws and razor blades on the recording console, or fucking neon lights on the walls.

As for chemicals, Chris was smoking pot, and I'm sure Marc and Ed were stoned, too. But Rich, Johnny, and I drank a couple of beers at the most, so we weren't drunk at all. It wasn't a "hanging out and getting stoned" vibe. It was a "kick fucking ass" vibe. Ultimately that's what the band was. Just listen to the record. *Southern Harmony* is the sound of a band that is simply fucking unstoppable.

While working out the songs, we communicated openly and easily. Double time here, half time there, eighth notes on the bridge, hold the wah-wah pedal for the back half of the solo—ideas were flying all around the room from every direction. Chris and Rich were the creative engines as far as songwriting went, but the band made it easy for them to write. We could play whatever they came up with in real time. All of the awkwardness and uncertainty that plagued the preproduction of *Shake Your Money Maker* was gone.

When Rich first started developing "Sometimes Salvation," we were swinging it: midtempo, kind of bouncing it around, actually. Rich then stopped, looked at me and said, "Let's do it slower. Like, a lot slower."

We started again, and he stopped. "No, like, *crawling*." He was attempting to air-drum while still playing guitar, hilariously, in order to show me where he wanted accents, and it wasn't making any sense at first. As we played the verse over and over, and continued to slow down more and more, Chris eventually broke it up and said, "I can't sing over that, it's too fucking slow, for fuck's sakes!" "Sometimes Salvation" found its way eventually, but for months that little moment meant something to me and Rich. We would share a smile as I'd count the song in. Little things like that are what keep a band's wheels rolling forward sometimes.

The drum pattern on the back half of Marc's solo on "Black Moon Creeping" was all George. I was playing straight through that part, and he heard something better. He was signaling me with fist pumps as we were playing: right hand for kick drum, left hand for snare. I couldn't make sense of what he was trying to get me to do. After the song he just said, "Walk this way." To this day, drummers tell me how much they love that change, and how it opens up the whole song at that part. Thanks, George.

The production credit this time around was shared: "Produced by The Black Crowes and George Drakoulias."

Chris felt George didn't do as much on this one, and therefore the band should share in the designation. While it was true George didn't do as much, it was only because the band was ready to hold up our end of the bargain. He didn't have to contribute entire parts to songs, he didn't have to hold our hands for tracking, he didn't have to give pep talks, he didn't have to nudge us to try harder. He could just *produce*, which is what he did. The credit should have been his and his alone.

We spent a couple of weeks in Chris's garage, and then we were ready to roll. We loaded into Southern Tracks Studio in Atlanta on a Friday in December. Brendan O'Brien returned to engineer the record. His production career was in full bloom by then, but he wanted to be there for the follow-up to the album that had changed all of our lives.

We started tracking late that night, and continued through the weekend. We were on fire. From Friday to Monday afternoon, we recorded all the songs that would become *Southern Harmony*. I left the studio on Monday night thinking, *Well, hang on, that was TOO fast!* After repeated playbacks, "Remedy" wasn't sitting quite right, so on Thursday we cranked that one up again to see if we could beat it. One take. Done. Now I really was finished.

The bulk of our second album was recorded in just eight days. Then George, Brendan, Chris, and Rich took the tapes to LA to finish. Some very minor tweaks, a few more overdubs, all the percussion, and then the mixing process.

Right away, we knew we had crushed it. That was the band at its strongest—the strongest it would ever be, really. Everybody doing what they did best, especially Chris. He was at the peak of his powers.

I drove home from Chris's garage, and then Southern Tracks Studio, on a high every night. The Black Crowes had truly become something special.

While I was initially hesitant to replace Jeff, there was no arguing that Marc completed the band.

Through no fault of his own, however, Marc's mere presence threw a real wrench into the dynamics of The Black Crowes.

Chris, Ed, and Marc were stoners.

Rich, Johnny, and I weren't, and that division was the first of countless splits that would follow in terms of the band's interpersonal cohesion.

There were many other constantly evolving subsets within The Black Crowes. Depending on the subject at hand, alliances would form and be forgotten within a matter of seconds. There were the four partners. There were the brothers. There was the rhythm section. There were Chris, Rich, and me, the longest-standing members. There were whichever five found themselves together with one odd man out.

The brothers would soon fully commit to the all-out, full-scale, head-to-head battle for control of the band that would largely destroy The Black Crowes. The rest of us would be caught in the cross fire—we were all ultimately collateral damage—but for now, The Black Crowes began to operate as a constantly shifting, amorphous being. You never knew quite what side or team you were on from day to day, minute to minute. Allies? Foes? Partners? Enemies? Adversaries? Blood brothers? Those labels blew back and forth in the wind. You grabbed whichever one you could get a grip on and hoped for the best.

14

Losing the Grip

The Southern Harmony and Musical Companion was released on May 12, 1992. It debuted the following week at number one, our first and only chart topper. We had four big hits off that album: "Remedy," "Thorn in My Pride," "Sting Me," and "Hotel Illness" all went to number one on rock radio. Other tracks, like "Sometimes Salvation" and "Bad Luck Blue Eyes Goodbye," were played in regular rotation on MTV. The entire album, save for a thrown-together cover of Bob Marley's "Time Will Tell," were staples of our live show for the rest of our career.

If The Black Crowes had been a normal rock band, this would've been cause for celebration. But as we have surely established by now . . . The Black Crowes were not normal.

A writer for *Guitar for the Practicing Musician* magazine happened to be with us when we learned *Southern Harmony* debuted at number one. You would think one of us had just died. The Black Crowes weren't a grunge band, but we certainly shared some of the anti-commercial politics of the grunge era, at least publicly. "The guys are pleased but subdued, even a bit somber," the guy wrote. And then there's a quote from Chris in which he compares The Black Crowes to Woody Guthrie, a man who would "never separate himself from folks." I read that out loud to Johnny and we both laughed, imagining Chris making the remark from the VIP section of a strip club.

Chris fully committed to presenting himself as both a populist "man of the people" type and a "serious artist." He bristled at comparisons to Mick Jagger or Rod Stewart. He wanted to be taken seriously.

As the frontman for The Black Crowes, he regularly risked making all of us look like insufferable clowns. He wanted to put a sticker on the cover of *Southern Harmony* that read "Within Contains No Apathy." No one else was on board with that one.

The truth is that Chris cared about money as much as any of us. When the chips were really down, and he was given the choice between his bottom line and virtually anything else in the world, the bottom line always seemed to mean more to Chris Robinson, no matter his public proclamations. The paradox of Chris's hypocrisy in regard to money was that his greed only seemed to benefit him at the expense of others, while his ego-driven and selfish crusade against "apathy" and tilting at other windmills prevented the band from enriching itself as much as it could have. Chris somehow failed as both a hippie and a capitalist.

By 1992, being in a band with Chris Robinson was like sharing a house with an arsonist. Every waking moment was spent putting out potential fires that threatened to burn up the rest of us.

The success of *Shake Your Money Maker* was in part due to our willingness to undertake whatever promotion was needed. Chris, as the singer and the most outspoken person in the band, shouldered the most responsibility when it came to doing interviews and pressing the flesh at radio stations. For our first record, Chris was willing to do that. For our second record, however, he no longer wanted to charm and woo industry people. In fact, he was openly hostile.

On the Shake Your Money Maker tour, Chris would visit every local rock station for live on-air segments with jocks, who universally loved him. He was a total live wire with a lightning-quick wit and tremendous irreverence, and that usually made for great radio. Yes, our music was also great. But our strong relationships with radio stations truly helped us get the kind of airplay we received.

For *Southern Harmony,* Chris would go to those same radio stations, and when asked to record station IDs, just like he had two years prior, he'd refuse. "Fuck that shit, I don't do those anymore." And the jocks would be stunned, thinking, *Whoa, what happened?* Things were different now. Chris was no longer a kid trying to make a name for himself and his band by any means necessary. Now, with two whole albums under his belt, he saw himself as an experienced, wise artist to be taken seriously, not one to be involved in the drudgery of promotion.

The jocks, of course, drew a different conclusion: Chris Robinson was just another rock star asshole.

Radio jocks talk. And promoters talk. So do publicists, journalists, venue owners, and label executives. None of this talk about The Black Crowes was positive.

Chris also stepped up his criticism of other artists, and not just the grunge bands from Seattle who had begun to overshadow us in the rock world. Chris took aim at everybody. In one interview, he slagged off Nick Cave, of all people, because he had supposedly been too rude to us backstage at the Pinkpop Festival in Holland. In the same interview, Chris also mocked Gregg Allman's girlfriend, in response to a harmless comment about how he was dressed like the rock stars of the 1970s.

It went on and on. Chris stepped on any and all toes, over pointlessly petty shit. That was fine when he was some kid in a small-time Atlanta band. But he was famous enough now for his words to carry real weight, and to slowly turn the world against us.

In fairness to Chris, there were times when we were all willing to act against our own best business interests in order to pursue what we stubbornly believed was a more righteous path.

Turning down one of the biggest stadium rock tours ever was one of those times.

In the summer of 1992, Guns N' Roses and Metallica hit the road together, right as both bands hit the peak of their careers. Metallica really wanted us on that tour as the opening act.

Lars Ulrich reached out personally, speaking several times with Rich about joining the tour.

But we said no. We never even considered it. Our thinking was simple. We're the best rock band on the planet right now. Why on earth would we go open for anyone?

We were set for multiple-night runs in theaters all over North America. There was one important order of business to take care of up front, however. We had to make up the dates in Japan, Australia, and New Zealand we had canceled because we were too exhausted at the end of the Shake Your Money Maker tour.

Oh, and I was also due for a life-altering, spirit-crushing mental and emotional breakdown.

But before that, we helped to usher America into the Jay Leno era.

After an album release party in Atlanta, we flew to Los Angeles for two weeks of promotion and rehearsals. We were booked to play *The Tonight Show*. It was Jay Leno's first week as host, after replacing Johnny Carson, so we knew going in there would be a huge audience.

Leno came to our room beforehand to say hello, which he would do every time we played *The Tonight Show*. Letterman, whom I worshipped, never did that. Jay was always really cool to us. I didn't care for his show, but he was a great guy.

That night we gave arguably our best TV performance ever. We called an audible and played "Sting Me" instead of the single "Remedy." We were totally dialed in. Afterward, we went to our usual LA headquarters, the Sunset Marquis, to bask in the glow of what we had just done.

Each of us had our own villa, but we all ended up in Chris's room, waiting around for three hours before *The Tonight Show* aired. (At that point, we weren't so cool that we wouldn't watch ourselves on TV.) It was a typical hang for that time—lots of weed, plenty of drinking going on, and a pretty chilled vibe overall. Well, it was typical until Chris's girlfriend showed up with some black tar heroin.

So, as we waited around to see ourselves on TV, we smoked heroin. I should say that I *pretended* to smoke heroin. I had no interest in that shit. But I'd already learned that saying "no thanks" was a fight waiting to happen. Chris couldn't stand it if someone didn't partake with him.

The show finally aired. We watched, cheered ourselves, told Chris his spot on the panel with Paula Poundstone was hilarious, and then split. But as I walked back to my room, I felt a real sense of dread. Heroin? Jesus.

During those two weeks in LA, we were out most nights. Not working, not hanging out. We were out specifically to be seen. Apparently, being seen in LA "as The Black Crowes en masse" was suddenly very important to us. In Stanley Booth's fantastic book *The True*

Adventures of The Rolling Stones, he writes about The Stones sitting in bars with everyone staring at them in awe. Chris loved that book and he had clearly decided to take inspiration from those passages.

I fucking hated that shit. I never, in a million years, wanted to be in a band that acted like this. It smacked of hypocrisy. Chris and Rich both railed against the fucking fame-whore bands and poseurs in the rock world, and yet we're all congregating at bars in Hollywood and pretending to be the fucking Stones in 1969?

One night, we were at a shitty Sunset Strip rock bar called the Coconut Teaszer. I saw a description online years later that called it a "hangout for mediocre wannabe rock star bands." I never forgot that, because it was exactly how I saw that place, too.

After an uneventful hour or two, Johnny went to take a leak. In the bathroom, some dude came up from behind and yelled "Black Crowes suck!" As Johnny looked back over his shoulder, the guy cold-cocked him. We all noticed the guy running out of the bathroom, and then a second later Johnny came flying out after him with a bloody nose. The whole band tore out of there, chasing this asshole down the street.

We had the number one album in America, and we were chasing a dude down Sunset Boulevard on foot. For those few fleeting minutes, I wasn't stressing or thinking about the absurdity swirling around me. Right then, on Sunset Boulevard, we really were a team. For better or worse, when shit got stupid, we still had each other's backs.

I was already dealing with my own personal issues, and the band dynamic was compounding the stress and tearing me apart inside.

I felt like I was going nuts, but it never occurred to me to talk to someone about it. Had I said to anyone I trusted, "Man, I just don't feel good about anything," they could have easily helped by saying something as simple as "It's not like there's a rule book to follow. You are dealing with a lot of new shit and it's normal to feel overwhelmed." But I couldn't do it. I thought I was too rational to allow this to get to me.

I really wanted to get out of Los Angeles for a while, but I couldn't. We had a full schedule and we were about to fly out to Japan. I felt trapped by my own band.

I loved playing. I loved the music. On stage, everything we did was great. But off stage, all this other bullshit, the flesh and blood rock 'n' roll cliché act where suddenly we're tough guys looking for fights, shitting on other bands, and puffing out our chests constantly? What the fuck was that? It went against every single grain in my being.

The next morning, we left for LAX. A cold sore had started forming on my lip, purely from stress and anxiety. It got bigger and bigger and bigger as I sat pounding beer after beer in the airport bar.

Pete asked me if I was okay. Clearly, I wasn't masking my struggle that well, and he was genuinely concerned.

Rich replied for me, "Steve's fine. He doesn't give a fuck about anything."

"Why would you say that?" I asked, dumbfounded.

"Because you don't. What could be bothering you? You don't care about the band like we do. You just do your own thing all the time."

"Go fuck yourself," I shot back. "I love this band with everything I fucking have, but I don't think of it as an extension of my fucking being. You and Chris think the band is *you*. I fucking hate how everyone acts and it breaks my heart."

He and Pete just stared at me, shocked.

"Dude, relax," Rich shrugged.

No one else paid any attention. More drinks were ordered.

There was nothing to do now but get on a plane to Japan for twelve hours with these people.

15

Splat

My plan was to drink four or five Jack and cokes and a couple of beers and then pass out.

We were flying first class, and the seat reclined flat to a full bed. It took a while, but I finally passed out and stayed out until we were about an hour outside of Tokyo. I had enough time to have a little coffee and get my shit together before landing.

Marc Ford was sitting across the aisle from me. I looked over to see he was drunk. Way, way drunk. I asked him if he'd slept. He slowly looked over to me and smiled, saying, "No, man. No way."

This was Marc's first tour with the band, and he was soaking up every bit of his new life.

The rest of us had worked our way up to this over a few years: the first class flight, the international tour, the hit album. Marc, meanwhile, dropped into this life overnight. He was determined to live it up. It must have been mind blowing to be the guy who just stepped right into it from a day job.

After clearing customs, we walked into the arrivals hall to find hundreds of fans waiting for us. We signed autographs and posed for pictures, and then it was time to move on.

But Marc didn't want to leave.

He was stumbling around, hugging every person in sight, playing up his new rock star status with a huge grin. He was overjoyed. We all thought it was great. Good for him.

A fleet of cars waited to take us to the hotel in groups of two. I hopped into the nearest one and assumed Johnny would join me. He knew I wasn't in great shape, and had been regularly checking in with me and offering support, always very subtly, so as not to draw attention from the others.

Johnny and I were developing a very close friendship that we would both lean on greatly in the coming years. We were often each other's sole support system through some very dark times.

But Johnny didn't hop in with me. Marc did. Our tour manager, Mark Botting, basically poured him into the car. Marc laughed, babbled incoherently, and then sat back with his eyes closed and passed out. Thirty seconds later, he suddenly lurched awake again.

"Holy shit, we're in Japan!" he yelled, laughing hysterically.

We had a ninety-minute drive to the hotel, which was plenty of time for Marc to throw up on me at the slightest provocation.

"Why don't you go to sleep?" I pleaded.

"I'm too excited!" he exclaimed.

Suddenly, Marc needed to take a piss, and he needed cigarettes. Right now! He started tapping on the driver's shoulder, begging him to pull over. The guy spoke no English. Marc just begged louder. "Come on, man, I need to pee! I need some smokes!" He was all over the place. The driver was confused and kind of scared, too. Marc was coming unglued.

I did my best to act out smoking and peeing for the driver to get him to understand. He finally got it, but we were traveling in a caravan and he didn't want to stop.

"Marc, how are you going to buy cigarettes, do you have any yen?" I asked, angrily.

"What's that mean?"

"It's Japanese money, it's called yen. Do you have any?" I knew he didn't. I was just hoping that would end it.

"No, man, I just got here," Marc snapped back, like I was the one making his life difficult.

Eventually, the driver pulled over so Marc could get his goddamn cigarettes and not piss his pants. Once he was back in the car, he started babbling again.

"It's finally happened—I'm a rock star now!" he said. I'm serious, he actually said that out loud. I couldn't believe it.

"Think you can get one gig . . . *just one fucking gig* out of the way before you decide you're a rock star now, dude?" I asked.

Ninety minutes in the car with Marc felt like ninety hours, but after the endless drive we finally arrived at the hotel. As soon as I got out of the car, I stormed over to Pete.

"Get that motherfucker away from me," I snarled. "I want to kill him!"

"Come on, Steve-O, he's just having fun."

There had to be a thousand fans waiting for us at the hotel; just an amazing turnout. Were all these people here for us? Who knew we were this big in Japan? Maybe Marc was right—we really were a big deal now.

As soon as our translator announced to the crowd that The Black Crowes had arrived, two-thirds of them immediately sat down and looked disappointed. Turns out they were expecting Status Quo, an English rock band I assumed had broken up at least a decade earlier. So much for feeling like a rock star.

The first couple of days in Tokyo were filled with press and photo shoots. I didn't do any interviews. I barely managed to stay upright for photos. Sobriety didn't feel like an option. It hurt too much.

As I was spinning out of control inside my own head, we launched our Japanese tour, which included a half dozen shows in and around Tokyo and then a few more dates in the rest of the country. During rehearsals at one of the Tokyo gigs, Chris called for us to play "Space Captain," from Joe Cocker's *Mad Dogs and Englishmen* LP. Apparently on the flight over, Chris had announced that he wanted everyone to learn it. That was news to me, but I had heard the song enough times to work my way through it. Ed hit the piano intro and, at some point during the first verse, I stopped to ask a question about the arrangement.

"You should fucking know it already!" Chris hissed.

We started to play again, and I knew the song as well as anyone else. It was shaky, but we were getting through it. But Chris didn't like what he heard, and stopped the band.

"Go fucking listen to the song, so you can know what you're fucking doing!" he yelled at me.

When I played the Joe Cocker CD in the dressing room, I discovered that I had played the drum part . . . exactly fucking correct. Chris insisted I was playing something different on the chorus, but it was just a straight beat, no matter what he heard. We'd had countless blowups like this over the past five years, but this one got to me. I was really rattled. And then I got more rattled about the fact that I was rattled to begin with. I couldn't snap out of it.

By the time the gig rolled around, I had my shit together. The countdown to downbeat—pacing around the hallways, warming up my wrists and forearms, shooting the shit with my drum tech, having a few drinks—all did its job. I was ready.

We walked onstage to polite applause, and then . . . silence. Unlike practically every other show we'd played in the last couple of years, there was no buzz in the room.

We learned the hard way that this is just how Japanese audiences behave, but at the time we didn't know that. We had to figure it out as we went.

The shows in Japan always started at six o'clock, which meant we were offstage by eight, and back at the hotel by eight thirty. That left a full night to hit the city. Every night, we would have a big dinner at a great restaurant with the promoter or people from the label, and I would drink my weight in beer. It was like Xanax at that point. My sole focus was trying to stay calm and not lose my shit.

I drank nonstop in Japan, which was easy because there were vending machines on the streets that sold half-gallon-sized bottles of beer. For the first five days in town, whether we were doing a photo shoot in Harajuku, or just walking around killing time in Rappongi, I was drinking beer 24/7.

Our hotel, the Roppongi Prince, was square-shaped. The elevators were in one corner, and had glass doors that faced into a center atrium. Everyone had the same room on a different floor, a corner suite directly opposite the elevator bank. Starting at the eighth floor, one of us would get out on each floor, and the rest of us would watch him walk to his door. And the guy walking to his room would look back and wave. Those left on the elevator would wave back. It was funny every single time.

Every time I entered my room, I was overtaken with dread. I couldn't sleep. The jet lag and the drinking were making it impossible. I could drink enough to pass out, but then I'd snap awake within a couple of hours. Every time. I started having nightmares. I actually believed my room was haunted. I don't normally think like that. I don't believe in rooms being haunted. Except for my room in Tokyo in June 1992. That fucker was haunted for sure.

I would call my girlfriend, Rose Mary, several times a day, just to check in. The time change meant I was waking her more often than not, but I didn't care. I needed to hear her voice. I'd hang up with her and call my brother, Jim, in Baltimore. I'd ask about the Orioles and try desperately to sound normal. I'd call friends from college whom I hadn't called in years.

My friendships have always been my ballast. My world was fucked up, but if it sounded like the outside world was normal, I felt reassured. I figured I could handle the stress of The Black Crowes as long as everything else in the world was still as I remembered it.

I finally hit the wall on the morning of our Yokohama gig. After another round of horrible nightmares, I walked over to the hotel window and noticed I could open it from the inside. For a moment, I thought about jumping out. Maybe then I would finally be at peace.

I couldn't believe it. "You're thinking about suicide!" I screamed aloud to myself. And then I threw up on the floor.

I sat on my bed and cried. I just couldn't make sense of anything anymore. I'd never felt anything close to that level of despair.

After a few minutes, I called Rose Mary again, and I couldn't get any words out. I just cried. I couldn't stop.

"You have to talk to somebody," she pleaded.

"I can't talk to anybody."

"Go talk to Chris."

"No chance," I said, sobbing. "Fuck it—he doesn't want to hear shit from me."

"Go talk to him," Rose Mary insisted. "Just tell him you're losing your fucking mind. Everyone probably feels the same way as you right now."

After we hung up I called Jim, who told me the same thing Rose Mary just had—it was imperative that I get the fuck out of my haunted, depressing hotel room.

I spent the next hour debating with myself about whether I should go to Chris's room. Finally, I splashed some water on my face and headed to the elevator.

Outside of Chris's door, all I could feel was dread at the prospect of having a breakdown. But he was fueling a large part of my anxiety, and I had finally hit the point where I had to clear the air or I didn't think I could stay in the band. I could hear music coming from the room. I stood at that door for at least ten minutes.

Fuck it, I don't want to do this. It'd be easier to jump off this fucking balcony right now. That was the second time I'd had that thought. *What the fuck is wrong with me? Knock. Knock. JUST FUCKING KNOCK!*

I knocked, probably a little too urgently. He opened the door, clearly annoyed. The look on his face said, *What the fuck do you want?* I walked past him and sat on the couch in his room. He could tell something wasn't right.

He finally said, "What's up?"

I started to cry. I couldn't speak. I just dissolved. I was full on weeping. I somehow ended up in a ball on his floor and laid there for a few minutes, sobbing uncontrollably.

"What's wrong? What's wrong? What's wrong?" he said frantically. He probably thought someone had died. "Who is it? What happened?"

"It's me. I'm losing my fucking mind. I can't do this anymore. I can't take it."

As soon as those words came out, Chris sat on the floor next to me. He put his arm around me and said, "It's okay, man." I lay there and cried for an hour. All of the worries, fears, and emotions I had bottled up were coming out. And not just from the past few months, or even the past two years. It was a lifetime of shit. It felt like I was leaking poison.

"How can you be this upset, man?" Chris finally asked.

"You! Fucking everybody! All of this!" I said. "I don't like any of this. I hate what we have become. I fucking hate that you're everything you never wanted to be. You literally look at me on stage in front of our band and crew and yell at me about what I'm playing on a song I've never played before. What's wrong with you? How can you do that?"

I let Chris have it on all kinds of shit—his moods, his raging ego, his escalating drug use, the way he was constantly dividing the band into different camps, his disrespect toward Rose Mary and all of us in the band who were in relationships, his unwillingness to listen to anyone else's opinions, and everything else that had built up.

I wrapped it up with, "Everyone feels this way, too, by the way. It's not just me. You're doing this to everyone! Why? Why are you always fucking with everyone?"

It was an honest question. I wasn't yelling by this point. I wasn't even crying anymore. Once the lid blew off, I settled down pretty quickly, actually. But I wanted some fucking answers.

Chris started to cry. Within seconds, he was crying as hard as I'd been. Jesus Christ, all of a sudden my breakdown was *his* breakdown? No, I wasn't having that. *You ain't taking this from me, asshole.* "Tell me why you think it's okay to act the way you act," I demanded. "Why do you get to ignore the most basic fucking rules of human decency?"

"Man, I don't know what I'm doing," Chris said softly. "This shit is really hard for me, too."

"We were on the cover of *Rolling Stone* last year and my first thought was, *Well, good for Chris.* I can't even appreciate that it's me, too, on that cover, because you're going to take that joy from everybody."

"I just feel so much pressure to do everything," he said, "and no one else understands that."

We were both talking quietly by now. There was no tension or anger anymore. I still felt like a raw nerve, but I could breathe at least.

"Well, how about you fucking communicate that to someone? You're not a solo act. It's a fucking band. Share the load, for God's sakes."

Chris and I talked for a couple of hours, just crying and hashing out the shit between us. He referenced a half dozen times I had hurt his feelings, badly. I didn't remember any of those things. But he did, and they mattered to him. I told him I was sorry, that I didn't realize he was still capable of having his feelings hurt. No one did. He was horrible to be around most of the time.

"For a few years, you were like the older brother that I didn't have," Chris confessed. "It's weird for me now to be in the lead position after you were like that those first few years."

Chris told me he knew I didn't like him anymore and it was really hard on him. I told him he was right, but it was only because he was such an asshole. We laughed about that, like we had in 1987, back when none of it really mattered.

As we were winding down and running out of things to say, there was a knock on the door. It was Rich.

"What's going on?" he said, looking at me. "Were you crying?"

"Yeah, for like six hours," I told him. "Some of this stuff is just really hard for me, man."

All of a sudden, Rich sat on the couch and burst into tears.

"Man, if you can't handle it, then I can't handle it," he said. "A lot of this shit is really freaking me out, too."

Now that Rich had joined our impromptu group therapy session, it really ramped up. The three of us sat for another couple of hours, unburdening ourselves of all the things that had ever upset us, pissed us off, or freaked us out about The Black Crowes. Instead of addressing any of this in real time, we had waited until the very moment when the weight of it all had driven us absolutely fucking crazy.

Chris ordered room service, and we sat together eating ramen noodles and trying to feel less broken for a while. We might very well have been crazy, but at least we weren't alone.

By the time we wrapped it up, everything was a little better . . . for a while anyway. Heading to the gig in the van later that afternoon, Chris made a point to sit next to me. I couldn't help but think, *He's just worried that I'm going to tell someone he cried, too.* But it was more than that. He felt bad that I felt so bad. I could tell Chris was making an effort to be nicer. At sound check, he wanted us to learn a new cover. But instead of starting in on the song and getting pissed if we fucked it up, he called us into his dressing room.

"Hey, let's listen to this song and talk it through before we go play it," he said. You know, just like a normal person would operate.

Within a few hours, everybody knew about my freak-out. Hell, by then the sore on my lip was the size of a half-dollar, so everyone already had a pretty good sense that something was seriously amiss. There was a general assumption that Japan itself was the problem. But that wasn't true. I just happened to be in Japan when I hit the wall.

What did me in was the impossibility of being in The Black Crowes. It took me years to learn how to cope with it. I was stuck in a maelstrom of other people's insanity, and I had no idea how to look after my own mental health.

I had to learn that Chris and Rich were always going to be who they were, and it was up to me to manage my life accordingly. I didn't know how to do that yet. It would be a long time coming.

16

High as the Moon

Two weeks after returning from Japan, Australia, and New Zealand, we kicked off the first America leg of the High as the Moon tour with four shows at the Orpheum Theatre in Minneapolis.

Before the run, we spent a few days in town doing preproduction. The launch of this tour was a big deal. Tabitha Soren was around, filing *MTV News* reports every night and hanging at the hotel bar. She was an ally for sure. All of MTV was at that point.

There was a definite vibe in town all week—any restaurant or club started buzzing as soon as we walked in. Chris had a bodyguard at all times. He legitimately needed one. Chris was fucking famous, but also because it was easy for him to get into trouble.

Walking down the street one afternoon, a woman wearing a wedding dress jumped him from behind. She threw herself on his back and brought him to the ground like a linebacker tackling a running back. "We're getting married!" she screamed. The bodyguard picked her up and carried her away. That was par for the course now.

That first leg of the tour was incredible, on- and offstage. The shows were rocking. Every single one of them. But equally as important was the fact that on the bus afterward, we were all hanging together, drinking beer, smoking weed, and listening to music. We mostly played live bootlegs by Humble Pie, Little Feat, Sly and The Family Stone, Zeppelin, and The Stones. We were breaking everything down. *How'd they get that guitar sound? What's up with that bass line? What is the count on that turnaround?*

Marc rightly gets a ton of credit from fans for his contributions during this era. But, to me, 1992 was still all about how high Ed Harsch raised the bar for us. His instincts were always so musical and perfect.

When Ed paid you a compliment, like "Man, that shit felt just right" after a jam during sound check, it was the greatest affirmation you could get.

We took a break from our tour in September to perform at MTV's Video Music Awards.

The 1992 VMAs hold a pretty notorious place in MTV history. For the first time, the alt-rock movement spearheaded by Pearl Jam and Nirvana was fully on display. (In fact, Nirvana's bassist, Krist Novoselic, literally speared himself in the head with his own bass after he tossed it into the air when they performed "Lithium.")

On the other end of the rock spectrum, Guns N' Roses went the full-on bloated pomp-rock route by performing their extravagant epic "November Rain" with Elton John and a huge orchestra. In between those extremes, you had this weird amalgam of rising stars and soon-to-be has-beens: The Red Hot Chili Peppers, Def Leppard, Bryan Adams, Bobby Brown, En Vogue, Eric Clapton. They even beamed in the king of pop himself, Michael Jackson, from a tour stop in London.

And then there was us. We actually kicked off the show with our latest single, "Remedy." The VMAs were the biggest night in music, and The Black Crowes were the opening act.

It should have been a moment of triumph. But it was . . . weird.

Of course, we saw ourselves as superior to every other band there. Whether it was true is a pointless debate for fans at this point. I only mention it because that arrogance played a large part in our self-imposed alienation from the rest of the scene.

The most memorable part of the VMAs, taped at Pauley Pavilion on UCLA's campus in Westwood, occurred backstage. As soon as we got out of the car, there was a red carpet where all of the performers were welcomed and got their pictures taken.

Right away, Tabitha Soren asked us about a "controversy" already brewing backstage. Apparently there was bad blood between Kurt

Cobain and Axl Rose, and people were concerned it might come to blows.

Seriously? We're going to sit here and have a conversation about whether two singers might have a fight? It was ridiculous, like in the movie *Anchorman* when the rival news teams have a street fight.

But, more than anything, we were just pissed that no one was talking about us. Not that we'd ever have admitted it at the time, of course . . . but it was true. We all sensed, quite accurately, that while we might think we were the best rock band on earth, Guns N' Roses and Nirvana were the main attractions.

We were led to our dressing room, which was the middle trailer in a set of three. To the right was Nirvana. To the left was Guns N' Roses. Now, that is what they call a real-life metaphor. We were too iconoclastic to fit in with the dinosaur stadium rock bands of the time, and we had no connection whatsoever to the ascendant alt-rock movement. In between the two biggest bands who represented the two biggest rock movements of the past five years sat The Black Crowes.

If Axl and Kurt were going to fight, at least we had ringside seats. We were in our trailer with the door wide open, drinking beer, listening to loud music, and doing our best to present an entirely inhospitable vibe to anyone passing by.

Of course, nothing happened. We were loudly mocking the entire situation. Some of the GNR entourage would walk by and we'd all start singing "Get in the Ring" in our best Axl voices.

Kurt and Courtney walked by and Marc Ford said, very deadpan, "Well, hang on now, he's just a little fella," and we all fell out laughing.

At one point, there were people milling outside both the other trailers, so I stepped out of ours and loudly announced, "The Black Crowes will happily kick the shit out of Nirvana *and* Guns N' Roses at the same time. Any takers?"

Nobody thought it was funny. MTV staffers were clearly stressing about the pending fight. It was tense.

Eventually, we headed to the stage. Dana Carvey was hosting, and he greeted us warmly. We'd met him when we did *SNL* and he was a fan. He asked if we could do an extra song, before the show

actually started, to warm the crowd up. We said, "Sure, no big deal."
We counted in "Sting Me" and did just that. It was a good warm-up,
actually. When the show started and we kicked into "Remedy," we
were already locked in.

I didn't stick around for the hang. I got right into a town car and
went to LAX to catch the red-eye home to Atlanta. Rose Mary met me
at the airport and we flew down to St. John for a few days.

Eighteen hours after opening one of the most memorable VMAs
ever, I was scuba diving a billion miles away. Had I known how the rest
of the decade was gonna shake out, I might have stayed around for a
bit. We never got that close to the center of it all again.

The good vibes that surrounded the start of the tour started to fade by the
fall, as cocaine became the front and center drug of choice for The
Black Crowes.

Rich was never going to do coke. That was a given. He didn't smoke
pot, and he rarely drank. He took a ton of abuse about that, but as his
entire life up to that point had been taking abuse from Chris, he didn't
give a shit.

I was the only other band member not partaking. I wasn't subjected
to overt pressure, but I could always sense that the other guys wanted
me in the back lounge with them. On a long overnight trip I finally
decided to give it a go. I ripped open the door to the back lounge and
said, "All right, let's have it!"

I had been around coke long enough to know it made anyone who
did it pretty fucking annoying. I was surprised I didn't really feel much
of anything. I guess I expected an edgy mushroom high or something.

"Honestly, I don't really feel anything," I told Rich in the front
lounge not long after, as I opened another beer. A few minutes later I
told him again, "I don't feel anything" as I opened another beer. A few
minutes after that I said, "What's the big deal about coke anyway?" as
I opened another beer. This happened again. And again. And again.

Finally, it hit me. *I am drinking a case of beer and talking about being
high. I'm like everyone else on coke. I sound like a fucking idiot.*

I did coke a few more times—maybe a dozen?—over the next couple of years. Once, in Spain, I did some blow that was supposedly

extremely pure, and the truth is that shit was *euphoric*. But other than that, coke did nothing for me.

For Chris, cocaine was probably the worst drug he could've taken, as it exacerbated all his faults. It's in Chris's nature to act like a cult leader. He wanted to be surrounded by people who loved him, feared him, and who would never challenge him. Add cocaine to that mix, and you wound up with a full-blown megalomaniac who lived inside a cocoon.

Our schedule was pretty consistent: four nights on, one night off. After the fourth gig, Chris, Marc, Ed, and Johnny would stay up all night on the bus doing blow. I'd drink with everybody until I'd had enough, and they would keep going. Those days off always turned into drinking binges.

I used to think a lot of this could've been avoided if we'd stayed in cheaper hotels. We were in Ritz-Carltons and Four Seasons everywhere we went, and those guys always hit the bar by noon. Why not slum it at the Hyatt or Holiday Inn? Those bars aren't nearly as inviting. Johnny and I had started paying more attention to how much we were spending on the road. Wasting money so recklessly was an affront to both of us. To the brothers, we were an arena-level rock band who chose to play theaters. But since we weren't actually playing arenas, we weren't generating that kind of income.

Still, the brothers had millions from publishing. They never understood that Johnny and I didn't have that kind of money. Spending $150,000 on hotels was a big deal to us. But Chris and Rich operated as if the band was an ATM card.

When the subject would come up, Chris's response was always the same. "All you guys care about is money. Money, money, money!"

"No, we care about wasting money. There's a big difference, man."

"Not to me! You're just greedy."

Whatever. Chris was preoccupied with perpetuating a bullshit rock 'n' roll lifestyle. Drug talk dominated all conversations. *Who is doing how much of what and with whom?* He talked about it nonstop.

I knew plenty of other people who did drugs. They were self-medicating, or simply having fun, or hiding from life. Whatever their motivations, the vast majority of those people used drugs discreetly. Not Chris.

The Black Crowes were a drug band now, exactly what I wanted to avoid when I left Mary My Hope and joined Mr. Crowe's Garden. By the time the High as the Moon tour concluded the following summer, half the band were daily users.

Another pivotal change was that Chris decided to move to Los Angeles. He didn't officially pull up stakes until the end of the summer of 1993, but he was already spending all his downtime out there.

We never had a conversation about the whole band relocating from Atlanta. It was just *his* thing. I guess I would have considered it, had the other guys wanted to go, too. But Rich made no bones about it. "No fucking way am I moving to LA."

I think Chris was, yet again, ignoring the more grounded voices in his head. He had long talked about getting a farm in Georgia and building a studio on the property, to give the band a permanent home to record. He was now in a position to do just that. Instead, he went straight-up cliché rock star and bought a house in the Hollywood Hills.

With Chris in LA, The Black Crowes were split among three cities: Chris and Marc in LA; Rich, Johnny, and me in Atlanta; and Ed in Detroit. At the time we justified this separation—that's what airplanes are for, right? But when you're all in the same town, you do shit constantly. You can say, "Let's jam tomorrow" instead of "Let's jam next week."

Back when the band started, Chris and I were out every night together. We ate together, drank together, and got in trouble together. Even in the moments when we thought we hated each other, we bonded. But now he was leaving Atlanta. How do you stay bonded with someone who lives two thousand miles away?

As destructive as Chris's relocation to LA and his growing coke habit were on the band, another change in Chris's personality possibly upset the apple cart even more than either of those developments.

He became a Deadhead.

In the 1980s, Chris fucking hated the Grateful Dead. He hated the music, he hated hippies, he hated the whole culture. Back then, when the Dead played a three-night stand at the Omni, he'd sit at Fellini's Pizza in Little Five Points during my shifts, mocking all the Deadheads congregating outside and occasionally asking for free slices. So it was a definite shock to see Chris *become* a Deadhead.

To be clear. I never had a problem with the Grateful Dead, or their fans. I had a problem with exactly *one* of their fans, and what that *one* fan did to his own band in his desperate efforts to emulate his new heroes.

Chris was warmly received backstage the first time he went to a Dead show in 1991. In fact, he was quite surprised at how well he was treated. He was already torturing himself with whether *real musicians* would take him seriously. He left that first Dead gig a much bigger fan than when he walked in, in large part thanks to the respect he was shown.

During the High as the Moon tour, Chris went to see the Dead a few more times, and that's when his burgeoning fandom started to influence his approach to The Black Crowes.

"They just stand there, man!" he told us one day. "They just play! That's it. *It's just about the music!* And they're fucking wasted! They don't have to worry about a fucking light show or performing for the crowd. *They're real musicians.*"

Oh, holy hell. Suddenly we're not real musicians. Suddenly it's cool to just stand there.

At the start of the High as the Moon tour, Chris was a fantastic performer. He danced, he pranced, he strutted, he *entertained*. He was fucking great. On the first half of that tour, we put on a real rock show. Every night, five minutes before showtime, we would cut the house lights and blast "Are You Ready?" by Grand Funk Railroad. And every time, the place went nuts.

At the end of the song, after sitting in the dark for three and a half minutes, the house would be screaming with anticipation. I'd start keeping time with a pattern on the ride cymbal, Rich would come at full volume with the intro riff, the whole band would fall into an up-tempo jam that segued into "No Speak No Slave" as the lights blew up. It looked and sounded like an explosion.

When Chris started singing, he stood perfectly still at the mic with sunglasses on. And he stayed there, just holding the mic . . . during the verse, then the chorus, then another verse. You could feel the tension build. Right before the guitar solo, he would sing something like "Why talk to me like this when you could be beautiful?"

And then he'd dramatically rip the sunglasses off, throw them into the crowd, and take off dancing. The audience always went berserk for it.

The show was over when that happened. Every single time. Four minutes in, and we had the audience in the palms of our hands for the rest of the night.

Pete designed that whole routine, by the way. Just incredible. But after Chris watched the Dead, all those theatrics felt phony to him.

When we picked up the second half of the tour in January 1993, after we had played *Saturday Night Live* for the second time the previous December, our intro music at the first gig was different. Instead of Grand Funk Railroad whipping the crowd into a frenzy, Indian music blasted out of the speakers.

"What the fuck is this?" we asked Chris, walking to the stage.

"I'm not doing that Grand Funk shit anymore," he said. "This is cooler."

Chris was quickly losing interest in acting like a frontman, and he had zero interest in discussing it with the rest of us. The process of dismantling what we had built had begun.

As we continued through the spring and summer, cracks were continually forming in the foundation. After guiding our career to tremendous success in just three years, it was Pete's turn to be the odd man out. Chris decided Pete should simply execute whatever vision Chris Robinson cooked up from now on. He no longer wanted Pete's input on creative issues of any kind.

This was a catastrophic turn for The Black Crowes. Beyond the business side of Pete's input, he'd been our greatest creative secret weapon as well. From directing our videos, to designing our live production, to helping Chris become the great performer he was, Pete's contributions were immeasurable.

Pete rarely talked to us about the music. He took it as a given that we would have our shit together in that department. He certainly had strong opinions on what the single should be, or he'd offer a suggestion on punching up a chorus on occasion. But those moments were few and far between. From the very beginning, it was fucking simple. Pete did his part. We did ours. We were successful.

But by the end of the High as the Moon tour, we were fully at the mercy of an unstoppable force, Chris, and an immovable object, Rich, who instinctively resisted whatever Chris wanted to do.

Once Chris started using hard drugs, Rich looked at it as an opportunity to seize control. But Rich has always been guilty of thinking he is a lot smarter than he is. Most of us are guilty of that, too, but for Rich it's truly egregious. He really sees himself as a businessman with a brilliant mind. But he has no concept of how business really works.

Rich was a savant when it came to playing guitar. When Rich and I were playing, we connected in a way that was life changing. We were responsible for the unique feel of The Black Crowes' music. But the idea that he could take the reins of The Black Crowes beyond that? Fucking insane.

This was where we finally found ourselves: between two brothers battling for control of something neither were qualified to pilot. The rest of us would be forced to pick one side or the other, which inevitably meant pissing off the guy you didn't pick. An impossible situation any way you look at it.

The problem with The Black Crowes—and this will always drive me crazy—is that we weren't some hard-luck story, like Big Star or The Replacements. If you are Alex Chilton or Paul Westerberg, people look at you and say, "Man, they should have had bigger careers." But we had a big career. And we had a big-time manager who knew how to maintain it. And then we threw it away.

17

Tall

The High as the Moon tour ended in the summer of 1993 with a festival run in Europe, including the headlining slot at the Glastonbury Festival. Robert Plant played right *before* us. Just three years earlier, we were opening for him.

As soon as we got back home, Chris started making plans for our next album, to be made in Los Angeles. He had just set up his new house in Laurel Canyon. It looked very much like something out of a late-'60s pipe dream. Rugs, lava lamps, dogs, cats, drugs, random local hippies, incense. It was everything he would have laughed at in 1990.

Before making our next record, it was clear to everyone we had some serious work to do on ourselves. Across the board, there was a lot of wreckage from the High as the Moon tour within the band.

Pete had an idea. Let's all go to Yosemite National Park and spend a few days with Ron Kauk, a close buddy of his. Ron is a world-famous rock climber who made legendary first ascents on El Capitan and several of Yosemite's most notable walls. He was featured on ABC's *Wide World of Sports* doing the first-ever live free climb of the Lost Arrow Spire in Yosemite. He doubled for Sylvester Stallone on his film *Cliffhanger* set in the Italian Alps, and was the stunt coordinator and double for Tom Cruise on *Mission Impossible II*. Whenever you see Stallone and Cruise climbing in those movies, Ron is the guy who literally showed them the ropes.

What Pete didn't say (he didn't have to say it, because it was obvious) was that we had to find a way to heal after the bruising tour we had just completed. For the most part, it was about Chris and Rich.

There was so much unpleasantness, so much fighting, and just general unhealthiness on the High as the Moon tour.

Pete was thinking *Let's put them in an environment where no one is in their comfort zone. Where they have to have each other's backs. No one's in charge in the woods, other than Ron and the black bears.*

Johnny and I were way into it. We went to the sporting goods store REI together, with the checklist Ron sent us. We bought hiking boots, headlamps, sleeping bags, a two-man tent, all that shit. A few more guys jumped in, too: Pete's brother, Chris; my cousin, Jeffrey; and Jimmy Ashhurst, one of Marc Ford's oldest friends who was playing in Izzy Stradlin and the Ju Ju Hounds. No one ever thought to invite Ed. No way that dude was hanging in the woods for three days.

Throughout this entire time frame, Rich had other things on his mind. He was getting married that November, so the Yosemite trip was about a month before the wedding. I thought it would be a great chance for him to clear out some bad vibes before what was sure to be a really happy time in his life. I was wrong.

Johnny and I went to the airport together expecting to meet Rich at the gate. He wasn't there. We boarded the plane, thinking Rich would come running on at the last second. Didn't happen.

We flew to LAX, where the rest of the group was waiting for us to get a flight to Sacramento, and then on to Yosemite in a van. Pete brought us up to speed. "Rich called me this morning and said he can't make it. He has too much going on with the wedding."

So that was that. Rich didn't want to be there.

We flew to Sacramento, grabbed a rental van, and started off on the drive to the park. Within ten minutes, we bonded around a common theme: Rich was a fucking dick for not being there. We tore that asshole a new asshole.

Chris of course loved this entire thing, because it was all on Rich now. By simply showing up, Chris looked like the good guy.

In spite of Rich's absence, Pete was onto something. Remove the members of The Black Crowes from the machinery of The Black Crowes and from society at large, and right away we were all getting along and having a blast.

We checked into a Yosemite hotel late in the afternoon, ahead of the hike to Half Dome in the morning. That night, I sat at the hotel bar watching the Phillies eliminate my Braves from the National League Championship Series. My fury was matched by the strength of a really strong local beer. I got pie-eyed drunk.

I woke up with a brutal hangover ahead of a long day of hiking. Oops.

We went to breakfast and I couldn't even eat. I was utterly miserable. But for the next eight hours, we did the hike all the way to Half Dome. Switchbacks, scenic views, streams you could drink from, the whole nine. By the time we got to our campsite, we were different people. Everybody had turned back into normal human beings. Surrounded by this incredible natural beauty, there really was no pecking order.

We woke up with the sun on Saturday, and after everyone had some coffee and steeled their nerves, we went up Half Dome. It's a nearly vertical rock face with ropes permanently affixed, so we used them to do a Batman-like crawl up the side. It was scary at first, but within a few hundred feet it became invigorating.

That night we cooked over a bonfire, drank bourbon, and had a great hang.

In the end, it was the best trip ever . . . but Rich wasn't there. By the time we parted ways at LAX on Monday, the one thing everybody remembered was that we were actually friends, and the one thing we all agreed on was that Rich was a fucking asshole.

Not long after, we all went to Los Angeles to begin preproduction on our third album. It would eventually be known as *Tall,* and the entire recording process would be an absolute, unmitigated disaster.

Rich immediately announced he couldn't live in a hotel while working on the record. He needed his own house and he wanted the band to pay for it.

"I can't be creative here! I have to be in my own space," Rich demanded.

Johnny and I, along with Pete, were astounded at the audacity. It's a band expense? But publishing is not a revenue stream for the *band,* is it? No, it's not. So go fuck yourself.

"It's bullshit," Rich pouted. "Chris gets to go to his own house every night, while we're in a hotel."

"Then buy your own house here, dude! If we were making this record in Atlanta, would you pay for Chris to rent a fucking house? No! So we are not paying for you to rent a house in L.A. Absolutely not!"

Rich finally accepted that we wouldn't pay for his house, so he demanded we pay for him to upgrade to a villa at the Sunset Marquis. Unbelievable. No fucking way were we paying for this asshole to spend a couple of months in a villa. Ultimately, he did end up in a villa, and he paid for it himself. We made damned sure about that. We had no doubt he would try to slide those costs onto the recording budget.

Chris had installed himself as our new producer, with assistance from an engineer named Jim Mitchell who had worked with Guns N' Roses on the *Use Your Illusion* albums. I love Jim Mitchell to death, but he didn't stand a chance, as Rich could never see him as anything but Chris's guy. And make no mistake—Chris Robinson was certainly not ready to be a producer, at least not for The Black Crowes in 1993. Unfortunately, Chris had long ago banished George Drakoulias from our lives.

During the recording of *Southern Harmony*, George hadn't changed how he interacted with the band. He recognized that we were a very different band than the one he signed, and he complimented us regularly for all we'd accomplished. At the same time, he made a point of saying, "You went on tour, you became a great band—that's your job. We still have to work just as hard on the new songs. That's my job."

He didn't bow to Chris's whims. He spoke his mind no matter what. And that is exactly what did him in. Chris decided before *Southern Harmony* was even released that he could no longer work with George. He felt we'd "outgrown" him.

The obvious choice to take over was Brendan O'Brien, who had gone on to great success working with Pearl Jam and Stone Temple Pilots. (We had actually recommended Brendan to Stone Gossard and Jeff Ament when we hung out after a Black Crowes gig in 1992, right before Pearl Jam made their massive second album, *Vs.*)

Brendan ultimately produced just one session for us, at Daniel Lanois's studio in New Orleans on a day off from the High as the Moon tour. At the time we assumed Brendan would do our next album. The songs we recorded that day were all written on the road, and the band was as locked in and as powerful as it would ever be.

We tracked all the songs live, no overdubs at all. Brendan wanted to get a sense of where we were with the new tunes. "Exit," "Bewildered," and "The Fear Years" were three of the heaviest tunes The Black Crowes ever came up with, and there were also a couple of other jams we played live for years in various forms. We also put down the first recorded versions of two songs from later albums, "Nonfiction" and "Girl from a Pawn Shop."

I loved what we recorded that day. We captured a moment that surpassed what we'd done on our second album. These songs, to me, seemed like the next step in our evolution. I felt they were even compatible with the more heavy-riffing aspects of alternative rock at the time, despite them being darker and heavier than anything on the first two albums. I wanted those songs mixed and released as a post-tour EP, a little something extra to hold fans over until the album.

But nobody else was on board. Everyone loved the tunes, but for whatever reason no one else thought putting them out was a good idea. They were rough, sure. The vocals weren't great, sure. But they were REAL. It was a live band in a studio playing like the world was about to end.

As I feared, Chris also decided that "Exit," "Bewildered," and "The Fear Years" weren't going on the new album, either. He hated using "old" material. Chris saw songs written on tour as "tour songs," and he thought albums should all be written off the road.

"We are starting over," he declared. "We're not bringing any old songs to *Tall*. The third album is going to be all written in LA when you guys get here."

Before we got to LA, though, Chris and Rich sat down with Brendan to discuss the album. They played him a few new tunes, and Brendan offered some suggestions on how to trim the length down to get them closer to four minutes, and therefore increase their chances with radio play.

"I'm not doing shit for radio," Chris said.

"Look, these songs are great, guys, and I think we can make a great record. But they're twice as long as they need to be," Brendan replied. This, by the way, is exactly what producers are there to do.

Chris lost his mind. He wasn't simply unhappy there was a dis- agreement. He was *offended*.

Chris thought we no longer needed to think conventionally. "Con- ventionally" to Chris simply meant anything other than what he was thinking. I think Chris also hated the fact that Brendan had become extraordinarily successful without us.

"He can go make bullshit Pearl Jam records," Chris declared. Of course, that's exactly what Brendan did, with the results of those ef- forts being self-evident.

Rich had his own issues, too. Brendan, like George, was sarcastic, witty, and incapable of kissing our asses. Brendan made fun of Rich's car during the recording of *Southern Harmony*—it was a BMW 850 and Brendan asked one day, "Who parked that Ford Probe under the hoop?"—and Rich never got over it. He thought Brendan "didn't show enough respect," as if we were royalty.

There was also the fact that Brendan played the guitar solo on "Hard to Handle," and Rich, feeling insecure about his own abilities at the time, resented Brendan for it. Rich was too thick to understand that his lack of guitar knowledge was his greatest strength. The fact that he taught himself to play, while already writing original music, made him unique. A guy like Brendan could whip off the guitar solo in "Hard to Handle" like he was sneezing, but Brendan could never do what Rich did instinctively. But Rich couldn't get over his own defensiveness.

With Pearl Jam and Stone Temple Pilots, Brendan demonstrated he could make exciting, live-sounding rock records that also dominated radio and the album charts. Not hiring him to produce our third album was one of countless lost opportunities at that juncture in our career.

In November of 1993, we began work on our third album without the help of a real producer. That decision cost us over $600,000 and the result- ing album ended up collecting dust in a vault for years.

We set up shop at a rehearsal studio in the San Fernando Valley called the Alley, and immediately hit one hell of a stride. We cranked out song after song after song. Within days we put together the tunes that made up the bulk of the album. "Wiser Time," "A Conspiracy," and "P.25 London" all appeared quickly.

"High Head Blues," another new one, was the first song Chris wrote entirely by himself. Rich immediately dismissed it, saying point blank, "That song sucks." But Chris kept it in the mix. To me, I didn't give a shit who wrote what. I was pro-songs. I wanted as much material as possible to pick through. So I was fine with "High Head Blues."

"Wiser Time" took a little while to find itself. Rich had the verse and chorus parts, and was playing them over and over, back and forth one day. I was playing a straight beat, just looking for the right feel and getting nowhere. Rich felt like he was onto something, but nobody else brought anything that clicked. So we moved on. Maybe tomorrow. That's how it worked. There was always another new song or idea to chase.

Chris and I were playing a game of h-o-r-s-e in the parking lot later and he said, "Hey, maybe think more about specific parts on some of these tunes. Like the verse beat in 'Ticket to Ride' or something. Not just a groove but a signature pattern. You know, just see if anything pops."

I was thinking about that the next day as I pulled a cowbell out of a box and attached it to the kick drum. I'd never used one before, and thought maybe it'd trigger some ideas. Of course, I immediately played the intro to Grand Funk's "We're an American Band," because that's what you do with a cowbell. Everybody laughed, and then without thinking I started playing a frantic pattern, double time on the hi-hat, double strokes on the cowbell, that would have sounded at home on the first Devo album.

Everyone laughed but Chris. He jumped off the couch and ran to me. "Play that exact part, but slower!"

I actually thought he was kidding. What on earth could he be hearing in that head of his?

I played it slower, and he turned to Rich. "Now play those changes from yesterday that you like!" Rich picked up a different guitar and began playing the verse changes to "Wiser Time." It sat perfectly over what I was playing.

The rest of the band felt it, too. Everyone jumped in. Rich stopped to suggest an idea for Johnny's bass line. Johnny ran with it and eventually found his part. Within ten minutes the song was finished. That was us at our best. Not forcing things, just waiting for the right inspiration to take an idea and blow it up into a fully realized song. Moments like that could always justify the rest of the nonsense to me.

Some songs were put together like a puzzle. For "A Conspiracy," Rich had four completely separate ideas he was messing with, and Chris simply put them in order. What Rich heard as a pre-chorus became the chorus, and vice versa. Rich complained a lot when Chris arranged the pieces like that, but nine times out of ten, Chris got his way. That wasn't at all unlike writing sessions in 1987. Rich provided the lumber, and Chris laid it all out as the architect.

For the first time, though, the arrangement process took precedence, in terms of time spent, over the actual songwriting process. At the Alley, the brothers weren't in a room with a producer and a couple of acoustic guitars, working out the finer points of the songs' structures. We were all in a room together, focusing on arrangements and grooves.

Songwriting with George was full of little finesses. What's a quick turnaround to set up the pre-chorus? How do we transition out of the chorus without simply hitting the verse again on the downbeat? Do the lyrics make sense? Do they fit the vibe of the music? We ignored all that shit on *Tall*. We had the meat and the potatoes. We were focused on vibe, tempo, and groove. Once a song felt lived in, we were done. Lyrics? Melody? Chris would get around to that eventually.

Look at "Wiser Time." It's essentially just two parts: verse-chorus, verse-chorus, solo over the verse, chorus out. It's a fantastic track, and definitely one of The Black Crowes' signature tunes. But it's not about the "song" in the classic sense. You won't hear buskers in Dublin whipping out "Wiser Time" for coins in their guitar case. Chris's lyrics "On a good day, we can part the sea / on a bad day, glory beyond our reach" are certainly significant in the overall arc of The Black Crowes, but they're not the sort of universal lyrics that automatically resonate with someone unaware of the context. It's the performance, the feel, and the mood that make "Wiser Time" special, not the craft of the songwriting.

That's not a knock on Chris and Rich. We had plenty of great "songs" in the classic sense. But now we were at a point where we could take some bare-bones pieces, craft something special out of them, and that would be good enough.

Once we began recording these new songs, *Tall* went off the rails. But preproduction for *Tall* was exciting, spontaneous, and productive. We were engaged fully, working well together, and for the most part successfully negotiating our way through Chris and Rich's power struggles.

The Red Hot Chili Peppers were set up in the room next door. We'd hear some noise coming out of their room, but not much. For days on end only Chad Smith and Flea, the rhythm section, would be in there. They'd pop into our room, drink a beer or take a hit off a joint, listen to us jamming for a bit, and then head into their room again. We'd hear them together, just digging into the same groove, over and over and over. We'd listen through the walls and say, "We've written three songs today, what the hell are they doing over there, just playing the same thing?"

Chad told me much later that Flea would be so stoned from Chris's (very strong) weed that he'd only be able to play one groove. They called it "Flea's Been Hanging with the Crowes."

A few times, they stopped by at the end of the day to ask what we'd come up with. We'd immediately play them whatever songs we had just written. A private little concert for two dudes on the couch in the corner. And they would always say, "Jesus Christ, you wrote that today? We can't even all get in the same room for an hour."

We were showing off, and they loved it. On the whole, those were good days.

Southern Harmony was a great album, in large part because there were very steady hands on the wheel. We really missed that input on *Tall*.

We began recording *Tall* in December at the Conway studios in Hollywood. We'd already been in LA for a month, had worked some really long hours at the Alley, and had a ton of songs to show for it. Preproduction is the hard part, when all the nuts and bolts are put in place. Recording is supposed to be the fast part. It's like making a film: you write the screenplay for five years and shoot the whole thing in a month.

In a perfect world, we would have taken a few weeks away from each other, come back in January fresh and recharged, and knocked out the recordings in a couple of weeks.

But Chris wanted this to be an *epic* album. So, in his mind, we needed an epic experience in the studio, like The Stones recording *Exile on Main Street*. They had spent a year in a French chateau, needlessly burning through millions of dollars, drug dealers coming and going, waiting for the right mood to strike, and every now and again capturing a great take.

To that end, Chris insisted on only rolling tape after dark and working until sunrise. He honestly thought the music would be better served by forcing a vibe down our throats that Rich, Johnny, and I found to be entirely counterproductive. I love The Rolling Stones, but I couldn't see the point in trying to do anything other than be ourselves.

I thought our greatest strength was that we could plug in and let it rip. The music itself was the vibe. We didn't need to wait until midnight to start working just to fulfill some ridiculous image of what a rock 'n' roll band was. We already were a world-class rock 'n' roll band with great songs. What else did we need?

Hard drugs and liquor were as integral for Chris as the songs themselves. I walked into the studio one day and saw a guy playing a French horn for the outro on "Descending." We were clearly in the weeds. *A fucking French horn? Jesus Christ, are we making a fucking Sting record?*

Even the title, which he had settled on before one note was written, was a drug reference. "Tall" was an old jazz term for getting high that Chris thought was cool.

The whole experience blew my mind. For a month at the Alley, we were clear-headed and focused. Now that we had moved into a studio to make the actual album, the focus was gone. Chris, Marc, and Ed were doing tons of blow, both in the studio and back at the Sunset Marquis bar. To Chris, not just our singer but also our producer now, coke was an essential part of making the record.

I had no interest in that.

"This is a fucking rock 'n' roll fucking band," Chris spat. "You're a fucking pussy!"

Those were his direct words right in my face: I was a fucking pussy for not wanting to do cocaine in the studio.

My response every single time was simple and direct: "You have the first punch—whenever you want it, take it. You can start it anytime, but then I'm gonna finish it."

At the risk of stating the obvious, that first punch was never thrown.

18

Björk, Hans Gruber, and an Earthquake of Note

Chris's belief that the making of our third album should be an epic endeavor of legendary hedonistic proportion was clearly refuted by the actual record we were making. The tracks for *Tall* sounded muted. They had no life. No energy. It just sat there on tape like a dry fart.

The main issue was unquestionably the performances. The playing was flat because we were tracking at midnight. There were three members of the band not doing coke every night: Rich, Johnny, and me. We were the three guys who needed to be the most alert, who provided all of the muscle, groove, and feel of the tracks.

Everything else can be overdubbed and fucked with. But the fucking rhythm tracks? They gotta be real. And we were just tired.

Chris was in way over his head. On stage, the band communicated telepathically: we could read each other. Making records is different. A producer has to be able to say, directly, "This is what I need" and explain it in short, digestible sentences.

Chris couldn't do that. His frustration over his own ineptitude would bubble over into overt anger. A quick chat about the setup to a chorus would somehow devolve into a thirty-minute negotiation where Jim Mitchell would end up trying to talk Chris off the ledge.

Every day was like that. The sessions were almost *deliberately* tedious. Chris really believed if we took weeks and weeks to make *Tall*, then that would make the record better. The days were so goddamn long, too. We would leave the studio every morning at five or six, drive to the hotel, try to sleep until two in the afternoon, and then wake up, have some coffee, and head back to the studio.

We did that every day, seven days a week. There were no days off. We took four or five days off for Christmas and then went right back to work. It was madness.

Chris referenced Steely Dan a lot that month. He was intentionally trying to push our band in that direction. His guiding principle was "we're not going to be some stupid rock band."

Of course, that mind-set was in direct opposition to the very essence of The Black Crowes. Our strength was playing live, as a unit, in the moment, instinctively, and without a lot of deliberation. Chris rambled on incessantly about the magic of music, and yet when he was surrounded by it, he never seemed to notice.

Rich was fucking miserable about all of it. Across the board, he was coming out on the losing end of his power struggle with Chris. One day during preproduction, I hopped into Rich's car to head back to the hotel. It was his Porsche, or his BMW 850 . . . I don't remember. I just know he had them both shipped out to Los Angeles so he wouldn't have to rent a car. Anyway, as we took off he cranked up the new Nirvana album, *In Utero*. Rich had it turned up so loud I was literally covering my ears.

"This is what I want!" Rich screamed over "All Apologies." "Why can't we fucking rock?"

I loved Nirvana. I was with him in that regard. I dug our new tunes, but there was a noticeable lack of straight-up rock involved.

A few days later, I mentioned that to Chris and he hit the roof.

"Don't ever fucking talk to me about Nirvana, please. It's embarrassing."

For Chris, as always, any band who was part of our generation was a joke. He hated Pearl Jam more than anything. There's a line in the song "P.25 London" about Eddie Vedder, in fact. Chris had read somewhere that Eddie often acted drunk to avoid having to deal with certain social interactions. He carried a wine bottle for added effect, but it was usually empty. That's where the "empty bottle saviors they crawl" line came from.

Chris went off the rails about how the Seattle music scene was already dead. It meant nothing, it never had, it was all just marketing, blah blah blah. His reticence to rock and his desire to soften all the edges was in large part a reaction to grunge. Hell, the entire first verse of "A Conspiracy" is about the Seattle explosion from 1992. He was mocking it, calling it a lost cause, and a cynical product of a briefly successful marketing campaign by MTV and radio:

Did you ever hear
The one about last year
It was all a lie
Ain't it funny how the time flies

Great. So Seattle sucks, and those bands are all posers, and the entire movement was created by MTV. And, oh yeah, you don't care about it at all. And you'll show how little you care by writing lyrics about it.

We took one day off that whole month: Sunday, January 16. I stayed in bed most of the day, watching the NFL playoffs, thrilled to not see anybody. As hard as I tried to clear my head, I couldn't stop thinking about the band, the record, and how far off course we had blown in just a matter of weeks.

By early evening, I was really wound up. I'd never had another breakdown like the one in Tokyo, but I had to admit to myself this was the worst I'd felt since then. It came on so fast, and I was starting to panic a bit.

I called Rose Mary at home in Atlanta, and she talked me down enough that I was able to fall asleep by midnight.

At 4:30 a.m., the Northridge earthquake hit.

It was a monster. From its epicenter in the San Fernando Valley, the quake hit the Los Angeles area with a magnitude of 6.7, causing the most intense shaking ever measured in an urban area in North America. It killed fifty-seven people, injured more than eighty-seven hundred people, and caused as much as $50 billion in damage.

I knew The Black Crowes had some karma. But I had no idea we had *that* kind of karma.

By the time the shaking stopped, I was wide awake on my feet in a pitch-black hotel room, confused and panicked. It felt like the world was ending. I somehow felt my way to the door. To my right in the hallway was an external exit door that opened to a stairwell. Johnny's room was to my left. There was absolutely no sound. Dead quiet. For a few terrifying seconds, I thought that maybe I was the only survivor in the building.

Finally I heard a voice.

"Steve?"

It was Johnny.

He opened his door and called out for me again. I was about two feet away, and we grabbed hands in the dark. We hugged; we were both shaking.

"Holy shit, are you okay?" Johnny asked.

"Yeah, I'm fine, are you okay? We have to get outside."

Johnny's girlfriend, Rosie, was with him. The three of us, and their pet pug, inched back to the exit door and then walked down three flights to the back courtyard. I realized I was holding three blankets. I was in some sort of shock and on autopilot, thinking like a Red Cross volunteer or something.

Outside, a handful of people gathered in the garden area that led to the back villas. I noticed a girl standing alone, wearing a little nightie. She looked about twelve years old or so, and she was shivering. I couldn't believe she was out there alone. Poor kid.

"Hey, do you need a blanket?" I asked. She turned to look up at me and said, "Yeah, sure, thanks." It wasn't a twelve-year-old kid. It was Björk.

I was taken aback. The only way to describe the whole scene is to say it was like a dream. As in *I had this weird dream where I offered a little girl a blanket and it turned out she was Björk.*

After a few seconds to calibrate just how weird my life suddenly was, I led Björk and a few other hotel guests through the gardens and into the lobby of the hotel. As we walked past the pool, a tremor shook the ground again. Everybody froze and reached out to hold on to each other. Everyone but Björk, anyway. She danced a little jig and squealed with delight. This was officially a *Twilight Zone* episode now.

"Come on," she said after plopping down on a couch, "sit with me. God, that was fun," she said. "It was like a roller coaster."

"Yeah, uh . . . no. I don't like this at all," I replied. "This shit's not cool."

Right then, the first really big aftershock hit, a four-point-something. It lasted over ten seconds.

"Woo!" Björk squealed, her face lighting up.

"Fuck this," I said, and ran out of the lobby and into the middle of the street. I looked down the hill and all the telephone poles were wobbling in sync with each other. The aftershocks started coming in regularly, and I stayed out there for a while, trying to calm down.

There was a break between aftershocks, at least ten minutes. I talked myself back into the lobby and sat on the couch again with Björk. Johnny and Rosie were there, too, and Rich and his wife, Emma, had come down from their villa.

I felt someone sit down on the couch next to me on the other side. I looked over and it was Alan Rickman. Holy shit . . . Hans Gruber from *Die Hard*! Could this night get any weirder?

He and I had what had become a standard conversation for everyone in the lobby: "Were you asleep when it hit?" "Did you know what it was?" "Ever been in one before?"

I finally started to relax a little. For the first time in a while, I was actually shaken out of my doldrums. The internal wars being waged within The Black Crowes weren't in the least bit concerning anymore.

By the time the sun finally rose, the lobby had become a refuge. Everyone was genuinely concerned for everyone else. There were real smiles, real hugs, real relief that everyone was okay. All of the hip-Hollywood-hotel vibe was gone. For a few hours, everyone sat together and comforted one another. It was really nice.

At seven thirty, the lights popped back on. A cheer went up throughout the lobby. Having the greatest scare of my life had actually been kind of great. I hadn't thought about the album in hours. I had to laugh at myself. A natural disaster providing me with relief was clearly a sign I was still running short on perspective.

There were minor damages to the studio, so we had a few days off. Johnny, Rosie, and I were on a red-eye back to Atlanta the next night. Rose Mary was waiting for me at the airport. By the time I got there, I'd been awake for twenty-four hours and was spinning a bit. I didn't get out of bed for two days.

Johnny and I flew back to LA, and after ten more days of recording, we were finished. We weren't gonna hang around for overdubs, so it was back home for us again.

Within a few weeks, the record was mixed and we all got copies to listen to.

I played mine on my stereo at home once or twice, and tried to talk myself into liking what I heard. It was a tough sell. It was stiff. Dead on arrival.

The battle over what to do next kicked off in earnest. I don't recall the label being too enthused. Rich hated it, Chris loved it, and the rest of our opinions were valid only if aligned accordingly.

There was a period of limbo for a month and a half. What do we think? Is this really the album? Chris took every comment personally. To suggest something wasn't quite as good as hoped was an insult to his vision. It was impossible to get a consensus on anything. All I knew was that every time I heard the fucking French horn I wanted to throw up.

And then, in a flash, it was over, thanks to The Rolling Stones.

The Stones had set up camp in LA to record their first album in five years, *Voodoo Lounge*. Don Was, their producer, invited Chris to come by the studio for a hang. He went over one night for a few hours. He heard two songs they had recorded, and they rocked.

Chris called Pete that night and said, "We have to redo the whole record. The Stones are making a real rock 'n' roll record, and we have to rock now, too."

That was it. Chris spent three hours with The Stones and decided to shelve our new record. His record. The album he pissed away $600,000 on.

The fun was just getting started.

19

Best Not Buy

As we regrouped in Los Angeles to make the record that became *Amor-ica*, we had a great idea. Let's rerecord the songs we did for *Tall*, but this time let's make sure the album doesn't suck.

We'll rock. We'll get aggressive. We'll reassert *our own* identity. We'll just be The Black Crowes. Genius.

Chris was not, mercifully, going to produce the second time around. He did, however, select his own replacement: Jack Joseph Puig. We'd heard about Puig from our buddies in Jellyfish, as he had coproduced both of their albums. He was experienced, though it's not like he had worked on a ton of cool records. His early discography was heavy with Amy Grant, Bette Midler, and Debby Boone LPs. But he was a professional who knew what the fuck he was doing.

We began work, for the second time, on our third album. Jack had booked us at Sound City, in Van Nuys. The first thing I noticed when I walked into the lobby was a platinum album on the wall for *Nevermind*. Cobain's suicide had occurred just two weeks earlier, and here we were loading into the same studio where he had recorded his breakthrough. On a day when I was hoping for clear skies, that struck me as a bit of a black cloud.

Luckily, from day one, the sessions at Sound City with Jack felt great. The drinking and the drugs were dialed way back. Everyone, even Chris, knew getting off on the right foot was essential. We also upended the daily schedule from *Tall*. This time around, we were all at Sound City no later than noon every day and out by midnight. The energy in the room subsequently improved dramatically.

By the second week, however, Jack's obsession with getting sounds "just right" started to bog things down. He could easily burn seven or eight hours chasing the perfect kick-drum sound. Mic adjustments, mic replacements, blanket positioning, choosing the right kick drum for each song: Jack came off like a mad scientist tinkering in a lab with no particular goal in mind.

Eventually, he would shout, "That's it! Let's do this!" after I'd been sitting at the kit, playing the kick drum, for hours.

"No, Jack, I'm about to fall asleep. Lemme get some fresh air and get out in the sun for a bit." I hated being the guy to complain, but it was making me fucking crazy.

Turns out my worries were mostly for naught. Jack really did keep the ball rolling. Toward the end of the last week, we revived "Nonfiction" out of Chris's forbidden "old song" files. It led to our first big blowup of the session. We got a take everyone dug and then it was time for some overdubs. Chris had a bug up his ass about my tambourine track. He insisted we bring in a professional percussionist to rerecord it.

"Dude, we don't need someone else to play tambourine. You can just do it, or I'll do it again. It's a fucking *tambourine* part." I couldn't believe this was an issue.

"No, that's bullshit," Chris said. "Am I the only one who fucking cares about getting it right?"

Jack and I were caught off guard. Where was this coming from? We'd played the song on *Saturday Night Live* a year and a half earlier, and for that version I'd played congas. For the first time ever. With twenty fucking million people watching. And now we needed a ringer?

"We don't need Tito Puente to come in and play a tambourine for fuck's sakes!" I said, laughing.

Finally, Jack stepped in and suggested we both take a pass to see if we could improve it.

I went first. The song played, I shook the fucking tambourine, and the song ended. It wasn't exactly rocket science. Jack said, "That's perfect."

"No! That's not real fucking tambourine," Chris complained. "I'll fucking do it."

Chris recorded a take. He listened back and still wasn't satisfied.

"Fuck it. We just need a real tambourine player."

Two days later, Jack came over and told me Chris had finally agreed to use my tambourine part.

Gee, great. Who cares? *It's a fucking tambourine part.*

We got through the sessions in one piece. But we had a world tour to plan. Singles to choose. Videos to shoot. Many, many decisions to make.

We were about to come completely unglued.

After Amorica was released, a mythology was spun yet again around the making of the album that wasn't anywhere close to reality. We played no small part in creating that narrative, of course, as we shot a promotional video of us performing some of the new music in the studio, which was filled with extras wearing all kinds of wild costumes. Midgets, strippers, drug dealers, members of the clergy, cops—it looked like a bizarre mushroom-fueled fever dream orgy was about to explode. The mushroom part was real. For the shoot, we handed out shrooms to the whole room like they were candy. Everybody was tripping. Well, everybody but Rich.

But the rest of the process was nothing like that. Hell, even *Tall* wasn't like that.

The vibe at Sound City for *Amorica* was pretty simple: "We have to go make a badass record, pronto."

On a sunny Saturday afternoon, the whole band ended up at Barney's Beanery for lunch. There were a few days of overdubs to do, then vocals, and then the mix. We knew we'd done it right this time. We were all in good spirits, with equal parts pride and relief.

Johnny and I had talked with Pete that morning. He suggested we do all we could to streamline the process. With Johnny and me finished, there was no reason to stay. It made perfect sense. We both agreed without a thought.

After we finished lunch, I started saying my goodbyes. I was gonna head back to the hotel, pack my stuff, and get a red-eye home. Chris couldn't believe it. He was furious.

"Why the fuck are you going home?" he yelled at us as we walked out the front door.

"Why would we stay?" I asked. It was an honest question. I wasn't antagonizing him. "Chris, you don't give a shit what I think about mixes, you never have. None of us were in the studio when the first two albums were mixed. Why should this one be any different?"

I was absolutely right, of course. Chris didn't want my input. What he did actually want was to accuse us of not caring about the band as much as he did.

"Fuck it. No, fine. Go ahead, man. Just leave. It doesn't matter," he said calmly. He immediately detached himself from the conversation. He turned around and walked away, leaving me and Johnny to wonder what kind of damage the seed he had just planted would bring.

By the middle of the summer of 1994, *Amorica* was finished. We loved it. A lot of Black Crowes fans think it's our best record. One could argue that *Shake Your Money Maker* or *Southern Harmony* have better songs, but it's indisputable that the playing sounds absolutely ferocious on *Amorica*.

We all assumed *Amorica* was going to be the ultimate ends-justify-the-means album. Pete was working day and night with the label on every last detail: the release date, the first, second, third single, video shoots, European promotion, press tours, radio junkets, tour dates. All of the pieces to the puzzle that would ensure building on our success worldwide. *Southern Harmony* had sold about half as many copies as *Shake Your Money Maker* domestically, but it had sold more copies in the rest of the world. We were poised to take our career to the next level.

That didn't happen. We never had a chance. As it turned out, *Amorica* was dead on arrival commercially, and Chris Robinson was the one who killed it.

Chris decided the cover image from the July 1976 bicentennial issue of *Hustler*, which depicts a woman's crotch with pubic hair sticking out of her American flag bikini, would be the cover of *Amorica*. He had also named the album *Amorica*, although he was never able to explain the same way twice what the fuck "Amorica" meant. He said something once about it being a "state of mind, free of judgment," which caused Ed Harsch of all people to say, "Well, motherfucker, you might wanna stop by sometime!"

We voted. "Who wants this as the album cover?" Chris voted yes. Rich, Johnny, Pete, and I voted no. *Nothing* speaks to the dysfunction of our band more than the fact that Chris got his way.

"Fuck all of you. This is what I do for the band. I'm the creative director."

Despite acknowledging *Amorica* was a better album than *Tall*, Chris was still furious about the fact we rerecorded it in the first place. He had failed miserably as a producer, and instead of taking his lumps and getting back on board as a member of the band, he doubled down on his need for control.

The record label hated the cover for obvious reasons: many retailers were not going to stock an album with pubic hair on it. But Chris refused to budge. He talked himself into thinking he was actually taking a principled stand.

To this day, I think the *Amorica* cover looks like a Mötley Crüe record. It's like when Spinal Tap put out *Smell the Glove*. Chris was our very own Nigel Tufnel, wondering, "What's wrong with being sexy?" It's juvenile. Embarrassing. And, most importantly, it has zero connection to the music.

The album cover was clearly going to hurt us with the big retailers but, actually, Chris had already done a good bit of damage on his own in that regard. Toward the end of tracking on *Amorica*, Pete and Mark DiDia, the president of Def American, dropped by the studio with an executive from Best Buy. Pete had mentioned to the rest of us they'd be over, and to simply be hospitable for a few minutes.

Pete, Mark, and Mr. Best Buy walked into the control room. Chris greeted them warmly. He was excited to play Pete and Mark a couple of the tunes.

"Hey, man, how are you doing?" Chris said, extending a hand to the guest.

He was doing his "we're just getting our vibe on" act, because he didn't know who this guy was. And the Best Buy guy was starstruck. *Oh, my God, it's The Black Crowes, and here's Chris Robinson!*

"What do you do, man?" Chris asked after a few minutes.

"I'm the music buyer for Best Buy," he said.

"What? What the fuck are you doing in here?" Chris was immediately on edge. "Fucking Black Crowes fans don't shop at Best Buy."

"Actually, you'd be surprised. We sell a lot of your records," the Best Buy guy said, not yet sensing that Chris was gathering a head of steam.

Chris killed the song. The party was over. It was time to clear out before it really got worse.

As Mark ushered the buyer out of the control room, he stopped and apologized to Chris for intruding. He was shellshocked. One minute he's an invited guest, sipping a Red Stripe and rocking out with the frontman of a famous rock band, and the next minute that same frontman is yelling at him about the purity of his fans' shopping choices.

Sure enough, six months later, Best Buy was not carrying *Amorica*, and Wal-Mart was not carrying *Amorica*, and a bunch of other stores didn't sell *Amorica*, either.

Kneecapped before the race even started. Great. Thanks, man.

Contrary to what Chris wanted to believe about our fans, many of them *did* shop at Best Buy and other big-box stores. A lot of them didn't live in towns with cool local record stores, not even in the '90s. The point is, if you have the chance to get your record into every major store in the country—most bands never get that opportunity—you don't squander it.

Chris told us one day we were all out of touch; we didn't really know and understand Black Crowes fans.

"I have a feeling I'm more in touch with them than you are, as you live in the Hollywood Hills and you spend more on weed than most people make in a year," I replied.

"That's not fucking true."

"How much do you spend on weed in a year?"

"I don't know, a hundred grand?"

20

Money

Amorica was released on November 1, 1994, just under a year after we started writing songs at the Alley. The ominous black cloud I had sensed rolling in when I noticed *Nevermind* on the wall, back on day one at Sound City, finally came to fruition. Nirvana's *MTV Unplugged in New York*, the band's first album after Kurt's death, was released the very same day. One of those two albums (not ours) became a cultural phenomenon, and the other (ours) went largely unnoticed by comparison.

We were in London for about a week doing promo for the album release. We actually agreed to do an in-store appearance for the day of release. We hadn't done one of those in years, but our UK label (now BMG, I think) begged us, saying creating a mob scene at a local megastore would go a long way toward creating buzz for the new album.

Walking into the store, we were immediately dispossessed of that notion. There were, at most, three dozen fans waiting for us. We signed their albums, took pics, and were walking back to the hotel within fifteen minutes.

Sixteen months earlier, we had headlined Glastonbury and the Phoenix Festival. As far as we knew, we *owned* the UK in the summer of 1993. And now . . . that's it? I guess the rest of our fans were all at home listening to the new Nirvana record.

A couple of weeks later, we went out for a short club tour in the States. The idea was to create a bit of pandemonium wherever we went by playing tiny rooms. Those shows were really good. The smaller rooms meant less volume onstage, and I just didn't have to hit as hard. We had a lot more dynamic in our playing, which I loved. We were still rocking, but we were also at our most musical.

But before long the same excesses that plagued the second half of the High as the Moon tour returned. In Minneapolis, we played First Avenue, the historic downtown venue where Prince and the Revolution hang out in *Purple Rain*. Between songs, Marc came around behind his amp, where his tech had laid out a fat rail of coke. Marc snorted it up in full view of the audience, and then went back around and started playing the next song.

This to me was a whole new level of stupidity. You want to be high onstage? Fine, I guess. But doing coke in front of hundreds of people was lame. That's the kind of glory-hound shit I imagined the guys in '80s hair bands did.

Back in the dressing room after the show, everyone was talking about it. Chris said, "Damn, dude, that was awesome." Awesome? I didn't get it. By the way, Marc played like shit for the second half of the set. His tone went straight to hell the second he shoved a rail of coke in his fucking gob.

Drug stunts aside, the shows did what we hoped. There were lines around the block everywhere we went, and the fans who actually did get into the clubs to see us were all raving.

Amorica entered the *Billboard* album chart at number eleven, and then dropped out of the Top 20 by the second week. Pete was sounding the alarms about the tepid response at radio and MTV, but we focused on the gigs. We told ourselves we were launching an eighteen-month world tour, and the album would find its audience.

I probably would have been concerned about all the various external red flags, had I not been raging about an enormous, all-encompassing *internal* red flag. Just before we left for London, Pete set up a conference call with me and Johnny. For the first time since we met Pete, he fumbled his words a bit. It was clear from the beginning of the call he would be delivering bad news.

Chris and Rich wanted Pete to renegotiate our partnership agreement. They had called Pete and explained that, from their perspective, since Johnny and I were not as involved in the making of the music, we should receive less money. And Chris specifically mentioned our decision to leave LA before the mixing of *Amorica* as a shining example.

Up to that point, all the money the band generated was split evenly four ways. That's record sales, touring, merch. Basically anything that wasn't songwriting, which went solely to Chris and Rich. Publishing is worth tons of money, much more than the band made. But Chris and Rich wanted still bigger slices of the pie. Greedy motherfuckers.

"Well, shit," Johnny said. "I guess we should've seen that coming."

Johnny was more reasonable than me. He was at least willing to discuss the situation.

Me?

No. Fucking. Way.

I had been with the Robinson brothers much longer. I was the first outsider who had ever fully committed to the band. I was the only remaining connection to Mr. Crowe's Garden. I had worked too hard, and put up with too much lunacy, to imagine being relegated.

"I'm out," I said.

"Hang on. You're not quitting the band," Pete shot back.

"Pete, I am absolutely quitting the band if they think they're going to change our agreement. Those two motherfuckers fight every goddamned day—they drive the fucking band into the ditch with their bullshit. They don't want my opinion on shit. Hell, Pete, they don't want YOUR opinion on shit. Everything has to be Chris's way or Rich's way. And now they decide, after making all the rules and choking everybody else out, that they're coming for our money, too? No fucking way."

"Look, this is a business," Johnny reasoned.

"No, it's not a business. It's a fucking *band* with a couple of assholes."

Pete eventually talked me off the ledge. Johnny remained calm, even though he was equally angered. We ended the call, as Pete told us he wanted to talk to the brothers.

He called back within twenty minutes.

He said, "I suggested we focus on the album release and the club tour, and then we can pick this back up in a few months, after the holidays. They agreed. Just trust me, here."

As far as I was concerned, the Robinson brothers could pick it up any goddamned time they wanted. I was fully committed to quitting the band before giving them anything.

So that entire chapter of the Robinson brothers shit show was lingering throughout the entire week in London and the Tiny Tour in clubs. I didn't confront Chris about it until December, when we were in Paris for some TV appearances and to shoot the video for "High Head Blues." Michel Gondry directed. He later made *Eternal Sunshine of the Spotless Mind* with Jim Carrey and Kate Winslet, but in 1994 he was known as the hippest music video director working. By 1995, all his videos were in constant rotation all across the world. Well, all except one.

It was a pretty wild concept. Chris Robinson plays Chris Robinson, and the rest of us are orange-clad aliens that climb inside his brain one night while he's asleep. We then assume control of his actions. Or something like that. I'm not entirely sure. I honestly don't know that I ever saw the finished product. Few people ever did. The single never got any traction at radio, and the video followed suit.

We spent three days in a warehouse on the outskirts of Paris painted orange, drinking wine, and counting the minutes until we could go home for the holidays. On our last night in town, we somehow ended up at Queen, a raging gay disco on the Champs-Élysées. Everyone in the place was on Ecstasy, dancing and losing their collective minds. It was like a Gianni Versace wet dream. Johnny was wearing leather pants with tassels, which was a normal look for him, but now at a gay disco in Paris, he didn't look raw. He looked *butch*. A steady stream of men came up to hit on him.

We were drinking straight vodka for hours, having a great time. We were leaving for the airport at nine in the morning, so there was no point in going back to the hotel. We walked out of there at sunrise.

When we were about two blocks from our hotel, I decided right then, blasted on vodka, to confront Chris about the money.

"Hey, man, let me tell you something," I slurred. "This thing, where you're trying to take our money, this is not right, man."

As drunk as we were, I could still tell I caught him off guard. I kept going. "I *have* to be an equal, or you can just go fuck yourselves. Call it 'The Chris Robinson and Rich Robinson Black Crowes' if you want. But *The Black Crowes* is a band."

"I know, man," Chris said. "You're right." He folded immediately. "Uhh, I mean, it's Pete. It was his idea, and we just went with it."

I knew that was total bullshit. Pete's life was consumed with trying to alleviate the tension in the band. He always fought for all of us collectively. He would never think of taking money from me and Johnny to give it to Chris and Rich. He would never create *more* conflict.

"I hear you, man," Chris said drunkenly. "We'll figure it out. It doesn't have to be that way. I love you, man."

Of course "I love you, man" didn't mean any of our issues were resolved. In fact, it was about to get a whole lot worse.

On January 3, 1995, we all flew to London, and then drove to Newport, Wales, to kick off the European leg of the Amorica or Bust tour. Unlike the "Tiny Tour," this was the real deal: a full-scale theater show with our own lights, backdrops, the works.

Pete had designed the lights and production for the High as the Moon tour. That production remains by far the best we ever used. It's still the one most people talk about: the thousands of Christmas lightbulbs instead of standard lighting, the moving mesh curtain around us, the backdrops . . . it was spectacular. The attention given to that light show was so overwhelming that, inexplicably, Chris decided to take control of the next one.

On our first day of production rehearsals in Newport, it was immediately apparent that Chris's stage production abilities were as disjointed as his album production abilities. The stage was fucking dark. There were very few lights at all. Chris didn't want "all that cliché shit." This was about setting a mood. Creating a vibe. There were several backdrops, including one with a Sherlock Holmes–looking character holding a lantern. None of it made sense.

Chris also tapped my cousin Jeffrey to wear three different costumes onstage during the shows: one was the devil, one was a cop with a pig's head, and one was a crow dressed up as Uncle Sam. Chris had hired the guy who makes costumes for Disney theme parks to design these getups. They cost a fortune.

In Newport, Pete was speechless. "Oh my fucking God" was all he could say. Which was more than anyone else could come up with. We were all in shock.

After a lengthy rehearsal, we met in the dressing room so Pete could explain to Chris just exactly how fucking terrible his stage design was.

Pete started gently, but soon enough couldn't hold back. "It's too dark! No one will be able to see you. No one will be able to see *anything!* And what's with these bedsheets that look like they were spray painted by learning-disabled third graders that are thrown over the amps? It doesn't make any fucking sense."

Chris responded to every point Pete made with rage, screaming that Pete just didn't understand. That none of us did. That we weren't a "stupid fucking rock band" and that "our music deserves to be treated with respect, not some Van Halen fucking ego bullshit."

The relationship between Chris and Pete was already seriously strained. They'd had a blowup just like this one a couple of months earlier at the Four Seasons Hotel in New York. Pete had read us a letter that Mitch Schneider, our longtime publicist, had written, saying he could no longer work with us if Chris continued to shit on other artists. The timing was horrible, as the album was about to hit the stores.

Chris had gone ballistic. "I'll say whatever the fuck I want! Fuck Mitch! I didn't get in a band to let a fucking publicist tell me a goddamned thing!"

Pete lost it that day. We'd never seen him that angry. I thought he was going to have a heart attack. He was beet red. "What the fuck is wrong with you?!? How can you hear those words from Mitch, a man who wants NOTHING but the best for you, breaks his back for you, and then tell him to fuck off?"

"I don't care. I don't have to ask their permission to fucking say what I want to say!"

"That's a hell of a stand to take. No one is telling you to ask permission, so stop with the fucking verbal smokescreens. I am telling you, as is your publicist, to stop criticizing other artists. It sounds fucking petty and makes you look like punks instead of musicians!!! You are fucking up, my friend."

Two months later, back in Wales, it was blowing up again between the two of them.

"Chris, this production is much too dark, it isn't going to work. I have designed shows for years—"

"Yes, for Van Halen. Fuck Van Halen," Chris interrupted. "I don't fucking care, Pete."

"Not just for fucking Van Halen," Pete fired back. "Now you have no fucking memory of the shows I designed for you?!"

Chris probably drank twelve beers during that argument. We all watched him open them, one after the other, and knock them back in just a few pulls. While Pete was talking, Chris would take a long slug off the bottle, as if recharging his batteries with anger. He'd scream for thirty seconds and then take another long slug. Over and over. His alcohol-fueled rage was clearly displayed on a daily basis but, still, this particular performance was impressive.

If nothing else, I felt relief that I didn't have a drinking problem. After all, I only drank eight or nine beers while this fight played itself out. That was fine. Nothing to worry about there.

Chris finally tapped out. "I'm not talking about it anymore. You'll just have to fucking trust me. It will be fine!"

He left the dressing room. Pete didn't take a breath. He turned to Rich, Johnny, and me.

"We're playing Royal Albert Hall in a few weeks. It's a historic venue, we're playing it for the first time, it's sold out and it can't fucking look like this! We are not going to have this bullshit on that stage! I'm going to London tomorrow, and I am going to design an entirely new show. Fuck this."

We agreed without hesitation.

So we would limp along with Chris's shitty light design until London. How Pete was going to explain a whole new look to Chris once we got there was his problem to worry about.

The next three weeks were rough. The tension on the bus, in the dressing room, and even on stage was hitting some all-time highs. There were regular shouting matches between songs, mostly between the brothers, but occasionally Johnny or I would get into it with Chris, too.

When we finally got to London and walked into the Royal Albert hall, the stage looked incredible. Pete had changed the entire production, and it was finally time for what we all anticipated would be a knock-down, drag-out fight between him and Chris.

Before sound check, Pete called Chris to the front of the house. He stood at the light board and talked Chris through every single change. He had lights everywhere. He showed him the many varied moods he had designed, and which songs he was attaching them to. He had various sizes of reflective, white painted stars and moons stenciled onto the monitor wedges, across the front lighting trusses, and all over the stage, all of which were glowing to define the stage. He had huge velvet curtains on each side of the stage. He had floor rugs with colors and patterns that complemented each other. He had hidden Chris's sheets high up in the trusses as a sort of tent-like roof that he had lit. He had a new Black Crowes logo hung and lit on the center of the front truss. It was awesome.

The rest of us were in our places onstage, nervously laughing to each other, just waiting for the mother of all time eruptions to kick off.

And then Chris said, calmly, "Cool, yeah. It looks great."

Pete simply said, "Well, I am glad you like it."

"Yeah, of course. I fucking told you my vision would work out. You just gotta trust me, Pete."

And then he walked to the stage for sound check.

Chris Robinson had officially lost his fucking mind.

The next day, Pete let me and Johnny know the brothers wanted to address the partnership agreement again. We were three weeks into the tour, together for twelve hours a day, and yet no one had ever discussed the ongoing partnership negotiation face to face other than when Chris and I drunkenly hashed it out in Paris.

A few months after our initial shock, Johnny had a much easier time with the conversation. He'd spent a lot of time thinking about it, and found he could clearly view The Black Crowes as a business. He later had tremendous success in the business world after he left the band, and his ability to survive was in large part thanks to his willingness to separate his feelings from the job.

That is one area where Johnny and I differed greatly.

"Pete," I said simply, "I'm done." I walked over to my shoulder bag and pulled out my passport. I held it up for him to see.

"I'm either going to Heathrow right now, or I'm not. You tell those cocksuckers to try me. Better yet, I'll go tell them myself."

Pete stood up, stopping me from heading to the door. He said simply, with a bit of a laugh, "Okay. They just needed a definitive answer and now they're gonna get one."

I could tell that as much as he wanted this issue to go away, he'd needed me to take a hard stand, without telling me to take one.

He walked out of the room. Johnny and I sat there for a minute. He finally said, "Okay, man, if you go, I go."

Pete was back within ten minutes.

He said, "Okay, it's over. I told the brothers that it wasn't happening. They accepted that." Then he added with a grin, "They did say, however, that you guys should show a little more enthusiasm for the band."

The three of us shared a cynical laugh. It wasn't funny, but there was nothing else to do.

The Robinson brothers had made it crystal clear that despite their inability to agree on any single other thing, if something benefited the two of them financially, they were on board. Together.

Greedy motherfuckers.

21

Just Leave.
Go Home and Be Done.

When they weren't conspiring to take more money for themselves at their bandmates' expense, the relationship between the Robinson brothers was a total disaster.

The European press tour for *Amorica* was infamously bad. Chris and Rich spent two weeks insulting journalists, photographers, and label reps for a wide variety of transgressions. In the evenings, at dinners with the regional record label bigwigs, they would loudly argue with each other over everything. One moment it was over who actually wrote the songs, then next it was about who made a better homemade marinara sauce. They literally threw dinner rolls at each other at a restaurant in London. They were a two-man clown car.

If you're selling millions of albums and dominating radio, you can get away with acting like an entitled prick. People are way more tolerant when you're making them a lot of money. But *Amorica* wasn't nearly as successful as our first two records, and behind the scenes everybody in the industry—the record label, radio, MTV, promoters—saw it coming. The only people surprised when the album stumbled out of the gate were the six people in The Black Crowes.

Pete told us many times there was never going to be a time when people worked harder for our band simply because we were *better* than other bands. All careers have peaks and valleys, and Pete knew that when our inevitable valleys appeared, we'd need the support of friends in the industry to carry on. The key was simple: don't make enemies.

You didn't have to make friends, necessarily, but you couldn't make enemies. We were *constantly* making enemies. And as the number of enemies inevitably rose, those valleys stretched out ahead, longer and lonelier with each passing day.

The Royal Albert Hall weekend, when Chris took credit for Pete's lighting design and I threatened to quit, is a classic example of disaster and triumph comingling within the world of The Black Crowes. The gigs themselves were actually triumphant, but it was after the second show that things really took off. Our old friend "Uncle" Robert Plant marched into our dressing room, bringing Jimmy Page in with him.

Robert was so happy as he introduced us to Jimmy that night. Hugs all around, genuine affection. "Look at my boys!" he yelled as he walked into the dressing room. I'll forever love him for that. Robert was still taking good care of us.

Jimmy jumped right in. "What a band! I really enjoyed it!" We were shitting ourselves. We were totally comfortable with the idea of Robert being our friend, but then you bring Plant *and* Page in, and it was an entirely new level of *can you believe this shit?*

Jimmy is a mystery to most people. *Who is he, really? Is he from this dimension? Is he an acolyte of Satan?* There's so much mythological bullshit with Jimmy Page. But with us he was immediately and completely charming. A normal guy. Relatively speaking, anyway.

"Do you guys always improvise that much?" he asked. He could tell right away what was improvised and what wasn't. There weren't a lot of people who would just dig right in with us and mention certain parts of a particular jam. But Jimmy was really into breaking it down.

"I felt like I was watching us twenty years ago," he added.

The day before, I had been fully prepared to leave the band forever. Twenty minutes earlier, I'd had to insert myself into a brewing fistfight between the brothers. And now, Jimmy Page had just told us we reminded him of Led Zeppelin. I wasn't going anywhere. I was in the best rock band on earth.

That's essentially how The Black Crowes stayed together. If the band hadn't been great, it would have ended years earlier. But you put up with all the bullshit because one day Jimmy Page says, "There just aren't live bands like you guys anymore. You really made me want to play. I want to join your band!"

A week later, Ross Halfin, the photographer, called Mark Botting, our tour manager.

"I'm coming to Paris with Jimmy," he said. Holy shit, Jimmy was coming back!

We played Le Zénith in Paris. It's a small indoor arena, about nine thousand seats. Jimmy and Ross turned up as we started our set. During the show, I'd look over to our monitor engineer and there was Jimmy, standing next to him on the side of the stage, all smiles. I watched him as he took it all in. He was really enjoying himself.

We finished the set and ran off to the dressing room. Jimmy was again very complimentary.

Chris asked, "So, uh, you feel like hopping up for the encore?"

Jimmy shot back, "Well, what would we play? I can't say that I really know any of your tunes."

"No worries, we'll just play a couple of old blues."

Jimmy said sure, he'd have a go, and off we went back to the stage. We played a couple of tunes while our techs prepared a guitar for Jimmy to use.

Finally, Chris said to the crowd, "Well, I can't believe I am saying this but . . . Mr. Jimmy Page!"

The place exploded. Jimmy walked out to join us, smiling ear to ear. I doubt there was ever another single moment on a stage where every member of The Black Crowes was that happy at the same time.

We ran down two blues tunes, "Shake Your Money Maker," the old Elmore James standard, and "Mellow Down Easy." As I started to count in the first one, Jimmy was watching my left foot on the hi-hat. He wanted to be sure to see where the beat was falling in case he couldn't hear it clearly. *I bet he used to look at Bonham's foot like that.*

Jimmy took a solo in each tune. I couldn't hear a note he played. I didn't care. None of us cared. We were all jubilant, which was ironic because on that tour, Chris and I had some major blowups over, of all things, blues songs.

At a gig in Munich, Germany, we played "Champagne and Reefer" during sound check for the first time. Chris lit into me. "What the fuck are you even playing? You sound like a fucking '90s rock drummer in some fucking grunge band. You have no fucking swing, no soul!"

"Well, I actually *am* a fucking '90s rock drummer. And I am playing a five-piece kit with a twenty-four-inch kick drum that's here specifically because it's fucking loud!"

Honestly, I was also annoyed that we were playing the song in the first place. Nothing against "Champagne and Reefer," but in my mind our German fans bought tickets to our shows to hear *our* songs, not our version of a Muddy Waters classic.

"Fuck you! You don't know shit about the blues."

"I'm done! Thanks, everybody!" I announced with a giant fake smile. I got up from the kit and walked off the stage.

The gig was in a giant sports facility. There was a basketball court backstage. Our opening band, Dillon Fence, were back there shooting hoops. I walked out to join them. Chris showed up seconds later. He had followed me there after our fight.

"Let's play," he said, angrily. "You and me."

He stepped out onto the court and called for the ball. He was challenging me to a game of one on one. He was dead serious. I couldn't believe it. *This* is how you want to settle an argument?

"Knock yourself out, dude," I said.

Chris took the ball, put up a shot, missed it, and I got the rebound. As I dribbled out past the free throw line (international take-back rules in effect, of course), Chris ran out on me like it was Game 7 of the NBA Finals. He was right up on me, talking shit. "Come on, motherfucker, let's go!"

Chris was a decent player. He played in high school. He had a nice shot, when left alone. But this? One on one? And with me already fucking pissed at him? Please.

I backed him down into the paint. Dribble, dribble, dribble, jump hook. Bucket. My ball again. Same move, bucket, my ball. Again. Same move, bucket, my ball. Again.

"You don't wanna be here, son! What are you gonna do? You think you can stop this?" I was letting him have it. He could yell all he wanted onstage at sound check, but on a basketball court, that fucking idiot couldn't begin to stop me.

I had fifty pounds on him, at least. He couldn't budge me.

"Yeah, back me down, that's all you can do, you fat fuck!" he yelled.

I laughed, stepped back, and hit a twenty-footer. Bottom. My ball again.

Two dribbles, twenty-footer. Bottom. My ball again.

A couple more possessions and the game was over.

Chris was fucking furious. He slammed the ball down and stormed off. Five minutes later, I walked into our dressing room and we talked as if nothing had happened.

Chris rarely, if ever, acknowledged when he acted like a lunatic. He moved on as if everything was normal. It was maddening. Finally, I came to accept that to Chris, those things actually *were normal*. I honestly don't know if he's ever had a still moment in his mind.

Two weeks later in Paris, with Jimmy Page blasting a solo right behind him, Chris and I looked at each other and shared an "isn't this great?" moment of recognition. We would scream at each other during sound check, threaten each other, and then share some genuine laughs onstage during the gig. You know . . . "normal."

The US tour began in March. We kicked off again in Minneapolis, although this launch bore little resemblance to that of the High as the Moon tour. There was no MTV, no citywide buzz. We were in and out in one night.

The mess in London definitely closed the door on a lot of bullshit for me. After that I was thinking, on a daily basis, about leaving the band. I had finally accepted that things were the way they were always going to be. Expecting or even hoping for a more positive culture within the band was a fool's game. That acceptance was liberating.

As the tour went on, Chris's complaints about our stage volume moved from an occasional flare-up to a daily conflict. He wanted us to play quieter, specifically Rich, and I agreed with him, actually. Rich played at full volume. All the time. The rest of the band was forced to try to keep up.

Jeff Dunn, our sound man, never put Rich into the PA. There was no need. He mixed the rest of the band around the sound coming out of Rich's amps. Trust me when I say that is fucking insane. Rich was always the loudest thing onstage by a mile.

No matter what Chris tried, he couldn't hear himself onstage. He was singing full voice at all times, and usually screaming more often than not. Now it was affecting his voice. But Rich didn't care. Not one iota. He focused on his tone and his volume at all times. Whatever anyone else did was secondary. Fans were regularly telling us they couldn't hear the vocals out front. But that was meaningless to Rich.

The brothers fought about it every day, and every day it played out the exact same way.

Chris: "Turn your amps down! I can't fucking sing!"

Rich: "You can't sing because you were up all night doing coke and smoking weed. Get some fucking sleep and you can be a fucking rock 'n' roll singer!"

They were both right. They were both wrong. We were all fucked.

In Albany, Chris announced at sound check that we were going to learn "Casey Jones" by the Grateful Dead and start adding it to the sets. This touched a nerve for two reasons. Chris was writing setlists with more and more cover tunes, which no one else in the band thought was a good idea. And now, for the first time, he wanted to do a tune by the Dead.

For the cherry on top, Chris strapped on a guitar and said he would also be playing on this one. Holy hell. If anything, that is always the death knell for any great rock 'n' roll band. When the frontman puts on a guitar, the party is over.

Rich almost had a heart attack.

"I'm not learning a goddamned Grateful Dead song."

He walked offstage. Chris carried on, leading everyone through the changes. It went nowhere fast. There were a lot more chords than Chris anticipated.

I walked over to Rich, standing off on stage left. "Rich, we're never going to play this song live," I said. "There is no way Chris will be able to learn it and keep it straight. And he won't do a Dead song unless he can pretend he's Jerry. Just indulge him and it'll go away."

"No, fuck that."

Johnny came over and backed me up.

"Rich, come on, let's just do it. You'll look like the good guy."

Rich gave in and joined us back onstage. We tried to learn that fucking Grateful Dead song for another ten minutes. No one could make sense of the changes, least of all Chris. No matter how much Chris wanted it, this just wasn't us.

Finally, Chris threw up his hands. "Fuck this!" he said in frustration, and walked off. Sound check over. Dead crisis averted.

I looked over at Rich. "Hate to say I told you so, but . . ."

"It's still fucking bullshit," Rich said, "because now he's just going to pick an easier song."

"One day at a time, dude," I replied. "Let's cross that bridge when we get there."

All of this was part of the buildup to an infamous five-night run at the Beacon Theatre in New York City. There was always extra tension in New York City, but for Amorica or Bust, it blew like a volcano.

That extra tension in New York stemmed from the fact that Chris always, *always* put too much emphasis on those gigs. He still thought New York *meant* something. Granted, it did mean that a lot of the music industry would be at the shows, but the gigs themselves? They were the same as anywhere else. A gig is a gig. Fans are fans. Our job is always the same.

Chris assumed everybody in the building was a card-carrying member of some counterculture taste-maker music illuminati. He looked out at the audience at the Beacon and saw twenty-five hundred beat poets from the West Village. Never did it occur to him that some dudes from Long Island were in town just to fucking rock. Or that a couple from New Jersey hired a sitter for the night, met some friends from college in a bar across the street for a quick one before the show, and were really hoping we could give them a special night away from the normalcy of their daily lives.

Chris always accused everyone else of fucking up the gigs in New York. He'd walk onstage, wound up like a top after two hours spent backstage warning everyone to keep their shit together, and then wonder why the gig felt different.

No matter the soft response we had gotten for *Amorica*, the fact that we had a five-night sold-out run at the Beacon spoke volumes about our live prowess. A triumphant week in New York was still well within our reach. We didn't quite get there, though.

We got off on the wrong foot, oddly enough, because Johnny turned up totally trashed from an all-night bender that was apparently still rolling in its second day. He was a mess. There was no mistaking the fact that he wasn't right as the minutes leading up to the show ticked away and, for once, Chris actually had a reason to be stressed out in New York.

The gig suffered mightily. Not just because Johnny was missing notes and dropping turnarounds, but because of the domino effect of playing music with someone who's suddenly not right. Confidence is everything up there, and his collapse was contagious.

Whether or not anyone in the house even noticed is beside the point. We all knew it. We all felt it. It was a bad show.

Chris was apoplectic about it. He was screaming at the top of his lungs as we walked up the stairs after the gig. Johnny apologized. Repeatedly. He swore it would never happen again. He wasn't even really that upset about Chris yelling at him. He was upset with himself, *furious* with himself. Beyond that, Chris was just hot air.

Johnny had been completely solid and reliable for as long as he'd been in the band. When he found himself, for once, on thin ice, the whole band crashed through it with him. If anything, his inherent value to the overall sound and feel of The Black Crowes was more apparent than ever when he didn't deliver for one night.

Johnny's bad gig really put Chris on edge. The next night, as we were walking onstage, Chris barked at all of us, "Everybody better fucking bring their A-game!"

Right away, we were off. Demanding that someone bring their A-game is a great way to distract them from their A-game. It was better than the night before, but not enough to satisfy whatever was making him crazy.

We sat in that pressure cooker all week. The gigs were fine. If not the best ever, they were perfectly acceptable. No matter. The rage was building. The lid finally blew off on the final night, just after sound check, when Rich saw the setlist Chris had written. There were too many covers.

"No one wants to fucking hear all these cover songs," Rich said. "People want to hear *our* songs."

It immediately turned personal. As they had been arguing for literally their entire lives without ever resolving a single issue along the way, there was never a buildup. There was no series of jabs leading to a haymaker. The brothers just launched full fusillades right out of the gate.

"You don't know shit," Chris screamed. "You don't go see other bands. You don't listen to records. You don't read books. You're a fucking slug. You know nothing. You sit at home with your fucking wife and you're getting fat."

Rich gave as good as he got. "Oh, okay, tell me about the real world you fake fucking hippie. You're the angriest fucking prick on earth, but you're all 'peace and love' when you're hanging with Deadheads. You're a total fucking poser. You think Jerry Garcia gives a flying fuck about you, speaking of fat slugs?"

This entire conversation was happening in a dressing room the size of a utility closet.

There was one chair in the room. I was sitting on it.

Pete stepped into the room, both to try to help them find a solution to whatever they were arguing about, and to let them know everyone in the entire fucking building could hear every word they were saying to each other.

"Guys, for fuck's sakes, what are we going to do here?" Pete asked. "How about if you stop yelling about what you don't agree on and focus on what you can agree on? What can we agree on?"

But Chris and Rich didn't hear him. Not one word. They kept on screaming at each other, and the volume somehow kept rising. Louder and *louder* and LOUDER!

But in my mind, it was getting quieter and quieter. I was lost in my own thoughts.

Stand up, shake Pete's hand, thank him for everything, and leave. Just leave. Go home and be done. I'm turning thirty this summer. It's the perfect time to leave.

As I weighed the odds of actually quitting right there, Chris picked up a Red Stripe bottle and tried to throw it at Rich's head. But the bottle slipped and hit the wall right above *my* head. That snapped me right back into the room.

"Fuck! I am so sorry, Steve," Chris immediately stammered. "I did *not* mean for that to happen."

I'm going to beat him and throw him out of this third-story window, and he's going to land on the sidewalk on fucking Seventy-third Street right where those fans are waiting by the stage door.

"Fucking stop!" Pete yelled. "You're so mad about a setlist, you're throwing beer bottles? What the fuck?"

No one moved. It was totally silent for a few seconds. It was as if someone had poked their head in and screamed, "Freeze!"

I stood up, slowly turned around, and walked out of the room. I walked downstairs and out onto the sidewalk where I had just imagined throwing Chris. I crossed the street, walked over to Broadway, and started walking north.

Don't go back. Don't say anything. Just leave. They don't deserve an explanation. Pete will understand. Johnny will understand. Marc and Ed will understand. Hell, everybody else on earth will understand.

Shit. Johnny.

He told me in London that if I go, he goes. I can't ditch on him now.

Fuck.

I walked around for an hour or so. I knew I couldn't quit. Maybe I was afraid, sure, and I knew I couldn't fuck Johnny over, but more than either of those things, I didn't want to let them beat me.

I walked back to the Beacon about forty-five minutes before our set. I honestly don't think anyone even noticed I was gone. Whatever happened while I was out must have been pretty fucking dramatic.

The brothers were standing together, looking at a setlist and quietly talking about it. When they noticed me, Chris said in a very conciliatory tone, "Hey, man, we're going to open the show, just the two of us, with 'Cursed Diamond.'"

I looked at them both and said, "Go ahead. I'm done giving a flying fuck about what either one of you does."

They both looked at me for a few seconds, and then we all walked into separate dressing rooms.

Three hours later we walked off the stage after playing what many fans, to this day, say was the best show of our career.

22

Peking Duck is Now
on the Menu

As The Black Crowes left New York City for Boston, I was struck with an unexpected new feeling. We were bulletproof. If New York didn't kill us, nothing could. If we could make it there, we could make it anywhere, I guess.

We finished the first leg of the tour in New Orleans, at the Saenger Theatre on a Sunday night in late April. Our old friend Peter Holsapple from The dB's turned up at sound check. He was living in New Orleans and had put together a new band, the Continental Drifters, with his wife, Susan Cowsill, and Vicki Peterson from The Bangles. He was playing a solo acoustic set in town at midnight and invited us over after our gig.

Chris and I were excited to see Peter play. What better way to wrap up a brutally contentious leg of the tour than hanging with an old friend, a guy whose music was an initial connection point for our friendship, and someone who was always an early champion of our band?

Johnny, Marc, and Ed weren't familiar with his music but were more than happy to have something to do after the gig. Rich, however, had no interest. He wanted to walk offstage, get right on the bus, and head home.

"Come with us, for fuck's sakes. It'll be fun. It's fucking Peter Holsapple!" I said.

"I don't want to sit around New Orleans until fucking three in the morning, and then get stuck in Atlanta traffic," he complained.

"Dude, we are going to see our friend," I insisted. "He starts at midnight, we'll be back by two."

"No! That's bullshit. You're just going because Chris wants to go. He's a fucking dick the whole tour and now he's in a good mood, so everybody just jumps on board with him. Fuck that, I want to go home. Why can't you ever respect my opinion?"

We went back and forth until Rich finally relented. We'd split at two. Though Rich still refused to go to Peter's gig. He said he was going to go to sleep on the bus. *Whatever, dude, knock yourself out.* Miserable prick.

The rest of us got a couple of taxis over to Carrollton Station, a club Mr. Crowe's Garden had actually played in 1988 on our lone trip to New Orleans. Peter played for about an hour. He did a few dB's songs, which Chris and I sang along with, together. Fucking music—it always makes everything better. As long as someone else is playing it, anyway.

It had been a rough six weeks. But we'd just had a blast in New Orleans, and we were all about to part ways on a good note.

That all went out the window the instant we returned to the Saenger Theatre and noticed our bus was gone.

"Oh my God, there is *no way* he took the bus," Chris said, laughing in disbelief. Chris was flying out to Los Angeles in the morning, so he wasn't directly affected.

I got out of the car and stared at the space where our bus had been. It was 1:55 A.M.

"He did not leave us behind, there is no way, it's not even feasible, *it's not even comprehensible,*" I said, with more shock than anger.

We walked onto the crew bus. Our sound man, Jeff, told us what had happened before we even asked. "Rich left over an hour ago," he confirmed.

I lost my mind. The most obvious of all the unwritten rules of rock 'n' roll, or fucking life for that matter, is this: you never leave a man behind. Or in this case, two men. Bandmates. Partners.

That prick didn't get his way, so he left. On *our* bus. Our luggage was on that bus. Other personal effects were on that bus. How were we supposed to get home? Did that asshole double-check that Johnny and I hadn't left our wallets with our IDs *on* the bus? He never would have screwed Chris over that way. This was a pecking-order decision. Johnny and I were "below" him, so he could justify leaving us behind.

I called Pete in Los Angeles.

"I'm going to fucking kill him!" I yelled. I could barely speak in complete sentences. "What kind of asshole does this? He didn't even wait until two!"

Johnny got on the phone. "Pete, this is the biggest breach of . . . *of fucking everything!* You don't leave a person behind. You just don't, no matter what, but *especially* on a bus that everyone is paying for."

All Pete could do was agree with us and try to talk us off the ledge.

Mark Botting booked us flights home at six in the morning. I told Pete that Rich would pay for our flights or else I wouldn't be back on the next leg of the tour. Johnny agreed. Pete promised us he would take care of it.

There was a lot of road construction on Rich's drive, apparently, and he made terrible time back to Atlanta. As it turned out, we got home before Rich did. That did nothing to take the edge off.

I called Pete as soon as I walked into my house. "I'm going over to his house and I'm going to kick his ass," I said. I wasn't kidding.

"Don't do that. Nothing good would come from you beating him up."

I lay in my bed seething. I felt radioactive. Rich lived only a few miles away.

Pete called me later that day after talking to Rich and, almost laughing, said, "He says you guys don't have any respect for him."

"Of course I don't have respect for him, he's a fucking toad. If Rich says 'no one likes me,' the answer is 'no shit they don't.' Even Chris, on his worst fucking day, would never take the bus. That's never happened in the history of bands. It's unforgivable."

We had a week at home. Rich never talked to me or Johnny. He never apologized or even acknowledged what he had done. Ever. To this day.

Instead, he demanded his own tour bus, saying he could no longer share a bus with Chris. He expected the band to cover the cost of a new bus, just as he had expected the band to pay for him to rent a house in LA when we recorded *Tall*.

Johnny and I refused. If he wants his own bus, he can pay for it. Why should everyone pay for an extra bus when there are only two people who can't get along?

Rich took a hard stand—another bus or he wasn't touring. Pete was the reasonable one, as per usual. He had Mark Botting price out a cheap bus, then we looked at the total cost of the bus for the final month of the tour and compared it to the losses we would all suffer if we canceled. His attitude was always "eyes on the prize." The total cost from the partners' pockets would be a few thousand dollars each.

Fuck it. Okay. Fine. What's one more stupid fucking expense in the grand, lunatic scheme of things?

Rich rode his bus from Atlanta to Dallas to start the next leg. Johnny and I flew. After sound check that day, Rich told everyone we were all welcome to ride with him, as there was no sense in him being alone on a whole bus. He pitched it as a positive thing for everyone to be able to spread out a bit. Yeah, right. Whatever, dude. No one ever got on that bus.

A few days into the leg, at sound check in San Antonio, Chris and Rich started arguing about Chris's plan to play five covers in the set. "Fuck you, you have no idea what our fans want!" and "No, fuck *you*, you hate yourself and don't want to play your own songs!" went back and forth a few times. And then it went way off script.

Rich took off his guitar to leave the stage. Chris yelled at him, "Go ahead, walk away, you fat piece of shit." Rich had put on a few pounds the last couple of years, but he's over six feet tall. It wasn't a big thing, but he was sensitive about it.

Rich spun back, yelling, "Go do some more drugs, you fucking poser, you fucking alcoholic! Go sit in the dressing room listening to the Dead, thinking about how high you're gonna be after the show tonight, you pathetic fucking loser!"

Rich walked off and they steered clear of each other for a few hours, but in the dressing room, minutes before showtime, it flared up again. Chris threw a beer can at Rich, flipping his switch. Rich charged at full speed. They grappled across the room for a few seconds, throwing short punches at each other.

Botting and I caught each other's eye from across the room. We shared a look that said, *Let's not stop this one. Let them kill each other.*

They were choking, grabbing, pulling each other's hair, and cursing one another. It was real. This was the big one. *Finally.*

It went on for about fifteen seconds until they crashed into a large mirror surrounded by lightbulbs. The mirror cracked and several of the lightbulbs exploded. Botting and I again shared a look, but this time it said, *Let's end it now before someone cuts open a vein and bleeds out.*

Mark grabbed Chris and I grabbed Rich. Rich threw a punch off target that hit me. *You motherfucker!* I put him in a headlock and started choking him. He wrestled out of it and suddenly we were facing each other.

"Go ahead, motherfucker," I screamed at Rich. "That skinny fucking asshole owns you, so what do you think you're gonna do to me?"

I turned to Chris. "And fuck you, too! You wanna be in a cover band? Do it on your own fucking time!"

They had both stopped fighting back. "Fuck both of you," I said. "You're both gonna quit? Bullshit. You're both pussies. When this fucking tour is over, *I am gonna fucking quit.* And this band won't last a fucking hour after I'm gone. And you both fucking know it!"

There was total silence. Mark finally said, "Chaps, it's time to head to the stage."

I grabbed my sticks and walked out. The house lights were already down.

On the way to the stage, Chris asked, "Are you really going to quit?"

"Yeah. Have a good gig, man."

On stage, Rich barely made eye contact with me. For whatever it was worth, they both got the message.

We opened with "P.25 London."

It rocked. Hard.

I wanted to kill both of them.

I wanted to kill The Black Crowes.

It was a great show.

Well, that's it. *I said it, so I guess I'm out at the end of this tour.*

As we headed to Houston that night, I felt relieved. I was out in four months. Piece of cake.

They kept the fighting to a minimum for a couple of weeks. I was dumb enough to think that maybe my threat to quit finally got through to them, but the lid blew again in Salt Lake City a couple of hours before the gig. No idea what sparked this one (not that it matters), but for the thousandth time Chris yelled, "That's it, I'm fucking done!" and stormed off to the bus. But this time he didn't mean *I'm done in September.* He meant *I'm done right fucking now!* He was out. Tour over. Band over.

We still had a three-night stand in Los Angeles, plus another dozen or so West Coast dates, wrapping up in Portland and Seattle.

Botting called Pete, and put Chris on the phone with him.

"You cannot cancel the tour like this," Pete maintained. "The answer is no."

"Pete, I can't do it. You can't ask me to come home to LA and then go back out. I'll play the LA gigs but that's it. I'm fucking done after that."

Pete wouldn't back down. "We can't cancel shows because of a band fight. It'll kill us in whatever markets we pull."

Chris drew his own line. "Fine, I'll go through Vegas. But I will not go to Portland and Seattle."

Pete had no choice but to give in on the Portland and Seattle shows. And we paid for it the next time we played those two cities. We slid backward in ticket sales. Significantly. Two of the best music towns in the world, and what did those fans get from The Black Crowes? A refund and a hearty "fuck you."

So now, instead of Seattle, the American leg of the Amorica or Bust tour was going to end with two gigs in Las Vegas at the Hard Rock Hotel, which had just opened.

We had a few weeks off scheduled after Vegas before heading back to Europe for festivals and some gigs opening for The Rolling Stones. We were going to follow that up with a headlining run on the H.O.R.D.E. tour, a jam-oriented festival tour founded in 1992 by Blues Traveler.

But there was no denying the album had stiffed. We had toured behind *Shake Your Money Maker* for twenty months. *Southern Harmony* sustained us for fifteen months. *Amorica* was seven months.

We were moving in the wrong direction.

In Vegas, Pete had an idea he felt would get media attention and guarantee years of word of mouth in Las Vegas and the music business.

"When the show ends, let's invite all the fans to join you at the roulette wheel right outside the front door. I'll get the promoter to bring out our entire show guarantee in a mountain of twenty-five-dollar chips, and you'll place it all on black! Whatever happens, the press and years of word of mouth will be worth much more than our guarantee could ever buy. One spin, red or black, win or lose, and The Black Crowes will instantly become part of Vegas history!"

I was totally on board. But Chris and Rich were instantly against it. They didn't like to gamble at all. They both hated anything they couldn't control.

"You'll blow off gigs in Portland and Seattle but you won't do this?" I asked.

But even Johnny was against it. Shit. Outvoted. It would have been a hell of a story, no matter how it turned out.

Years later, Pete and I would still talk about how we should have put our money on black. We needed all the luck we could get.

Labor Day. I just had to get to Labor Day. Five weeks in Europe, four weeks on H.O.R.D.E., and then home. Done. Free.

Our two weeks at home flew by. I was back on a plane to London before I knew it. But, once in Europe, back in the festival groove, there were a lot of easy days. Playing in front of tens of thousands of fans always put us in better moods.

During that summer run, we had an inordinate amount of days off in Amsterdam. Chris always loved it there, of course, as he could openly smoke weed and hash all day and night. But in 1995, weed and hash were the least of our concerns.

Heroin had finally arrived in full force. Ed and Marc were snorting regularly, and now Chris jumped on board with them. They had dabbled here and there before, but it was becoming a more common fixture.

In July we did three nights at Wembley Stadium with The Stones. There were two dressing rooms for the band: one for me, Johnny, and

Rich, and another for Chris, Marc, and Ed. There was a sign on their door that read: "Peking Duck." That was their code word for heroin. "You have to order Peking Duck twenty-four hours in advance, same as this shit," Chris explained backstage, all but bragging about their use of heroin.

They thought it was funny. And they thought it was cool. We were playing with The Stones, so they were doing heroin because Keith Richards did heroin in the '70s? I guess that was their logic. You can't really rationalize the behavior of those who dabble in heroin, especially the ones who flaunt it like little boys with a new bouncy ball.

But I can't throw Ed under that bus, actually. With Ed you couldn't tell whether he was fucked up or just weird old Ed. He was, at all times, under the influence of some combination of drugs and it rarely, if ever, was even noticeable. It certainly didn't affect his playing. That dude was great no matter what.

With Chris and heroin, there was always more talk than action. People always assumed he was a full-blown junkie, and he did nothing to dissuade anyone from that line of thinking. He dabbled with heroin to be sure, and he talked it up as if it were a daily part of his life. But it was never a serious thing for him. Not so for Ed and Marc, unfortunately.

Unlike Ed, heroin most definitely affected Marc's playing. A few years later, after Marc was fired from the band, Rich claimed Marc was so strung out that he would on occasion be playing a completely different song from the rest of the band. That was bullshit. But Marc struggled, and he missed notes, and he was a bit of a zombie. And because this was The Black Crowes, instead of being seen as a weakened and wobbly soul in need of support, he instead became a target for blame.

But back in the summer of 1995, we were all playing great. We had a great run of festival shows, opening slots for The Rolling Stones and Page/Plant, and, of course, a few of our own shows. There were very few arguments and absolutely no actual fights. I guess that's the upside of half your band being strung out.

Nonstop touring—the cause of, and solution to, all our problems.

23

"Know 'Em?
Hell, i Wrote 'Em, Baby!"

The Black Crowes owe a sizable debt to The Rolling Stones. Many people accused us of ripping them off over the years. Those people were right, of course, but they often overlooked the fact that of all the bands who raided The Stones' larder, we did it best.

The Stones themselves saw us for what we were: a proper rock 'n' roll band unafraid to tip our collective cap to many of our heroes. They certainly recognized us as kindred spirits, to be sure. Nobody from their world was ever anything but cool to us. On the Tiny Tour the month of *Amorica*'s release, we played The Opera House in Toronto. The Stones were in town rehearsing, and Mick Jagger, Ronnie Wood, Bobby Keys, and our old buddy Chuck Leavell came out to the gig. Woody and Chuck sat in for the encore, which consisted of The Allman Brothers' "Statesboro Blues" and "Shake Your Money Maker." Mick remained at the side of the stage. Chris gave him a nod that said, *Come on out, man!* but Mick stayed put. The entire crowd could see him there, though, and that seemed to be enough for him. The man can read a room, to be sure, and I think he properly calculated that his appearance onstage would have caused a riot.

Afterward, we had a great hang in the tiny dressing room underneath the stage. Mick was great. "Oh, you guys are fantastic, what a band," he told us. As for Woody . . . well, Woody is always Woody. Lots of laughs, great stories. As highly as we thought of ourselves, hanging with those guys was always a thrill.

Keith Richards never came around to our shows. I don't think he ever saw The Black Crowes other than when we were their opening act.

Our first three gigs with them were at Wembley Stadium in London, and then we continued through Europe. In Montpellier, France, we played a triple bill with Bob Dylan in the middle slot. We were loving life that day. Just seeing the posters and billboards with The Rolling Stones and Bob Dylan next to our name on the drive into the stadium was mind-blowing.

The Stones' backstage area was called the "Voodoo Lounge," after their current album at the time. There were snooker tables, dart boards, giant-screen TVs, sushi chefs, a full bar the size of a standard pub, and grill tables with filet mignon and lobster. It was a level of opulence that barely computed with us.

We were milling around taking it all in when Chuck Leavell appeared. Big smiles, hugs all around. Phew. We didn't feel like intruders anymore.

"Pretty amazing back here, isn't it?" he said. "Look, our world is your world, make yourselves at home!" Chuck still saw us as "his boys" and we were more than happy to be thought of in that regard. Within a few minutes, Keith walked in, making his way across the room.

"Hey, Keith, you know The Black Crowes?" asked Chuck.

Without breaking stride, Keith looked us all up and down. "Know 'em? Hell, I wrote 'em, baby!"

We all fell out laughing. Best line ever. We loved it. My first time around Keith, and damned if he wasn't better than advertised.

At one gig, Rich and I watched a few songs together from just behind Charlie Watts, out of the crowd's line of sight. As they fell into "Monkey Man," Keith stood with his back to the audience facing Charlie, and as the groove locked in he decided there was no need to go anywhere else. He played the entire tune stuck in place, locking eyes with Charlie, about eight feet in front of us. It was ferocious. I didn't blink once for five minutes. It felt like standing in a wind tunnel, or riding a giant wave, or both somehow. As the song ended, Rich and I stared at each other in acknowledgment. All the personal bullshit aside, that thing . . . that connection that Keith and Charlie had? We had that,

The corner of Sunset and Alta Loma, spring of 1995, up the hill from our home away from home, the Sunset Marquis. © Ross Halfin

Flyer from my first gig ever, May 30, 1987. Mary My Hope opening for Mr. Crowe's Garden. Hours after the show Chris and I were walking in circles, drunkenly talking over each other, establishing a decades-long policy of ignoring warning signs at our own peril.
Courtesy of the author

Chris, perpetually hung over, standing in front of the Oakdale rock 'n' roll flophouse, 1987. **Courtesy of Jeanne-Marie Greiner**

Rich and me outside the Cat's Cradle, Chapel Hill, North Carolina, with Kevn and Tim from Drivin N Cryin, taking part in a faded-jeans, white-shirt hootenanny of sorts. 1988. **Courtesy of Randy Blazak**

Me at CBGB, 1988, suffering through one of the worst Mr. Crowe's Garden shows. **Courtesy of Paul Tyson**

Mr. Crowe's Garden perfectly summarized. Me having a good time, Chris having a better time, and Rich hanging back with equal parts disdain and envy. 1988. **Courtesy of Elizabeth Lenihan**

George Drakoulias, the catalyst. He saw and heard what we could be, long before any of us had a clue. Without George, The Black Crowes don't happen. Period. **Courtesy of George Drakoulias**

Robert Plant and his band with us on the final day of the tour, October 1990. We were a very different band than the one who had started with him six weeks earlier. **Courtesy of Jeff Cease**

Ed Harsch and Jeff Cease having a drink and a laugh as we flew to Europe for the final and devastating leg of the Shake Your Money Maker tour. **Courtesy of the author**

Ed Harsch, the greatest musician and the biggest heart in the band. England, 1991.
Courtesy of Jeff Cease

The haircut that actually made me feel normal again, 1991, Frankfurt, Germany. **Courtesy of the author**

Tokyo, 1992. I was in a complete blur. Jet-lagged, drunk, confused, and miserable. This shoot was two days before I hit the wall. © **Neil Zlozower**

Moments after a gig in Tokyo, 1992. I was, most likely, actually passed out. © Neil Zlozower

Marc Ford, the wonder boy, with every bit of it still ahead of him, in Chicago, 1992. He was an extraordinary, almost mystical musical addition to the band. © Paul Natkin

Outside the Aragon in Chicago, summer of 1992, slowly putting the pieces back together. © Paul Natkin

The Pot Festival, Atlanta, 1992. That was a hell of a day. Two years earlier, just before *Shake Your Money Maker*'s release, we played a free show in Atlanta for 49,988 fewer fans. © Neil Zlozower

Just before the release of *Southern Harmony*, we had no idea how ominous those black clouds actually were. © **Neil Zlozower**

Somewhere in Europe, fall of 1992. By that point, there was no question we were the baddest rock 'n' roll band in the world. And those faces reflect quite clearly how it felt most of the time.
© Ross Halfin

The brothers Robinson, August 1991, heading to Europe, coming apart at the seams.
Courtesy of the author

Johnny Colt, fist ready to fly if need be, onstage at Wembley Stadium, London, 1995.
© Ross Halfin

Johnny and me at the Beacon Theatre, Halloween 1996. All six of us rocked Elvis suits that night as we opened for ourselves as "Jelly Donut." Safe to say, Johnny made for a much better Elvis than I did. Courtesy of Karen Durkot

Losing the plot, slowly but surely. 1996. © Ross Halfin

Me and Chris caught in career no-man's-land, shooting the "Only a Fool" video. "Weird Al" Yankovic directed. I'd add more context, but there isn't any. I've apparently blocked the entire day from my memory. Courtesy of Karen Dusenbery

London, 1999, after what we thought would be our lone rehearsal with Jimmy Page. Despite having left Ed behind in a Belgian hospital the night before, we were all in great spirits. © Ross Halfin

Having a beer with Rich and Sven in Japan, 1999, protected around the clock from my own neuroses by the wrestling mask. Courtesy of the author

Rehearsals with Jimmy Page at the Congress Theater in Chicago, 2000. Don't let the look on my face fool you. I was having the time of my life. © **Paul Natkin**

Pete Angelus. The only one who always held up his end of the bargain. **Courtesy of the author**

End days, 2010, at the Riviera in Chicago. © Paul Natkin

too. We recognized something between them, and between ourselves, in a way that very few other people could have. We never said a word about it. We didn't have to. Moments like that keep bands together. Or, at the very least, moments like that kept our band together.

Our run with The Stones ended with two stadium shows in Basel, Switzerland. We took a photo of both bands together before the last gig, and I wound up standing next to Keith.

"Oh, you're the drummer," he said to me. "You're the one who always hides."

"Just trying to keep a low profile," I deadpanned.

"Probably for the best with these people," he said. "Well, it's a good fucking group, man."

That's all I needed from Keith Richards.

Woody invited us to come to their hotel after the gig for a hang. Now, The Stones' hotel was not like a normal hotel. We stayed in five-star hotels all the time. This one was way beyond any kind of star rating system. It was more like an unmarked fortress in the middle of town. I imagine it's the kind of place where only The Stones or the royal family would stay.

We left the gig that night as part of The Stones' motorcade. Their nightly egress was executed with military precision. They closed the gig with "Jumpin' Jack Flash," and as they waved farewell to the crowd, a massive fireworks display erupted. As the crowd watched the fireworks, the band ran offstage and into a fleet of idling Volkswagen vans (tour sponsor) that immediately took them out of the stadium before the house lights had even come up.

We piled into our designated van and waited for The Stones to come down the steps a few minutes later. We didn't realize there were two dozen police cars and motorcycles surrounding the vans until they all hit their lights. Without any real warning, the whole fleet of vans and police vehicles roared out of the stadium onto a side road, then onto the highway. All the exit and entrance ramps were blocked. The entire caravan flew along at a hundred miles per hour surrounded by more flashing lights than I'd ever seen.

This was their normal exit strategy. Everywhere they went. *This was their life.* And we thought we had it all going on because we had a bus. Holy shit. Until we saw it firsthand, we couldn't have quite understood how odd or awe inspiring it would be to see an operation like The Rolling Stones had, up close.

In a matter of minutes, we were unloading in the courtyard at The Stones' hotel. Immediately, it felt casual again.

"Come on, lads!" Woody yelled. "Let's go to my room."

Woody's "room" had two floors, probably three or four bedrooms, a kitchen, a fully stocked refrigerator, a fully stocked bar, an enormous stereo, and a pool table. It was the size of my house back in Atlanta, but with way better stuff. He had personal effects scattered all around the place. Books, CDs, albums, VHS tapes, journals. It looked like he'd lived there for years. As far as I could tell, he'd been there for three days.

Chris said, "Jesus, Woody, nice place!"

"This is nothing!" Woody replied. "You should see Keith's room!"

We stayed until sunrise drinking, throwing darts, shooting pool, playing records, and watching old Tommy Cooper videos. (Cooper was an English comedian who'd died about a decade earlier and Woody loved him.) It was pretty much exactly what you'd hope a night with Woody would be. Chuck and Bobby showed up, along with Darryl Jones, The Stones' new bassist. Mick and Charlie never made it by, but after a few hours Keith actually rolled in. He had a drink and then asked, "All right, guys, who's got a little something? I could use a pick-me-up."

"Wait just a minute!" Ed drawled. "Did you just come down here and ask if any of us had some blow? Now, you might not be aware of this but, motherfucker . . . *you're Keith Richards!* You ask the *opening band* for cocaine? Dude, what happened to you?"

There was a moment of silence. It felt like the scene in a movie where the needle drags across the record. It was awkward as hell. Keith sized up Ed for a few eternal seconds, and then he burst out laughing. Everyone fell in with him.

Only Ed could get away with that. Keith knew full well that Ed had played with Albert Collins and James Cotton, and he fully respected him for it.

"That's a good point, man. I must be slipping," Keith said, laughing.

"Lucky for you I got you covered, motherfucker," Ed added. Of course he did.

Being around The Stones had been an incredible experience, and we talked about it regularly over the following month. It was a glimpse of what was possible if we could just get our shit together. They were twenty-five years older than us, and they were still doing it. We all knew about the infighting in The Stones—*everyone* knew about it. It was arguably the biggest part of the band's mythology. Watching them interact, we could see ourselves.

"That's going to be us in twenty years," Chris said a few times.

We could all see it. And despite anything Chris would later say as he tried to rewrite history to fit whatever current bullshit narrative he was spinning, he wanted it. Badly. We all did. It made me reconsider my vow to quit the band after Labor Day.

We decided that month that we were going to do thirty years as The Black Crowes. We meant it. And we stuck with that plan for a while. A few years later, in the summer of 2000, Chris, Rich, and I bought Pete a Rolex watch with the inscription "10 down, 20 to go."

In 1995, Chris and Rich both believed they would be where Mick and Keith, then in their fifties, were. And that The Black Crowes would be where The Rolling Stones were. All we had to do was keep grinding for twenty-five more years.

In a little less than two years, it was patently obvious it wasn't ever going to happen. The whole fucking thing was about to unravel.

24

Three Snakes and One Honorable Man

We flew home on Labor Day. The plan was to take the rest of the year off, then in January head to South America for the first time, for a quick run of shows, and then start the fourth album upon return. We had four months off. *Four fucking months!* By our standards, that felt like ten years. I was thrilled.

Rose Mary and I were in a new house in Atlanta that was just one block from Piedmont Park. I walked our dog, Clementine, a few times a day in the park and started playing basketball again at a gym downtown. I felt happier and healthier than I had in a few years. I could breathe again.

Too bad it only lasted four weeks.

Chris called on October 1. He said he was heading to Atlanta in a few days to start writing with Rich. The plan to wait until 1996 was out the window. Apparently, we still didn't know how to not be The Black Crowes, even temporarily.

In short order we had a plan. We'd rent a house for Chris, Marc, and Ed to stay in throughout the entire album process and also use it for preproduction. We'd save money on hotels and a rehearsal studio. This was some serious progress. Chris had clearly decided not to repeat any of the financial mistakes from the *Tall/Amorica* era.

We found a house that was, as it turned out, right across the street from Chris's first Atlanta house, the one where we had put *Southern Harmony* together four years earlier. It was north of town, on a large lot in a heavily wooded area with endless, winding roads, and completely hidden from the street. Pulling up the driveway every day was like leaving the city behind.

Jack Joseph Puig was hired to produce again. He came to town almost immediately to hear what the brothers were coming up with and as soon as he saw the rental house, we added another element to the plan. We decided to build a studio in the house and actually make the record there.

As they were writing, I saw for the first time ever a willingness from both Chris and Rich to try each other's ideas without judgment; to really give an honest effort at understanding what the other was trying to do. We talked a lot about Mr. Crowe's Garden, how quickly the past five years had flown by, and how far we'd come. And we talked a lot about how our future could go on for decades. It was totally laid back, and it was genuinely exciting. I drove home each night in happy disbelief.

The first two new songs we put down were "Good Friday" and "Under a Mountain." I loved both tunes. "How Much for Your Wings?" also fell together very quickly. The demo was loose and pretty weird, actually. Initially, we thought it was unfinished but the more we listened, the more it felt perfect as it was.

It was amazing. We'd never really committed to the demo process before. So many of the steps that were completely normal for most artists were still foreign to us.

Jack was great this time around. He was right in the middle of the writing process from the jump and his encouragement and cheerleading was paying off. Within ten days or so, we had the outline for our fourth album. There hadn't been a single fight. Just a dozen or so demos that felt great.

Johnny was stopping by every couple of days. Chris and Rich, with Jack's blessing, had decided to record demos without Johnny. The idea was to streamline the process, which was working, though I could tell Johnny had mixed emotions about it. The first round of recordings was just guitar, drums, and vocals. As we continued, Rich started adding bass lines. I thought it was time to bring Johnny in. Why not?

Jack pushed hard to keep things as they were. His thinking was "fewer minds, fewer distractions."

To me, it felt like the old days. One of the new tunes, "Everybody Has Scars," sounded very much like something from 1988. I loved it. I nicknamed it "the Runt" because despite my affections, we all knew it wasn't quite up to par with the rest of the tunes, and would be left off the album. I still have the original demo the three of us cut. It's not exactly great, but I still dig it.

There were a couple of other tunes I thought would have been right at home in Mr. Crowe's Garden that did make the album: "Better When You're Not Alone," a jangly, straight-forward indie pop song, and "One Mirror Too Many." It felt like we were going back and picking up on ideas we had attempted as a local band but could never quite pull off.

We were trying all kinds of things, from straight psychedelia like "Evil Eye" to our version of a funk tune, "Halfway to Everywhere." Nothing seemed out of bounds. We even toyed with a double-drummer configuration on some songs. My buddy Tom Osander, the drummer from God Street Wine, came down for a week to vibe it out. We decided it wasn't really adding enough to warrant continuing, but even that decision was made in a low-key manner, and without tension.

Working out of a cheap rental house was relaxing and totally freeing. Our only expenses were groceries and electricity. We originally planned to wait until February to start recording, and yet by the end of December we had most of the album done.

The cold weather contributed to the overall vibe. We were all dressed like mountain men for the most part, and the facial hair was coming on strong. I had an old beat-up 1982 Toyota Land Cruiser that could handle the snow and ice easily. Chris and I would make regular grocery runs together and, more often than not, we were laughing at everyday life as we would have six or seven years earlier.

It all felt . . . normal. We never had anyone from the record label stop by. There were no photographers or journalists in the house. Our only visitors were our wives, friends, and Pete.

I don't recall a single day when I drove up to the house steeling myself for whatever battle might lie ahead. I didn't have to give myself pep talks like the ones in the past. I knew, finally, that whatever drama did actually come at me really wasn't about me on any level. That carried me through the sessions. There were days when I turned up in the early afternoon to find no one was awake yet. I'd hang out for a bit with Rich and Jack waiting for Chris to get his shit together. After a few hours, if nothing had started to happen, I'd just go home. No big deal.

A few years later, in our *Behind the Music* TV show episode, Chris talked about the making of *Three Snakes* as a dark, drugged-out experience. While that is certainly true—the drug usage was considerable—the darkness didn't consume me this time around.

Smoking weed and drinking were as much a part of things as plugging in an amp and making noise. They never registered on anyone's radar as a concern. But now, Marc and Ed were using heroin every day. That was a different story.

Even Chris was a little concerned with the depth of the hard-drug usage in the house. It wasn't a problem musically, yet. Marc and Ed both played great. They'd need a little more prodding, or guidance, on occasion, but we couldn't look at them and say honestly that their performance was suffering.

We couldn't say the same for our longest-standing crew member, Johnny's tech, Paul. He'd been with us since the summer of 1989 and ridden on the Junkyard bus on our first-ever tour. But now, after all we'd all gone through, we had to admit he was falling well short of his responsibilities. We told him one day that he needed to go get clean or we wouldn't be able to keep him around.

He said, "But I'd take a bullet for you guys."

I responded with a laugh. "That's great, but last I checked, no one is shooting at us, dude. We're asking you to stop using heroin."

It still bugs me that I said that to him. Under the best circumstances, kicking heroin is a rough road. The last thing he needed was me being an asshole to him about it.

Paul left for about five days and then returned, claiming he was sober and ready to work. He lasted less than an hour. When it was apparent that he was again high, we told him he had to go. Six years as a dedicated crew member, and now we had to show him the door. He was despondent. He drove off crying.

I never saw him again.

For "Halfway to Everywhere," Chris invited Garry Shider and Gary "Mudbone" Cooper from Parliament-Funkadelic to sing backing vocals. They turned up, busted out a crack pipe, and Chris's plans to spend the day living out his P-Funk fantasies went sideways in a hurry. I missed that whole thing. I called over to ask how it was going and Jack told me to steer clear. I laughed and thanked him for the heads-up. They got the track, and the vocals were great, but apparently it was a total shit show.

Suffice to say, life in The Black Crowes obviously still had its challenges.

No matter how positive the vibe was during the *Three Snakes* sessions, we couldn't ultimately overcome the fallout from a horrific mistake made early in the process. We left Johnny Colt in the cold.

Rich had played bass on the original demos. The brothers fell in love with his playing and decided he should do the same for the album, too. Usually, when they were in agreement it made life easier for everyone else. This decision, however, was anything but a relief. It was pure ego and stupidity. The core of the band's feel was Rich, Johnny, and me playing off of each other. It made no sense to me to take that feel away.

To risk sacrificing Johnny's commitment to the band so Rich could stroke his ego was nothing short of insane. But that kind of thinking never entered the brothers' minds. They saw something they wanted, and they went after it. It was just that simple.

"The music trumps everything else," I heard them say a few times.

"Keith played bass on a few Stones tracks," I heard them say a few times.

Bullshit. It's not like Keith ever told Bill Wyman he was out for an entire fucking album.

It wasn't even a musical conversation to me. The conversation was entirely about jeopardizing the band unnecessarily. I made the strongest case I could that Rich, Johnny, and I should record each track together, with Marc and Ed laying down overdubs later. It was all for naught. Chris and Rich, along with Jack Puig, were in agreement. Rich and I would track the tunes, Rich would overdub the bass, and then we'd move on to the rest. I was really caught in the middle. I had found a new level of contentment I didn't want to fuck with.

Puig sat down with Johnny and told him the plan. He took the news, expectedly, like a pro. While he wasn't happy about it on any level, he promised to be ready whenever he was needed.

Johnny was making his own very concerted effort to get his shit to-gether. He had jumped fully into yoga and meditation. I talked myself into thinking it was all going to work out fine. Or, I should say, I lied to myself unreservedly. But as we tracked the songs as a two-piece, the cost of appeasing the Robinsons at Johnny's expense became increas-ingly apparent. It was awful for Johnny. Fucking terrible.

Every day, without fail, he walked into the house ready to go. He would read, he would meditate, he would practice his yoga, and he would wait for a chance to play bass. It was demoralizing for him, and it was demoralizing for me, too.

We stood in the front yard one day with Clementine and his boxer, Knuckles, and he said, unprompted, "I am having a hard time trying to come up with a reason to stay in this band. I am here to play bass. If I'm not doing that, then I'm just wasting my time."

I tried to give him a different perspective. "Dude, you are a huge piece of The Black Crowes beyond the music. You do as much, if not more, for the band off the stage than anyone else around here."

"Right. So why spend valuable time here when it's not appreciated?"

I had no answer to that. He was right. And I knew right then that he was gone. Whether he stayed around for the tour or not . . . hell, if he stayed around for twenty more years, he wasn't ever gonna be the same. Which meant The Black Crowes weren't ever going to be the same.

We recorded a lot of tunes and we recorded a lot of overdubs. Lay-ers upon layers of tracks.

Most of those tracks ended up in the final mixes. Jack Puig could mix the hell out of an album, and *Three Snakes and One Charm* is a ster-ling example of that fact. It's dense, man.

When I first heard the final mixes, I was shocked. I was expecting a much more raw, live-sounding record. It seemed like every idea any-one had tried out was left in place on the record. I liked it overall, and

I saw it as a progression. Still, I preferred the leaner versions of the songs.

As *Three Snakes and One Charm* was being mixed, mastered, and ultimately turned in to the label, we looked ahead to our touring plans. There was a sense of optimism. We congratulated ourselves for learning how to get along. We talked about the fact that we'd turned a corner, and how we were all on board with the direction of the album. Finally, The Black Crowes could be the unified force we should have always been!

If we were unified in anything, it was abject denial. We had two full-blown junkies and a bass player who had completely, and justifiably, checked out. The end of the road for the band as we knew it was flashing like a giant neon sign. We just didn't wanna see it.

25

Things to Do in Denver When Your Band is Dead

Three Snakes and One Charm was released on July 23, 1996. A few weeks before that, we hit the road for a three-week run called the Hooked or Bycrooked tour with BR549, a honky-tonk band from Nashville. They were as good a live band as any on the planet at that time, and we loved having them with us.

On the Hooked or Bycrooked dates, we were jamming a lot, but we were well rehearsed and the jams still had definite structures. We were working in new covers throughout, like "Torn and Frayed" by The Stones. Neither the jams nor the covers felt excessive, though. The band was playing great.

The rock 'n' roll crowds from five or even three years earlier were nowhere to be found. In their place that summer was an unmistakable hippie vibe. A lot of people were traveling to see us, coming to multiple shows in a row, and we did our best to connect with them by starting a fan club, Taller, and publishing a semi-regular newsletter.

We could feel a groundswell, just one year after we played H.O.R.D.E., of fans who wanted different sets each night and who were coming to hear new things, not the same old songs night after night. A noticeable percentage of our audience was suddenly down for whatever we threw at them. Ever since the High as the Moon tour, we had allowed fans to tape our shows, and that also played a part in our changing audience. A lot of our fans evolved right along with us, moving away from the straight-up rock 'n' roll band we'd been in the early 1990s.

In the summer of 1996, though, we saw a whole lot of new people who were responding to what we were doing live right then. They hadn't been around for *Shake Your Money Maker* and *Southern Harmony*. They were recent converts. What they lacked in longevity, they made up for with intensity. They were *into it*, and there was a genuine, organic feel to what was happening.

We were successfully straddling both sides of the fence. We had rock fans and we had jam fans.

There's a big chunk of our fan base that believes the undisputed "golden age of The Black Crowes" is a one-year span from the summer of '96 to the summer of '97. In a way, it probably is. The band was certainly as ambitious as it had ever been.

Still, I preferred the *Amorica* era, when we still played more of the hard-rocking stuff. There were nights on the Amorica or Bust tour when we were like Led Zeppelin. Louder, more bombastic, more dynamic, and just badder than anybody else. It was the good kind of heavy. Where it's inherent, built from the ground up. On Amorica or Bust, we were like an oak tree. The tallest and widest tree on earth, and everyone else knew it. I think it was the best of all worlds.

To say I prefer '95 to '96 is not to dismiss the latter in any way. There was a new level of confidence to our playing. Whatever arrogance we had thrown around onstage the year before had given way to a much calmer sensibility.

The flip side to the great shows from the summer of '96 was everything else that was happening offstage. Drugs had completely enveloped the band by then. Coke, heroin, mushrooms, and acid were omnipresent.

Rich was pretty unhappy, as he wanted to rock more.

Johnny was having a daily conversation with himself about whether or not he was gonna stick around.

Me? Hell, I went with the flow. I looked for the positive wherever I could, and that new batch of passionate fans, more than anything, represented longevity to me. Maybe we actually would make it for thirty years if we kept them happy.

The suits I had worn for the past four years were long gone. I was wearing shorts and tie-dyed shirts onstage. I felt pretty damned good, actually. Or as good as I could feel considering I was drinking like a fish.

After the record was released, it was back to the old grind in theaters. Longer legs, shorter breaks. On the summer run, we focused heavily on the new material, with some of the old hits sprinkled in to close out the sets. With the album now in stores, the plan was to go out with full production and put on more of a proper rock show.

Of course, Chris had to fuck with the plan as soon as we started production rehearsals in Berkeley.

"I'm not playing 'Hard to Handle' anymore! I'm not playing 'She Talks to Angels'! Fuck that!" he whined. "We need to jam. We need to experiment. That's what our crowd wants now."

The notion that we could effectively give both sides of our fan base what they wanted wasn't something he was willing to consider. Sure, there were some great new fans who loved the idea of us learning new covers every single day and incorporating them into the shows, but there were still far more fans who wanted to hear the songs they'd loved for years. Giving them both enough of what they wanted wasn't rocket science. I could write a setlist in ten minutes that covered all our bases. Anyone in the band could have.

Chris wanted us to meander out of songs into noise: dissonant-by-design feedback-laden noise with no discernible rhythm underneath, and then find a way out of that into the next song somehow. As he wasn't actually playing an instrument, he saw himself as our conductor in these experiments. We did our best, but more often than not he was dissatisfied.

For The Black Crowes, it was a waste of what we were great at. It was self-indulgent, and it was stupid. We were a fake version of the Grateful Dead. It simply wasn't authentic.

Chris could never admit how much the drinking and the drugs had poisoned his thinking. "It's not the drugs, this is my vision," he would say, offended at the suggestion he was anything but a hundred percent together.

It spoke to the cocoon he was living in. Always drunk, always high on something, caught in the webbing of his own design. He was well past the point of tapping out for a reality check.

We started the Three Snakes tour in Berkeley and then went up the West Coast. We played Portland and Seattle for the first time since we canceled on the Amorica or Bust tour, and we didn't sell out either show.

"Fuck them! We're not coming back. We're *never* coming back here again," Chris seethed as we walked offstage in Seattle. We had fucked over our fans in both those cities by canceling dates without proper cause, and now we were facing the consequences. Cause and effect.

As Chris was ranting about the crowd, Rich went at him about the setlist.

"We need to play more songs," he said. "No one's coming to hear us do three twelve-minute jams."

"Fine, Rich, you write the fucking setlist and you watch when the fucking crowd leaves," Chris shot back.

The next night in Vancouver, Canada, Rich wrote the setlist. Two jams, four songs off the new album, an unreleased fan favorite, two covers everybody knew, and the rest from our first three albums, with "Remedy" to finish it off.

Voila! It felt like a party in that theater. The whole crowd was standing from start to finish, having a blast. From the stage, viscerally, it was the best crowd we'd have that whole tour.

We walked offstage to thunderous applause and Chris went right after Rich in the hallway.

"See? What'd I fucking tell you?"

"That crowd was amazing!" Rich said.

"That crowd fucking sucked!" Chris insisted.

"What are you talking about? Listen to that!" Rich yelled back. The audience was stomping in unison, begging us for more.

"So fucking what? If you wanna be in a stupid fucking rock band kissing everyone's ass, then you can fuck off! That's the last goddamned setlist you're writing!" Chris yelled.

Argument over. There was nothing else for Rich to say. Chris was denying, vehemently, something everyone else in the band plainly saw and felt.

Chris went back to writing the setlists. Initially, he followed an outline very similar to what Rich had done. The first handful of shows had some real energy again. But, before long, we were floundering, playing long-winded fucking jams and obscure covers that very few people, if any, truly wanted to hear.

Again, there's a real disconnect here, because our hardcore fans— the ones who collect bootlegs and have heard every concert we've ever played—revere this period in the band. And, yes, some of those recordings are fucking great. But onstage in the moment, more often than not, any hint of a collective spirit was dying.

We had a night off in Denver, and in an earnest attempt to cook up a little band unity, we all went to a strip club.

There were eight of us: the band, Mark Botting, and Brian Sarkin, the band's general assistant. It was the same old shit. All of us sitting there, drinking and talking about nothing much. Once we settled in, a naked stripper came over and started dancing in front of us.

"Are you guys in a band?" she asked.

"Yep."

"What's the band called?"

"The Black Crowes."

"Oh, my God, my mom loves you guys."

It was only 1996. It's not like we were in our fifties. I was thirty-one years old. And this stripper only knew the band as someone her mom liked. Damn. Life comes at you fast.

I sat next to Marc, who was in rough shape on several fronts. When he first joined the band, he was already married with a young son. On the surface, joining a successful rock band probably seemed like the answer to his prayers, but things hadn't been easy for him and his wife, and now the marriage was on the rocks.

Marc and I weren't very close, but I still felt like I should check in with him.

"Dude, are you okay?" I asked.

"It's not easy, man. It's not like I can just go home and fix it."

"Dude, you need to save your fucking marriage. The Black Crowes aren't worth you getting a divorce if you don't want one."

"No, it's okay, man. I need to feel this. All great art comes from pain, man. I need to feel this pain. It comes out in my playing."

"You want to feel pain?" I replied, incredulous. "Dude, what are you talking about? You're completely anesthetized. I could perform surgery on you right now. If you want to feel some pain, get your ass sober."

"I love you, too, man," Marc said spacily, looking at me with affection.

Anybody watching us from across the room would have thought, *Those guys in The Black Crowes have the life! Hanging out together, drinking beer all day long, checking out strippers.* I doubt anyone would have thought I was actually lecturing our guitar player about saving his fucking marriage.

I was waiting for Rich to give me the signal to bounce. Neither of us were ever strip-club guys. Finally, I caught his eye, we nodded to each other, and both stood up.

"We're out. See y'all back at the hotel."

We walked outside and were immediately approached by the driver of a white stretch limousine. He said he'd run us back to our hotel for twenty bucks. As we were negotiating with him, an old 1960s Ford Bronco pulled up to the red light on the corner. The driver looked like a big grizzled mountain man. He glanced over at me and Rich and yelled, "Hey, nice white limo, you fucking faggots!"

Rich and I fell out laughing. It was so random.

"Why don't you come back around and I'll show you who the faggot is," I yelled back.

The guy gunned it when his light turned green, taking a hard left and driving past us. He pointed at us, laughing wildly, then took another left at the next light. He was apparently taking me up on my offer.

The moment he disappeared from sight, the door to the strip club opened up and the rest of the band walked out. Rich and I told them we already had a limo lined up to go, and as we all piled in, we told them about the crazy-ass redneck driving around looking for a fight.

As the limo driver started to pull away from the curb, the Ford Bronco came roaring back up and cut him off, blocking us in place. He expected two long-haired "faggots" to be inside. He had no idea there were actually eight "faggots" in that limo, and he most certainly couldn't have imagined that Mark Botting was one of them.

Mark was six feet tall and weighed about 230 pounds. He was the loveliest, most jovial man you could ever meet and also the last person on earth I'd ever fuck with. He was a giant English bulldog—a thick beast of a man. And if there was one thing we all knew, it was that Mark always had our backs.

I looked through the front windshield to see the driver of the Bronco and his buddy standing in the street, demanding we get out of the car. I couldn't fucking believe it.

"Open the door, mate," Mark said, his voice rising. "OPEN THE FUCKING DOOR!"

I opened the door and Mark pushed past me. He jumped out onto the street and the whole band followed, spilling out of both back doors. Whatever was about to happen, no one was gonna miss it. Nothing brought us together like an honest-to-God external threat. And this one seemed tailor made for a little team unity.

The Bronco dude was about six foot three, and he was ripped. His buddy was much smaller, only about five foot ten, and nowhere near as built. The two of them were standing side by side, preparing for battle.

Botting never broke stride. He came around from the side of the limo, walking quickly, making a beeline for the bigger of the two dudes.

As he approached, Mark said, "Is there a problem, mate?"

As the word "mate" came out of his mouth, Mark's right fist landed square in the guy's mouth. Right on the downbeat. I heard the word "mate" and the sound of that giant fist smashing into the dude's face perfectly in sync.

Words could never do this punch justice. I mean, it was perfect. A thing of pugilistic beauty. It landed so squarely, and with such force, that for a split second nothing happened. It looked like something out of a movie—the guy stood there, dazed for a moment, and then another, and then another . . . until his knees buckled in toward each other. He was still on his feet, but not for long. His body crumpled and he fell forward, already unconscious, breaking his fall with his forehead. He lay there in a heap. He was out cold, right in the middle of the street.

"Holy shit!" the guy's friend said.

"HAVE YOU GOT SOMETHING TO SAY???" Mark screamed, turning toward him.

"No! It was him! I didn't want to come back! I don't want any trouble!" the guy screamed as he turned and started to run away.

Johnny Colt was a man looking to blow off some steam. He wasn't about to let that dude get away. He and Brian took off in pursuit, running down the block. As Johnny gained on him, we could hear the guy screaming, begging to be left alone. Johnny caught him, put him in a headlock, and Brian started throwing punches into the guy's midsection. They dragged him back toward the limo, where Johnny put him in an honest-to-God sleeper hold. That thing worked, too, as the dude went limp and collapsed on the street alongside his friend.

I couldn't believe it. Two dudes, both out cold, in the middle of downtown Denver. All in less than sixty seconds.

I looked over at the Bronco. It was sitting directly under the traffic light, still idling. My first thought was to hop in and take it back to the hotel, but I thought better of that. No need to risk being jailed for grand theft auto. So I settled for taking the keys. When those two idiots woke up, they wouldn't be going anywhere.

We were having a bit of a laugh about all of it when the limo driver said, "Guys, here comes a cop, let's go!" A Denver city cop car was about a block away at a red light. He'd be there in no time. We all piled into the limo.

The cop did in fact arrive on the scene as we were pulling away, but he didn't think to stop us. He had no idea what had happened. He just saw two bodies lying in the middle of the street near a cool old Bronco.

We ended up at the hotel bar, drinking and reliving the entire event for hours. We were a mess, but for a few hours we were a united mess.

That night in Denver was one of the last times it felt like Johnny was really part of the band. His isolation steadily grew during the Three Snakes tour. For his own good, he was pulling himself away from The Black Crowes.

Early on in the tour, we had a two-day drive from Chicago to Boston. Our gig the night before at the Navy Pier had been a barn burner, and we were all still jacked about it. We left Chicago around noon, and as we blasted the new BR549 album on the stereo, the party got up and going quickly. It was a long drive so I figured, *Fuck it, I'll jump in for this one*. Most of us were drinking, smoking, and shrooming the entire drive.

Johnny decided to join in as well. He'd been sober, as far as I knew, for a few months. But, hey, what else are you gonna do on a thousand-mile drive? We were all glad he was with us.

It didn't turn out well. Johnny got drunk, and high, and then he fell apart. His breakdown seemed to go on for hours. He'd walk up to the front lounge to clear his head a bit and then return to the back, only to hit a wall again.

Even in our various states of intoxication, we felt bad for him. Well, everyone except Chris.

"You're fucking up my buzz!" he screamed at Johnny.

Johnny's meltdown didn't ruin my buzz, but Chris's rant certainly did. I wanted to say something but I couldn't find any words.

Rich, thankfully, was stone-cold sober. When he walked to the back lounge to find Chris yelling at Johnny, he laid into him. "What the fuck is wrong with you? Jesus, man, could you be any less cool?"

Chris turned his anger to Rich, and they yelled at each other for what felt like an hour. I eventually stood up, walked out of the back lounge, and crawled into my bunk. So much for a fun ride to Boston.

I could be wrong, but I am fairly certain that was the last time Johnny ever had a drink or did a drug. That was his final straw. He just said, "Fuck it. I'm gonna white knuckle myself through this shit." And he did.

When I look back and think about him staying sober through his final year in the band, I am amazed. It must have been incredibly difficult, but he did it. He was reading, meditating, and practicing his yoga. He stayed in his own head, which had become the safest place to be when stuck in the orbit of The Black Crowes.

In the early 1990s, Johnny was the tattooed guy who would swig Jack Daniels onstage. He loved motorcycles and muscle cars. He wanted all of the classic rock 'n' roll stuff, and he got it. But along the way he was smart enough, and brave enough, to admit to himself, *This isn't what I wanted it to be.*

By the end of that summer, when Johnny got sober and stayed sober, the writing was on the wall. For the rest of that tour, Chris didn't talk to Johnny. Ever.

To Chris, Johnny was a dead man walking because he wasn't fucked up. End of story. Johnny was becoming a fully realized person and setting his own path, and it seemed to me Chris fucking hated him for it. Johnny, thankfully, was in such a new and healthy head space that he honestly no longer cared what Chris thought.

Johnny was, at this stage, beginning to live a life in direct opposition to the narrative of The Black Crowes. As a band our best days were behind us. We had taken great success and destroyed it. Not that we knew it, but by the fall of 1996, The Black Crowes had entered their death spiral.

Johnny Colt, on the other hand, was at the very beginning of his personal ascent. He was constantly learning, constantly growing, constantly seeking something deeper. Something better and more fulfilling than what life in The Black Crowes had turned out to be.

By the time Johnny did officially leave the band, in August of 1997, he was untouchable. He was truly prepared for life without The Black Crowes. He didn't need the band. Not on any level.

Johnny Colt is the greatest success story of The Black Crowes.

Johnny Colt *won* The Black Crowes.

26

To Hell and Band

The European tour started in early January 1997 in England and finished at the end of February in Ireland, hitting sixteen other countries in between. There were very few fights on that tour, but not necessarily because everyone was getting along. We were experiencing a collective shutdown of our central nervous systems. We were emotionally and mentally numb. We could still play great, but we were zombies otherwise.

It makes sense that in retrospect those shows are so beloved by the die-hards. We had nothing to feel good about but the gigs themselves. Frustration, melancholy, regret, dimmed hopes, realized fears . . . it was all on display in every show. Like Marc said that night in Denver, the pain came out in the playing. We played beautifully, with tired eyes and sad hearts.

Chris and I were getting along pretty well. We still, amazingly, had a pretty romanticized view of touring in Europe, and especially in the UK. We might not like each other much in Kansas City, but as we were both die-hard Anglophiles, we could always hang in England. In Cambridge, we went to a pub together for lunch. We walked in looking for a pint and a shepherd's pie and walked out with a new understanding of just how far Marc Ford had fallen down the well.

Marc was a fucking mess. We all knew that already. He was drinking and drugging heavily, well past the point of any initial concern. His playing was suffering now, too. He found himself in the wrong key occasionally. He had trouble with some of the intros. He'd come into a song dragging, or rushing, or sometimes it seemed like he was somehow dragging *and* rushing.

As Chris and I sat by the fireplace with our beers, Marc walked into the pub, alone. He went straight to the bar, with his head down. He didn't take a look around, so he had no idea we were there. Chris and I watched him drink four pints and six shots of whiskey in about twenty minutes. He finished off his last pint, stood up, spun around, and walked out. He looked no different than he had when he walked in.

"We have to do something, man," Chris said as we walked back to the hotel.

"That fucking guy is going to die," I replied.

Marc already looked half dead as it was. His skin had no color. All I could figure was that he and Ed were out of heroin, so he was trying to drink through his withdrawal.

A few hours later as we were on the bus heading to the venue, I asked Marc if he was doing okay. He smiled and said he was great, thanks.

Something's gotta give. We gotta do something. This guy might honestly drop dead.

A few days later we played in Hamburg. We stopped the gig in the middle of the set after a few beers were thrown onto the stage. A promoter rep told the audience, in German, that we weren't going to finish the set unless they stopped throwing cups at us. When we finally returned to the stage, we felt a little out of sorts. It's always weird to have an unexpected interruption in a show. We started up again with The Byrds tune "Mr. Spaceman." It was off-kilter from the jump, stayed wobbly for a bit, and then straightened itself out. It wasn't great, but it was fine. It was *acceptable*. But I guess Marc blew it somehow. Who gives a fuck? Look, if Marc blew "Cursed Diamond," I'd wanna nail him to the wall. But this was "Mr. Spaceman," for fuck's sake, and there was not one person in Hamburg other than Chris Robinson who wanted to hear that song anyway.

Walking into the dressing room that night after the gig, Marc said, "Sorry about that, guys" and then plopped down on the couch.

The rest of us were standing in a bit of a circle, facing Marc. It was a tiny dressing room.

Johnny started. "Marc, we're worried about you. This isn't about your playing. This is about you. You look like you're about to die."

Marc broke down immediately. "I'm so sorry," he cried.

The man was miserable. His home life was in shambles, his band was a mess, and he was strung out. And now it looked like it was time to face all of it.

Johnny said, "You don't have to apologize. You just gotta get healthy again."

Marc couldn't compose himself. He wept and wept.

Ed didn't say a word. I don't imagine it was a comfortable situation for him, as he was also strung out, of course.

I was lucid, but hardly an appropriate voice to carry the message we were trying to convey. I drank beer throughout the gigs, so I had at least six in me at the time. I simply nodded and seconded the points the other guys were making, and made sure that whenever Marc looked to me he saw a supportive face.

Chris was agitated. He tried to offer support initially but the longer the conversation lasted, the angrier he got. He was starting to pace a bit, and it was clear he was having a hard time keeping the lid on. I looked over to him and gave a silent head nod toward the door. *Go on, man, get out of here, we got this.* But he ignored me.

Johnny had the most to say. He pulled a chair over and sat face to face with Marc.

"I know exactly where you are. Marc, I'm you. I've been right where you are. You can do this and I'll help you as much as I can."

Marc was alternating between feeling attacked and feeling horrible about letting us down. At one point, I said, "Believe me, Marc, we're not piling on you here. We all need to get our shit together. Every one of us. You're just a little ways ahead of the rest of us."

That did it. Chris exploded.

"This isn't about the rest of us! We don't have to get our shit together! Some of us can handle our shit! This is about *you* and the fact that you're too fucked up to play!"

He was standing over Marc, screaming at him. Chris took every bit of this personally. His greatest fear was circling the room. Soon enough it would be *him* sitting on that couch.

Marc apologized again. He looked up at Chris and all he saw was rage.

"What the fuck are you gonna do without this gig? Go back to Orange County and work at a fucking record store again? You better wake the fuck up!"

Johnny stood up and faced Chris. Calmly, he said, "Chris, you're not helping."

Chris went at Johnny. "Fuck you, Johnny! Oh, you know something about this now so you're gonna save the day? Get the fuck out of here with that shit!"

He was completely out of his mind. Johnny ignored him and sat back down with Marc.

Rich and I stared at each other. We were both boiling, but we stayed quiet. We were hoping Chris would just shut the fuck up. Anything from either of us would have made it worse.

Marc cried even harder. "I'm sorry man . . . all my heroes . . . they all did drugs, man . . . Clapton, Keith, and Jerry . . . I just, it is just . . . I'm so sorry . . ."

Marc was totally exposed. He had no defenses left. So Chris went for the kill shot.

"*Keith? Jerry? Are you fucking kidding me?* Keith and Jerry are fucking artists, motherfucker! You think you're like them? You aren't shit!"

The room fell completely silent.

Anybody else would have realized they'd gone too far.

Not Chris.

He just held his fucking toxic ground, glaring at Marc.

It was the single worst moment in the history of The Black Crowes. Marc was helpless, flailing, lost. And Chris let him know in no uncertain terms what he thought of him. *You're just the hired help, boy. You're weak. You don't matter.*

"You're going to the fucking doctor tomorrow," Chris declared.

Marc looked up at him desperately and said, "I love you too, man," just like he had said to me in Denver, trying to find something, anything to cling to in a tough moment.

"I didn't say that I love you, motherfucker!" Chris shot back. "I said you better get your shit together!" And then he turned and finally walked out of the room.

Marc was heaving. Johnny had his hands on Marc's shoulders, telling him over and over that it was going to be okay. As soon as the door shut, Rich walked over and sat next to Marc. He looked him in the eye and said, "Fuck him, Marc. Don't listen to a thing that fucking asshole says. You're gonna be okay."

We walked out to the bus a few minutes later. Chris was already in the upstairs lounge, blasting music. No one went near him. He was glowing with rage.

Marc went to a doctor the next day with Mark Botting. They put him through a comprehensive series of tests. "Marc is staying overnight, he's in bad shape," Botting told us. His liver was shot, and overall he was a mess physically.

The doctors had him stop heroin cold turkey, but gave him a homeopathic remedy to smooth over the withdrawal. Whatever it was, it worked. Marc was stone-cold sober for the rest of the tour. A week after Chris and I had spied him in the pub in Cambridge, Marc came back to the tour a different man.

Within a week he had color back in his face. He was talking about feeling connected to his instrument again. Hell, he was reading a book. I'd never seen him read before. I don't remember what it was but I said to him, laughing, "Damn, man, if you wanted to read a book you could have just asked me for one. You didn't have to go through all that." He laughed really hard. Genuine laughter.

It only took a few shows for him to completely regain his touch. He was playing like Marc Ford again. He was smiling onstage. I'd never seen that. The entire thing was mind blowing.

By the time the tour ended, he said he was afraid to go home. "I don't know if I can stay sober. It's easy on tour when I have my guitar with me all the time."

We got to London about a month after Hamburg. Marc was on cruise control by then. Hell, we all were. The end was in sight. One week to go and then . . . well, we didn't know actually. There were no firm plans in place, which was fine with me. All I knew was I wanted to get the fuck back to Atlanta.

We played two acoustic shows on the same night at a tiny London club called The Garage. To die-hard Black Crowes fans, both shows are legendary. Several fans told me at the time that we were the coolest band in the world to do something like that—to play two gigs on the same night in a tiny room for them. I said I loved the intimacy of those small gigs, which was entirely true. The part I left out of the conversation was that we originally hoped to pull two nights at the Royal Albert Hall out of this run, and when it was clear there was only enough demand for one, we had to improvise. We already had a night off in London scheduled, and we couldn't afford to take another. So, feeling a bit cornered, we threw The Garage gigs together. It was to our collective surprise that we all enjoyed them as much as the fans.

Despite all of our troubles, we could still get onstage and for a few hours on the best nights, it was still worth it. All of it. All of the pain, all of the anger, all of the confusion, all of the abuse, all of the fear, all of the chaos . . . it was all still worth it when the show was great.

We were playing Neil Young's "Big Time" on that run. It was my favorite part of every set in which it appeared. I sang along, without a mic but in full voice, during the choruses every time. "I'm still living / in the dream we had. / For me, it's not over."

I didn't want it to be over. I just wanted it to make sense again.

On our day off, Ross Halfin called to say Jimmy Page was around and wanted to get a drink if we were up for it. Chris and I, in Anglophile cahoots again as we were back in London, met him at a pub right across the street from our hotel.

We were still blown away by the fact that we were hanging with Jimmy Page. That feeling would always disappear as soon as we got together, though. He was just a regular guy. He never played up his rock icon persona. We spent a couple of hours with him and it was not unlike a drink-up with any other friend. We talked about records, movies, history, politics, and most memorably, *The Simpsons*. Jimmy had just discovered the show and loved it.

"Did you see the one where Homer sings 'Born Under a Bad Sign'?" he asked.

No Jimmy, we haven't.

"No? Oh, it's brilliant!" Jimmy replied . . . and then launched into a full-on impression of Homer Simpson singing Albert King.

Chris and I shared a look. *I cannot believe we're watching this.*

We finished up with Jimmy and crossed the street back to the hotel. We walked up to the bar and ran into Sheryl Crow's band. We joined them for a few drinks and at some point Sheryl came walking by with her new boyfriend, Eric Clapton.

I was never a card-carrying Clapton fan but, still, it jolted me to see him like that. He didn't stay long, though, and after he left Sheryl joined our group for a nightcap. We sat for a while talking about our childhoods in small towns, and then Sheryl and I, plus a couple of the guys in her band, went up to her room. We drank a few bottles of wine and talked about everything and nothing until sunrise.

I went back to my room eventually, and fell asleep thinking about the fact that I had seen two of The Yardbirds that night and one of them sang like Homer Simpson.

I was still living in the dream I had. For me, it wasn't over.

The night after our Garage shows, we played the Royal Albert Hall. Two years earlier, on the Amorica or Bust tour, we had met Jimmy for the first time and left London the toast of the town. The 1997 gig, in contrast, was anything but triumphant. You could hear a pin drop between songs. It was clear that a lot of the audience were disappointed, because they expected us to be the band they'd seen two years earlier. As for the people who knew exactly what to expect . . . they weren't loud. They were stoned out of their minds and taking in every little thing we did in awed silence. It was the worst of both worlds: the respectfully quiet and the angry speechless.

We'd had plenty of shows with mixed responses on that tour. In Lyon, France, it was so quiet in between songs that Chris had Noodles (my drum tech) make his famous cricket sounds into the mic. But this was the Royal Albert Hall. It was a real benchmark, and it illuminated quite brightly just how far we'd stumbled off the path.

A few nights later we played the Apollo Theatre in Manchester for the third-to-last show of the European tour. We had played this venue many times, going back to the Shake Your Money Maker tour. We'd always had stomping shows. The after show in our dressing room was always like a gig in London—so packed we had to bring in extra beer to accommodate everybody. But for the Three Snakes gig, it was a ghost town backstage.

"Well, there's not one person on the guest list, mate," Botting told me before the show.

The party is over.

Just before the gig, Mark asked everyone to come into the main dressing room. It was totally quiet. We weren't listening to any music. Even the venue was quiet. There was literally no buzz coming from the crowd. It was 8:59 P.M. We always hit the stage on time. The misery ended—or at least the misery had a chance to end—as soon as we hit the first downbeat.

"All right, chaps, it's about time to go," Botting said. "But first, why don't we sit here together and have a beer before we start. Let's take five minutes. Just us."

He's quitting. That's what this is. Fuck. Fuck. Fuck.

Marc and Johnny had a sparkling water and the rest of us had beers. We toasted ourselves, and then we all stood in place drinking our beers, not saying a word. Mark checked his watch a few times. We waited for exactly five minutes.

"All right, boys, let's do it," Botting said finally.

We walked to the stage. As the house lights went down, I gave him a hug. He hugged me back, hard.

The Black Crowes were never good at sitting idle, even during our darkest moments. For once, that was a godsend. Chris finally called after we'd been home for a month or so.

"Hey, you know all these songs we've been writing? Let's start recording some demos."

We all agreed that we had some really good new songs, mostly put together at sound checks on the European tour. "Another Roadside Tragedy" and "Peace Anyway" were two of my favorite songs we'd ever written.

Johnny found a little hole-in-the-wall studio in Atlanta called Purple Dragon that was cheap and available, and we booked a session for early April.

Pete called with the news that Def American had essentially ceased to exist. Because *Shake Your Money Maker* and *Southern Harmony* generated so much cash for the label, Def American (renamed "American

Recordings" by Rick Rubin in 1993) had expanded into a full-fledged operation. They had signed a ton of bands, none of whom ever sold a damn thing. When *Three Snakes* tanked, they were suddenly out of money. They closed down their offices and let just about everybody go.

"There's no label anymore, but we're stuck with Rick," Pete explained. "He's going to find a new home and wherever that home is, we're going in and starting over."

Starting over? We're The Black Crowes!

The full extent of our situation hadn't sunk in. We assumed, as always, that Pete would figure out the best solution. And yet our instincts told us to get back to the basics. We were going to record in Atlanta on a tiny budget. No hotels. The three of us who lived in town would each take on a house guest. Ed stayed with Johnny, Marc stayed with me, and Chris stayed with Rich. Chris joked that "The Three Stooges were crashing with the three boy scouts."

The day before Marc got to town, I drove over to Rich's house. He and Chris were in the den playing acoustic guitars. I felt instantly that there was no tension in the air. They couldn't wait to play me their new tunes.

They went through them, one by one, and I was blown away.

They had somehow stumbled into a huge burst of creativity and efficiency. By the next day, we had ten songs ready to record. The choruses were great, as were the lyrics in general. The new shit was awesome.

We set up at Purple Dragon on a Friday. We cut "Another Roadside Tragedy" first. Just us and the house engineer. We played through the song once and Chris said, "That felt pretty fucking good!"

We listened to playback and it *sounded* pretty fucking good, too. We were off and running. Everyone got along great. We cut one of the new ones, "Predictable," and then "If It Ever Stops Raining," a tune Rich had written back in 1991 but Chris had never put lyrics to until that week. Its working title for six years had been "Teabaggin'." I was sorry to see that title go.

We tracked throughout the weekend. We were loose, playing like a real band. There was no pressure because of course these were just demos. By Monday, we had ten tracks recorded.

We sat together and listened to them straight through. I flat-out loved it. To me, these weren't demos. This was the next album.

At some point, though, Chris said, "Does anyone else think this shit sounds pretty great already?"

Everyone jumped in—we'd all been thinking the same thing.

I was so relieved. I still felt like we'd missed a great opportunity with the Brendan O'Brien sessions from New Orleans in 1992. I couldn't stand the thought of that happening again.

The way the album, which we later called *Band*, was recorded didn't leave a lot of room for fixes. We couldn't properly rerecord the backing vocals because they all bled into various other mics. We hadn't set up with separation, so everything was basically bleeding into everything else. We did add some horns, courtesy of the Dirty Dozen Brass Band, and we called Ziggy Marley's backup singer, Erika, who lived in town. Donnie Heron from BR549 came down to add some fiddle. A three-day demo session turned into a ten-day album session.

I was over the moon about this record. We did it in a hole-in-the-wall studio, on our own, and it felt amazing. We spent a few thousand dollars. Around one hundredth of what we'd blown on *Tall*.

All that playing, all those gigs, all that jamming, all that everything. Suddenly, we were able to condense it all into four-minute, well-crafted songs. You could feel the musicianship on that record more than anything we had ever done up to that point. The interplay between both guitars, and with the rhythm section, and with Ed and me, was just next level.

We were all pretty astounded, and all shared the same feeling. *This is the band we always wanted to be.* I still believe that to this day. We finally got there. We sounded like a real band, a proper band, an all-time great band . . . which is why it was simply called *Band*.

We were all on board. We were in sync.

Somehow, from the depths of our dysfunction and suffering, we pulled it together and created something incredible. It was a new beginning for The Black Crowes. Or so I hoped.

27

"Put On Some Fucking Clothes, Will Ya?"

In June, Pete told us that Rick Rubin had signed a distribution deal with Sony/Columbia.

At first, we thought this was all great news. We were excited. We already had a record finished that we loved. The only thing for Columbia to do was figure out when to release it. And, hell, it's Bob Dylan's label. What could be better?

We were long overdue for a painful lesson in reality regarding the music business.

Our first album was produced with zero interference from the label. Def American existed pretty much only on paper when they signed us. Well, they actually did have an office with a skeleton staff above a hair salon on Sunset Boulevard, but they were just getting started. It was rinky-dink.

We had always operated on our own terms. Our initial success coupled with Pete's renegotiation of our deal put the reins in our hands. Whatever problems we encountered along our career were all internal. The label never forced us to do anything.

But Columbia was a real corporate record label. They were part of what we'd always called the "Evil Empire," Sony Music. It truly was a whole new landscape, one in which we were ill-equipped to maneuver.

Before we could focus on any of that, however, it was time for the Further tour with a few Grateful Dead offshoots: Mickey Hart's Planet Drum and Bob Weir's RatDog. Bruce Hornsby, who had toured as a sideman with the Dead, was on the bill as well. He was a monster. Ed had a hard time watching him, in fact. Hornsby was the only guy I ever saw who shook him.

It is safe to say that overall, our sets were not well received by the Dead's audience. We got regular complaints about our volume. Nothing makes you realize you're still a rock band more than surrounding yourself with real, bona fide hippie jam bands.

Chris was thrilled to be in that world. He was convinced the Dead community was going to embrace us. But that was hardly the case. This was only two years after Jerry Garcia died. The Deadheads were still very much interested only in the guys from the Dead. They didn't give a shit about The Black Crowes.

The second show of the tour was in Atlanta, where two memorable things occurred: (1) Chris Robinson wore shorts and a Lakers jersey onstage, a clear indication of just how little he gave a shit about being a proper rock 'n' roll frontman at that point; and (2) Marc Ford claimed he was dosed. He was tripping *hard*, barely hanging on. He swore he hadn't consciously taken anything. We made it through the show, but it was a harbinger of things to come.

Within a few weeks, it was obvious that Marc had fallen off the wagon. We weren't sure what drugs he was doing, but he regularly reeked of alcohol. There was no slow decline. It was as if someone snapped their fingers and he was down the rabbit hole again.

In Detroit, the drummer from moe. approached me at the side of the stage and said, "Marc came by our dressing room and asked for a beer. We said, 'Sure,' and now he's down there just pounding them. He said, 'Hey, guys, don't tell anyone about this because I can't drink,' and I just thought you should know."

Sure enough, Marc walked into our dressing room before the set and was obviously wasted. That night after our show Chris started talking openly about firing Marc.

"He's never going to get his shit together," Chris said.

Clearly, Chris thought it was preferable to fire Marc than to try to help him. I wasn't surprised. In my mind, Chris knew one thing very clearly: Marc going to rehab might lead to Ed going to rehab, and that might lead to the worst possible result of all . . . Chris going to rehab. And that sure as hell wasn't an option.

The mood in the band had turned pretty grim within the first ten shows of the tour. We were playing some of the same venues as we had on H.O.R.D.E. two years earlier. The response from the crowds, and the outlook for our future, couldn't have been more different.

Pete was with us in New York City the day we played Forest Hills Stadium in Queens. During a band meeting at the hotel, he reiterated the poor outlook for our touring business. Chris asked about doing a club tour, saying we could spin the story into us simply wanting to do something special for our die-hard fans and only offer tickets through our fan club.

Pete shot it down immediately. "That's not a bad idea as a short promotional tour. But it's not real. You're not doing it because you genuinely want to give something special to your fans, you're suggesting it because you have nothing else to do."

"Look, there aren't any good offers," he continued. "But I'm not putting you in clubs for a full-length tour—if we do that, regardless of how you try to spin it, it means one thing: we're announcing to the world that we're done, and I am *not* willing to do that."

He had our full attention now. We might have pulled a rabbit out of our ass by recording *Band* that spring, but once Further was finished, we *really* had nothing to do.

"I have a lot of work to do with Columbia Records," Pete said. "They have to feel that you are their artist, their signing, and a priority. What I need from you guys is simple—just don't get in the way of that."

Pete turned to Chris. "There will be people from Columbia Records at this gig. They need to see a fucking great band and a fucking great show. If you walk out there wearing shorts and a basketball jersey, and jam for most of the show, believe me when I say it will make my job impossible."

"I wore shorts once," Chris laughed.

"Yeah, well, one time was too many. Just do me a favor—put on some fucking clothes, will ya? Something that looks like you give a shit. Oh, and I don't know if you've noticed this, but they have free shampoo and soap in hotels. It'll be near the water."

Pete was laughing and keeping it light, hoping a little levity might crack the code of whatever forces were in control of Chris's mental and emotional barometer at that particular moment.

"I'll think about it," Chris said.

Apparently he didn't have to think long. On the drive out to Forest Hills, Chris wrote a setlist that was a fucking monster.

He walked into the front lounge of the bus with the setlist in his hand. "Let's go fucking kill these people," he said.

Yes, please!

The thaw between Chris and Pete had begun.

We went out that night and rocked. It was great. The crowd loved it. We loved it. Go figure. After the show Chris and Pete sat on the bus, in the front lounge, quietly talking. They had been butting heads for years, thanks to Chris's insatiable and thoughtless desire for control. Now, with Chris sensing that we had played every card in his deck and were in dire need of some better luck, he was willing to let Pete guide us again.

"See, slim? We work really well, when we work together," Pete reminded him.

"I know, you're right," Chris admitted.

I sat right across from them for the whole conversation. They spoke for an hour. At a few different points, they were smiling at each other. And then laughing with each other. It felt like years since that had happened.

Pete summarized his overall view of things and then asked one very simple question: "Can you just go be The Black Crowes and be great again?"

"Yeah, man, I guess we probably should," Chris said.

Holy shit. Pete just moved a mountain.

Of course, there were still all kinds of major fucking concerns.

Marc and Johnny were very clearly both slipping away. One too sober to stay, the other too wasted.

I was drinking more than I ever had.

We had no idea what Columbia was going to think about *Band*.

We weren't going to be on the road for quite a long time, and we were wrapping up this touring cycle soon with very little money to show for it.

Chris would more than likely feel completely different about the future within a week. Or a day. Or by the time we got back to the hotel that night.

August 3, 1997. The final show of the tour was at Irvine Meadows in Orange County, just a few miles from Marc's house.

Chris wrote another rocking setlist. But the crowd wasn't digging it. A lot of them had their fingers in their ears. At one point Chris said, "For all the people with fingers in their ears, it's not gonna get any less loud. I'd hate to see what a bunch of young hippies would do if Jimi Hendrix was playing. He played fucking LOUD!"

If this was our final show for a while, Chris apparently wanted to leave behind a little piss and vinegar on the way out. It was very "un-Dead-like." Otherwise, we played our guts out that day. From top to bottom, the show was on fire. We finished the set with "No Speak No Slave." Put that in your pipe and smoke it, hippies.

Marc walked offstage, got right into a car, and took off. The next day, Rich, Johnny, and I flew home. The band was finished for 1997. Actually, the band, as we knew it, was finished forever.

After a few days home, the four partners had a conference call with Pete to discuss Marc.

"He's out of the band," Chris said.

For the past couple of weeks, every single day Chris had been saying, "He's gone, get rid of him." So that wasn't a surprise.

"I never want to see him again. I thought he could get it together, but obviously not," Rich said. He had never cared much for Marc personally, so that was also expected.

"If that's what you guys think is the best thing, then, yes, okay," Johnny said.

I hadn't expected Johnny to vote Marc out. He hadn't voted, actually. He kind of just abstained.

I was now the only dissenting voice. "Well, I know I've said it before," I finally offered, "but I'll say it again. I think we should put him in rehab."

"I would completely agree if Marc was open to it," Pete said. "But I have talked to Marc twice this week and he has no interest in going. He just asked that we send him his gear."

"Well, if he's unwilling to go get help, then I guess we have to let him go," I admitted.

The decision still didn't sit well. Marc was a mess, granted. But he was a pivotal contributor to the band. I hated the idea of treating band members like disposable parts. Saying farewell to Marc would permanently change how The Black Crowes sounded. It would also change how our fans saw us. I felt that at the time, but Marc's fate was already sealed.

Pete said, "I'm not closing the door. He may very well change his mind and if he does, we're going to try to help him."

Pete called Marc back and told him as much. "If you decide you want to get clean, then you call me."

"I just need my gear," Marc replied. That's all he fucking had to say.

Pete talked to Marc again a few days later and reiterated his offer. Pete really didn't want to see it end like this. He understood very clearly the value of a consistent lineup. He also understood, more importantly, that addiction wasn't a sign of a lack of strength, or a lack of character. Pete knew that Marc was in real trouble. Far greater trouble than simply losing a gig. *Call me, tell me you want help, and I'll help you.*

Marc said, "Okay, thanks." He never called, he never asked for help, and that was that.

I saw something Robert Plant said once about how he felt when Bonham died. Led Zeppelin pulled the plug, of course, and Plant said he felt like he was standing on a street corner for a few years with his ears ringing, and he just couldn't figure out which direction to go. That's exactly what it felt like to lose Marc.

I love bands. I love consistent lineups. I think a band that stays together always has an inherent strength and power that can't be replicated or duplicated by replacement parts.

I *hate* it when the bands I love change members. I didn't want The Black Crowes to be what The Allman Brothers eventually became, which was a few mainstays with a revolving door of side pieces. We had lost Jeff in 1991, but that was ultimately for the best.

I couldn't imagine that losing Marc would ever be seen as anything but a crushing loss.

I was right.

28

The Three-Headed Monster

Pete scheduled another conference call for the Monday following Marc's departure. He just needed a few minutes to update us on some conversations he'd had with Columbia. But before Pete could get into it, Johnny interrupted him.

"I'm going to say something, guys, and after I'm done I don't think you're going to want me on the rest of the call," he said.

Fuck, is this it?

"I'm quitting the band. I'm done," Johnny said. "I don't think I have to explain why, we all know this has been coming for a long time. If there is anything, at all, that I can help with, I will do it. I don't expect to hear from you, but I hope you know I mean that. Thank you all for everything. It's been great. But I have to leave The Black Crowes now."

As I listened to Johnny pulling the ripcord, I could hear my heart pounding. A voice in my head was screaming, *Quit! Do it! Do it right now! Just go with him!*

Johnny stopped talking, and there were a few seconds of silence.

"Well, all right, man, we got business now," Chris finally said. "Later."

Fuck you, Chris. Fuck your alcoholic drug-addicted narcissistic fucking life! The man just quit his own goddamned band and you have nothing to say except "Later"?

"Okay, thanks, guys," Johnny said. And he hung up.

"Um, did anyone know that was going to happen today? Steve?" Pete asked.

"No, I didn't," I said. Which wasn't entirely true. As Johnny said, the writing had been on the wall for a while now. I'd thought a hundred times over the past year that he would be gone soon. But knowing something is going to happen and then something *actually* happening are two very different things. The reality was numbing. I was just as shocked as anybody.

"Well, I'm sure we all agree that he means it. This wasn't a snap decision," Pete said.

Rich didn't say a word but I could tell, somehow, that he was reeling just like I was.

Chris said, "Okay, fuck it. Let's just get a new bass player. He's been out of the band for two fucking years anyway."

"Chris, I don't think this is the time to start making plans," Pete said. "I think we should all just take a minute here and think about this."

"I don't have anything to think about," Chris insisted.

"Well, I do," Pete replied.

"I sure as shit do, too," I said.

"Are you serious? Who fucking cares?" Chris said incredulously. He saw no difference between Johnny Colt quitting The Black Crowes and Mr. Crowe's Garden firing a couple of bass players back in the '80s. It meant literally nothing to him.

"Well, I think it's a big deal that we just lost a third of the band in a week," I said, pointing out the fucking obvious.

"The *band* is just the three of us anyways," Chris said. "That's all it's ever really been."

Rich still said nothing. I was done talking, too.

"Guys, let's talk again a little later," Pete said finally. "I need to talk with Johnny, to go over everything that we'll have to deal with, legally."

Pete sounded deflated. We'd been through an awful lot of tough moments before, but this time I could hear something different in his voice. I don't think he was worried that we wouldn't figure it out. Hell, he never would have allowed anything to knock him down for long, but I think he was keenly aware of the damage and deterioration drugs were causing the band, regardless of who was doing them, and our future. The whole thing was just . . . sad.

Rose Mary walked into the room halfway through the phone call. I hung up and said, "Johnny just fucking quit. He's gone. For real." I was crushed.

"I gotta go see him," I said.

"No," Rose Mary countered. "Not right now. Give him a couple of days. If you had just quit, the last thing you'd want is anyone coming over right after."

She was right. Shit. But I needed to do *something*.

After almost two years, the inevitable had finally happened. And there I sat, stunned and helpless. What the fuck had I been doing the past two years? What the fuck had I been doing the last *seven* years?

I could handle Marc not being in the band. I didn't like it, but firing Marc didn't take the wind completely out of my sails. Johnny's resignation? It buried me. It felt like the end.

Despite what Chris said about the band being the three of us, everything he and Rich had ever done showed how they really felt. Chris thought it was *his* band and Rich thought it was *his* band. It was never *our* band.

I knew all of that. I had known it for years.

And still, I didn't have a plan B.

The Black Crowes were my life's work, and my life's passion. I didn't have anything else lined up to pursue. As I sat there processing a million thoughts, one thing became crystal clear within a few minutes. I could handle anything this situation threw at me. What I wasn't prepared for was a *new* situation. I was institutionalized at that point. A company man.

The next afternoon, I called Johnny. We only talked for a few minutes.

"Dude, you and me are good," he said. "I need some time and you need some time, too. Don't worry about us, we don't have to say a thing to each other. I love you. We're fine. Let's just take some time, and call me back when you're comfortable."

And then he hung up.

I didn't call him again until December 21, 2001.

A few hours after Johnny quit, Rich called me. He was really upset.

"Man, we're fucked," he said. "Chris is insane to think this doesn't matter. I think we're done."

My first thought was, *Well, I hope you enjoyed playing bass on that last album, you fucking asshole.* But I kept that to myself. I was at least relieved to hear he was talking sense now.

We talked for a half-hour or so. It was the longest phone conversation we'd ever had. Two years earlier, we'd made plans to follow in The Rolling Stones' footsteps. But by now, the summer of 1997, it felt like we'd already been out of fashion forever. It had been forever since we *mattered*.

With *Southern Harmony*, we survived grunge. We were still strong. By the time *Amorica* came out, however, there was the fucking Dave Matthews Band. And then the second wave of grunge wannabes. Bush and Live were selling millions of records. Then there was Matchbox Twenty. And Third Eye Blind.

Jesus, every couple of months there's a new fucking thing and we are officially ancient now. That's how we felt. We were five years removed from feeling cool.

There had been a steady trajectory from opening in clubs, to headlining clubs, to headlining theaters, to headlining amphitheaters and a few smaller arenas . . . and then we slid back into theaters. And they weren't selling out.

You feel all of that. You can't help *but* feel it.

"The revenue streams from all areas continue to flow, as long as we grow, but the minute you stop growth, they all start slowly going away." Pete told us that from day one.

Your next record sells less but you're still staying in nice hotels. You're selling fewer tickets but you're still getting two buses instead of one. You get used to a certain lifestyle and the minute you slide back, if you don't adjust your spending with it, then you're doubling your losses.

We eventually made some cosmetic changes to our spending and touring expenses, but the brothers could never really accept downgrading. We had lengthy conference calls regarding touring costs in 2013, for fuck's sake.

By the summer of 1997, it was time to tighten up. Hell, it was past time to tighten up.

But not for Chris and Rich. That wasn't how they wanted to roll. They were famous. They were rich. Cutting costs was for other people.

We were about to find out just how far they were willing to go to maintain their lifestyle.

I turned thirty-two a couple weeks after we lost Johnny and Marc. I was down, but not defeated. If anything, I was still young. I was well on the way to being more focused and clear-headed than I'd been in years. I cut back my drinking considerably.

I had finally decided it was okay to allow myself to think like a rational human being with self-interest. That had always been forbidden in The Black Crowes. To think about one's own needs, or to think about anything other than the songs and the band was somehow selfish. Chris set that template early on, and eventually it just became a way of life. It was fucking cult-like groupthink.

I talked to Pete about all of this one day. I was explaining my struggles with thinking first and foremost about myself. I could see the problem, but I couldn't easily define it. I didn't have the proper language.

He listened for a long while and finally said, "Okay, Steve, lemme make a recommendation. Go to the bookstore right now and find a book called *Codependent No More*. Just trust me. Read it a couple of times. Be honest with yourself while you read it. I think you'll see yourself on every page."

I laughed and said, "Pete, I don't think I need the self-help section of a fucking book store."

"Well, you can't explain the problem because you don't understand the problem, and if you don't understand it, you can't participate in a solution. If you won't help yourself, who the fuck will? Chris? Rich? I don't think so. Steve, you need to educate yourself and seriously consider changing your approach to the band. You are a codependent dealing with addicts. That's not a judgment call. It's just the reality of this situation."

I bought the book. I read it right away and then I read it again. I'd love to say everything cleared up right away and I was a much healthier person, but that wasn't the case.

I did, however, recognize myself completely.

I was beginning the slow and painful process of making myself better. It's ongoing. There'll never be a day when I'm a hundred percent truly free of this shit. It's a lifelong work in progress, but it's not a stretch to say Pete really saved me that day.

The Black Crowes was officially a three-headed monster now. I had to step up and use this to my advantage. As shitty as it was to lose Johnny and Marc, I also saw an opportunity to reclaim some of my power in the band. We had a real vacuum now and I had a chance to take up a lot more of that space.

Pete said, "I'll open the door for you to have a stronger voice, but you're gonna have to speak up and hold your ground. You can't back down, regardless of the pushback. You gotta be the third band voice now."

With Chris, Pete had learned he had to always start with the money. *You might not like the sound of A, but if we do it, then we can afford to do B, which will then benefit the band long term. It requires X amount of time, etc., etc.*

It was always important to show Chris the carrot first. If you presented a concept he didn't like and hadn't presented the financial upside already, it was game over. After Pete had his attention, then we talked about time commitments and artistic rewards. But it was always in that order: money, benefit, time, art.

To this day, Chris complains that Pete was always about the money and never about the art.

You're right, Chris, art was in fact fourth on the agenda. YOUR agenda.

Rich didn't require nearly as much work. He was happy to know we had good money coming in. He might bitch and moan in the moment, but if the money was there, the answer was almost always yes.

If Pete thought something was a good idea for the band, I signed off on it. Simple.

I'm not suggesting that I didn't care about money as much as anyone else. This is a business, a *fucking* business. The music we made was undeniably world class, and we never did that with commercial intentions. But once the music was turned in and finished, my attitude was *let's go sell the fuck out of it.*

Chris insisted that playing the songs our fans wanted to hear was bullshit, and doing a lot of promotion made you a sellout. More than anything, he just hated doing the work. Pete would always say, "Thirty years from now, nobody's going to remember if we went to radio stations or not, they're going to remember the song." And he was right. There's only one thing that ultimately matters: the fucking song. Anything else is just a tool to get to that place where you're an integral part of people's lives forever.

Pete constantly preached permanence.

Chris continually chose convenience.

29

Reality Bites

In May 1997, I was walking Clementine through Piedmont Park when I saw a dude approaching with a Doberman pinscher. As he got closer I realized, *holy shit, that's Sven Pipien!* I hadn't seen him in five years.

I had heard over the years that Sven was a bit of a mess, so I was surprised by how good he looked. We both lit up as we recognized each other.

"Sven! What's up, man? You look great!"

"Hey, man! So do you!" he replied, which was really nice considering I was in overalls and a long-sleeved tie-dyed shirt. I also hadn't shaved in weeks, and was probably thirty pounds heavier than the last time I'd seen him. I looked like a defensive lineman who'd been kidnapped by some angry Deadheads and held hostage for a few months.

I asked him if he was still playing, and he told me about his former band, Needle. (The band name tells you everything you need to know about why they'd split up.) It hadn't been a pretty scene, but in the aftermath he'd gotten clean.

"I'm still drinking, but I don't really do drugs—no *hard* drugs. I was doing some speed for a while, and some heroin, and it was really bad."

"Damn, I hate to hear that. But you look amazing now! I can see it in your face."

He had just gotten a new place on the opposite side of the park from us. We made plans to meet and walk the dogs together.

Now, three months later, The Black Crowes were down a bass player, and a local guy we all knew and respected as a great player was not only available, but drug free.

On our next conference call, I reminded the brothers that I'd seen Sven a few months earlier and said I thought I should give him a call.

They both said, "Yeah, he's the only guy I thought of."

"Does he do drugs?" Pete asked skeptically.

"Well, he did," I explained. "He was in a band called Needle for a while."

"Do *not* call that person," Pete said.

"No, he's totally clean now and he's a great player."

"Then you better keep a watchful eye," Pete replied. "But I think it's time to prioritize bringing in guys who don't have a history with drugs."

I called Sven and asked if he wanted to jam with me and Rich. I didn't tell him Johnny had quit. I didn't want him to think it was an audition, so I told him Rich and I were thinking of putting together a knock-around combo to play in bars around town for fun.

"Oh, man, are you serious? I'm in!" Sven told me.

We met at our storage/rehearsal space. Playing with Sven again immediately took me back ten years to the Mary My Hope days. The first time I ever set up a drum kit in Atlanta, in 1987, Sven and I locked in. Now, a decade later, it felt like no time had passed. Rich was playing through some rough ideas, and he seemed into it, too. We played for two hours, barely stopping to take breaks.

Finally, Sven stepped outside to smoke a cigarette.

"Jesus, that dude is in the band," Rich said the second Sven was out of earshot. "No question. He's fucking great!"

It was shocking how quickly it happened, but I felt the same way.

When he came back from his smoke break, Rich and I asked him if we could get together again the next day. He said he could, and I asked him to learn a few of our songs.

Rich and I called Chris. We gave him the rundown and told him he should really think about flying over to Atlanta to check this out.

Chris said, "I don't have to. I know he's great, and if it feels cool to you two, then fucking hire him."

The next night the three of us ran through "Thorn in My Pride" and "Gone." After two songs, we took a break.

"Okay, here's the deal," I said, "Johnny quit . . ."

And that was it. Sven was in the band.

A week or so later, Chris came to town to jam with our new bassist. Sven was over the moon. He had a job waiting tables in a nice restaurant, I think, and now all of a sudden he was in The Black Crowes. His excitement gave us all a boost.

He and I had always gotten along great, even though on the surface we had very little in common beyond a love of soccer. We were from completely different worlds. Sven was born in Germany. His father was German but his mother was Spanish, so he spoke both languages growing up. The family moved to the States when Sven was ten, and that's when he picked up English as his third language. His dad was a Lufthansa executive, so they lived south of Atlanta, down by the airport. Both he and his sister went to public school down there. He was only twenty miles from downtown Atlanta, but it might as well have been another planet. He got killed in school for being German, and therefore weird, to those crackers down there.

He's super intelligent, well read, and very refined. He's got a completely dignified and respectful demeanor. On the other hand, he's a fucking social miscreant because he endured so much bullshit during his teen years. So it was only natural that he turned out to be a world-class bassist. Melody and rhythm. Thunder and harmony. The best bass players are all a little nuts.

I hadn't spent any real time with him in forever, but it was like reconnecting with an old high school buddy. We knew each other on that level that's really only accessible when you're young and are able to get to know someone very quickly. We'd played together in Mary My Hope for only six months, but we lived together the entire time, too. And when you're that age, six months is like five years.

With Sven in the picture, my Johnny Colt cloud went away quickly. I could accept that Johnny wasn't coming back, and it sucked. But I could also accept that Sven was a bad motherfucker and that the band, for now at least, was off life support.

After being outsiders in the music industry for so long, we were suddenly attempting to crash a party filled with the biggest insiders of all.

Don Ienner, the president of our new label, Columbia, sat second only to Tommy Mottola in the Sony Music hierarchy. Hell, even I knew who those guys were. They weren't producers turned label heads. They were born executives. They wore suits. They *were* suits. They were the living embodiment of everything we ever called the "machinery."

The more we learned about our new home, the less it made sense. Our initial reaction was to ask Pete how long he needed to get us out so we could be free agents again.

"We don't get out," Pete said. "Columbia is putting out our album."

Well, okay.

"Don is excited about The Black Crowes," Pete promised. But Ienner hadn't met us yet. He hadn't heard any music yet. And we knew that Ienner was the kind of guy who made snap decisions on what he heard, and those decisions were final. You gave him what he wanted or you were fucked. We'd heard stories about him locking members of his staff in closets for hours at a time when he got unfavorable reports. He was the kind of guy people write music industry books about. You know . . . assholes.

But apparently he loved rock 'n' roll music.

"I can tell you already, when he hears the name The Black Crowes, he thinks of *Shake Your Money Maker*," Pete warned.

This was an immediate red flag for all of us, but especially for Chris. And yet Chris in the moment was calm.

"I'm not making *Shake Your Money Maker 2*," Chris said reasonably.

"No, we're not," Pete said. "I'm simply giving you information. Your job is to help me navigate the situation to the best of our abilities, so that Columbia prioritizes and promotes our record. They can put a lot of muscle behind us, and with the strength of that machine, we've got a shot."

For now, Chris was listening—because he had no choice. He was desperate, as we all were. The label looked at us like Rick Rubin's leftovers. Ienner, and Columbia, had no incentive to do anything with us because they hadn't signed us. We weren't *their* band. They could, theoretically, put out our record and not do any promotion, effectively burying us.

"Putting out an album that dies is worse than not putting an album out at all. You have to understand that," Pete stressed. "We have to make Don feel like you are his band."

Pete was heading to New York to meet with Ienner. He wanted to play him only three songs from *Band*, our impromptu album from a few months back, because he knew Don had a very short attention span. He brought "If It Ever Stops Raining," "Only a Fool," and "Peace Anyway."

Rich asked him to bring along "Paint an 8." I suggested "Another Roadside Tragedy."

Pete shot us both down.

"Guys, they think about radio, they think about sales. Those aren't radio songs," Pete argued.

"But those songs are fucking great!" Rich said.

"Rich, stop," Chris said, again very calmly. "Those are album tracks. We have to give these assholes the simplest, straightest melodies and lyrics we have."

It was just beginning to dawn on us, the degree to which we'd been sheltered until then. We made our first album with George Drakoulias, and it was a hit. George never made us think he was looking for hooks, or singles. We just thought we were making a great rock 'n' roll album.

Pete had suggested, once, that Chris try to rework the chorus for "Gone." But that was it. We'd never had any interference while recording. Now we were almost a decade into our recording career, and we were starting over from scratch. And we had no leverage.

Soon, Pete reported back from his meeting with Ienner.

"Hear me out on this and then we can discuss our options. It's not happening," Pete said about *Band*. "I played the songs for Don and he didn't listen to an entire song. He liked the vibe, he got into "If It Ever Stops Raining" at first, but finally all he said was 'Let's find them a real producer and make a real album.'"

To Ienner, *Band* sounded like demos. It did *not* sound like an album that could produce radio singles in the late 1990s. And he was right—it sounded like something from the '70s, maybe even the '60s. It's a live band playing together with very few bells and whistles. It has soul and grit and *heart*. But Ienner wasn't interested in any of that stuff.

"We'll just wait him out," we argued.

"We're not waiting him out," Pete maintained. "We have to keep Don's head in the game. Forcing our hand will end up with him feeling disrespected and we'll end up with them doing nothing, which they have the legal right to do."

And like that, a record I loved and believed in and wanted to share with the world was dead. Don Ienner wanted a completely different record, so that's what The Black Crowes had to give him.

The funny thing about Chris Robinson is that when he has no options, he's a good little soldier. Give him an inch and he'll take a mile. But when there are no inches, he turns around and says, "Yes, sir."

Don Ienner was not Rick Rubin—part producer, part mogul, part pop culture icon. Ienner was a motherfucker in a $5,000 suit saying, "No, boy. Ain't gonna happen." He was not impressed with us on any fucking level.

Fresh out of inches, Chris threw up his hands. "Well, fuck it. Let's find a producer."

Chris got a good tip from an unlikely source: Joe Perry, who'd been less than hospitable to us when we opened for Aerosmith in 1990. In the meantime, they'd fired their Svengali-like manager and apparently they were an entirely different band to be around. Chris went to a gig in Los Angeles and was welcomed like a family member.

Aerosmith were back with Columbia by then, and when Chris told Joe what was going on, Joe said point blank, "You wanna make Don Ienner happy, call the Caveman." The "Caveman" was Kevin Shirley, a South African by way of Australia madman who'd just produced Aerosmith's *Nine Lives* album.

Calls were made, flights were booked. Don Ienner, as Joe Perry had suggested, loved the idea. Kevin was heading to Atlanta in a matter of days. During our first meeting with Kevin, the band was dialed in. We were all clean shaven, sober, clear headed, and ready to work. We knew what was at stake, and we were serious about making this new chapter in our lives work.

Kevin wanted to hear some new tunes. We'd sent him *Band*, but he hadn't listened. "It's important that we start from scratch," he said. "I can go back and listen once I've heard you in the room if I need to. Just gimme what you got right now that's fresh."

After three or four tunes, he waved for us to stop.

"Okay, I just have to tell you what I think, because if we're gonna work together, this is how it is," he said. "You guys have gotten too far away from rocking, I don't think you realize how midtempo everything is. You guys can groove like nobody's business, but lately it's all just sluggish."

Kevin turned to Chris. "I know you love the Grateful Dead," he said, "but you've taken this too far. You gotta bring it back to a place where you're playing to your strengths."

Those words were manna from heaven to me. Rich and I looked at each other and smiled. And then I thought, *Chris is gonna throw a chair at this guy*.

"No, I totally get that," Chris agreed, to my utter surprise. "I hear that. Yeah, we gotta rock some more."

"Be seventeen again," Kevin implored us. "Just have fun! It's okay to just have fun! Did you guys ever like punk rock?"

"I saw Black Flag at the Metroplex!" Chris barked, happy to show off his punk cred.

"Bring that back around," Kevin replied. He motioned over to me. "Just play a beat, Steve. Play a fast beat!"

I started a basic straight beat in 4/4.

"Faster!" Kevin yelled. I sped up. "Come on, faster!" he yelled again.

I sped up more. I had to laugh. I hadn't played that fast and that straight in years.

Kevin was pumping his fist in time with me. He was grinning like a maniac. His energy was infectious. Within a few seconds, we were all laughing.

"Don't stop!" Kevin hollered.

He turned to Rich. "Just play the first riff that comes to mind! Something fast and fun! Don't think! Just play something and keep playing it!"

Rich jumped right in. He threw something out that everyone immediately responded to. "Do it again, and again!" Kevin kept screaming.

Sven started playing, Chris started scatting lyrics, and suddenly we were writing a rock song. We stopped after a few minutes, and Chris was laser focused. He made a few suggestions to Rich about where to go for a middle part, they went back and forth, and in under fifteen minutes we had the arrangement finished for "Kicking My Heart Around." Chris had the lyrics written within another ten minutes. We played the whole thing straight through three or four times.

"That was kinda fucking cool!" Kevin beamed.

We were all sweating. We were having a good time.

Kevin Shirley, as it turned out, was a fucking lightning bolt.

We liked Kevin, and the label liked Kevin. So far so good. What really sealed the deal, though, was when he said, "If we're gonna make a record it's gonna be in New York."

Perfect. We needed a new producer, we needed new energy, and we needed a new city in which to work. We'd never even considered working in New York City before. Suddenly, it made all the sense in the world.

After the holidays, we got the official green light to move forward. When Pete told Ienner what we wanted to do, he said, "Kevin Shirley? Done. Here's your money."

Fucking amazing. We had gone from "we'll never put another one of your records out again and you'll die on the vine" to suddenly being very much back in business.

We needed help getting set up in New York, and Chris suggested his friend Amy Finkle, a vice president at Arista Records he knew from the Grateful Dead world. At first we all laughed. Amy? The Deadhead? How the fuck was she going to handle anything?

"She's like the most together person in the world," Chris said.

"She smokes more pot than you," Rich responded.

"So what? Just trust me, she can do anything."

It was true. Amy smoked more pot than anyone I'd ever met. But she did handle our lodging needs very quickly and efficiently. In fact, she quickly became indispensable to the operation of The Black Crowes. It would be a year before we officially hired her to be our tour manager, but that felt like just a formality at the time. She was already knee deep in everything.

Once she came in as our official tour manager, we never looked back. The replacement for Mark Botting that once seemed impossible to find? She turned out to be a slightly neurotic Jewish stoner pitbull from Long Island.

By the time we were booking flights to New York, it was obvious Marc wasn't going to come back. The best-case scenario was that he'd call and ask for help, at which point he'd probably go to rehab for at least three months. And then it would take, what, a year of sober living before Marc might have the strength to stay that way on the road?

By January, Chris and Rich had already written Marc off. Once we got a plan going, and felt momentum, it was hard not to. I had to let it go, too. I think Pete was the last one to give up on him. Like he promised Marc, Pete never closed the door. Marc just never picked up the phone. It was time to turn the page.

Ed hadn't been around much that fall, but in January he was needed for preproduction. We had some real barn burners, some midtempo stuff, some dark and weird things. We were digging it. A couple of the songs from *Band* made the leap with us: "If It Ever Stops Raining" and "Only a Fool." Kevin loved both of them.

Before we left for New York, Chris and Rich had both told me separately that they were planning to sell their publishing. The idea was to sell the mechanical portion of the publishing, which is the royalty paid each time the song is copied, like on a CD. They would still get money as writers, and it would also keep our music out of commercials.

Before they made the sale, I wanted to find out how much they valued my contribution to the music we made. So I sat Chris and Rich down, with Pete, and made a pitch.

"I'm not suggesting that I've ever written a single song," I began. "I haven't written a lyric, I haven't written a note, but I've been there for the majority of the arrangements. More often than not, you guys write songs with me in the room keeping time, helping you flesh out your ideas.

"I'm not asking for a share of your publishing," I said, "but I would like a tip of the hat. A percentage. A point. One single point. Something that tells me you acknowledge and appreciate the part I've played in all of this."

I could see that Chris was about to crawl out of his skin. He was instantly furious but I continued.

"I'm asking that you consider the fact that after everything we've been through, I'm still here. And I'm not going away. This isn't an ultimatum. If you tell me no, I'll still be here tomorrow. I'm just putting it on the table, now that you're cashing out a giant chip—a chip that is directly linked to the band's success, which I've played a part in building. I have no idea how much money you guys are about to receive. I'm not asking how much money you're about to receive. I am just asking for one percent as a sign of respect."

Pete sensed this was going nowhere fast. He said, "Okay, Steve, I think everyone understands what you're asking. Let us talk about this and we'll get back to you." Pete called me, like the next day.

"Steve, this will be a disappointment but not a surprise. They're not going to give you anything," he said.

I wasn't surprised.

It was a little sad, but far more than that, it was . . . great. The clarity their decision gave me was fantastic.

There was no gray area anymore. They really were *those* people. Cool.

Let's go to New York and see if we can turn this fucking thing around.

30

By Your Side

I was so happy to get to New York City for a couple of months. There are plenty of worse places to be in the spring. Amy found two apartments for the six of us: me, Chris, Rich, Sven, Ed, and Derrick, our guitar tech. Rich, Derrick, and I stayed on the northeast corner of Fifty-seventh Street and Seventh Avenue, across from Carnegie Hall. Chris, Sven, and Ed were a few blocks south at Fifty-fourth and Seventh. Both apartments were about a fifteen-minute walk to the studio, which was over on the West Side.

By that point, we'd been playing with Sven for a little over six months. He was clean, at least from hard drugs. Nevertheless, I was a little worried about him. He had stepped from a restaurant job right into a giant rock band, and his first duty was to go to New York City and make an album for Columbia Records. He'd made records before, but we truthfully had no idea what to expect from him in the studio. Would he cave a little? Freak out?

As we set up on our first day in the studio, Kevin laid down his golden rule. "I'm done at six P.M.," he announced. "The day is for work, and the night is for fun. So we're here at ten, we're working by twelve, and by six, I leave every day."

"Are you fucking kidding me?" Chris said.

"Daytime energy, man," Kevin replied. "This record will sound better if we're drinking at night and if we're wide awake when we're recording during the day."

Fucking thank you!

We started day one with one of the holdovers from *Band*, "If It Ever Stops Raining."

"Let's make a fucking record, guys!" Kevin shouted. "Isn't this fucking great? Isn't this amazing that this is what we get to do?!" He was genuinely *that* guy. It was infectious.

We counted in and blasted off. For about ten seconds. Then Chris burst out of the vocal booth.

"Come on, man, fucking stand up!" he screamed at Rich, who was sitting on a stool while tracking.

"I'll fucking sit if I wanna sit!" Rich screamed back.

Fuck, man, here we go. These cocksuckers were already at each other's throats.

"Yeah!" Kevin said, bounding over. "Everyone stand up! I'll stand in the booth! It's a fucking rock 'n' roll booth! See? I'm standing, too! Energy! Fun! Let's go!"

His enthusiasm was so over the top that we all had to laugh. It instantly diffused the situation.

"I think that's what you meant to say, Chris," Kevin added diplomatically.

"Yeah, that's what I meant to say," Chris grumbled, but the tension was gone, at least in that moment.

Kevin was clearly in charge. He was very decisive in the studio. There was never any guesswork with him. He would say, "That's the take, you're finished, put down your instruments, we are not going forward, that's the one!" And we'd be done. There wasn't a lick of doubt with Kevin Shirley. I loved that.

We had gotten great results with George Drakoulias and Jack Joseph Puig. But the actual process? I was happiest with Kevin. He understood that he was coaching us. Coaches blow whistles and yell. A lot. When the player isn't second-guessing what he's doing, he'll play better. When the musician isn't second-guessing the song, or the part, he'll play better. It's both very simple and very complicated. And Kevin got it, perfectly.

Columbia assigned John Kalodner to handle our A&R. He was, without exaggeration, a fucking legend. Years earlier, Kalodner had signed AC/DC and Foreigner in the same week. He brought Aerosmith back from the dead in the 1980s. He had just worked with Shawn Colvin on her breakthrough album. He had worked with XTC. He convinced Atlantic to sign Phil Collins as a solo artist. He'd even worked with Cher. And a million artists in between.

He was also, quite famously, a real fucking weirdo. I don't know where the line between schtick and reality was for him, but he'd clearly crossed it years earlier. He only dressed in either all black or all white. He had very long straight hair, a long beard, and spoke with a nasal Philly accent that could peel paint. Anyone who has ever met him does a Kalodner impression.

More than anything, Kalodner was a stone-cold professional. All he cared about was making hit records. I went in fully prepared to hate him, as he represented everything The Black Crowes were supposed to be against. But the truth is we loved him. He was fucking hilarious. And he had a track record you couldn't argue with.

And, oddly enough, he thought we were the shit.

We first met him in Atlanta during preproduction. He walked into our rehearsal space with Pete and was clearly thrilled to be there. It was like a fan getting to hang with his favorite band. He didn't have any airs of authority at all. It was disconcerting. He was such an odd person that we couldn't tell at first if he was sincere. He sat on the couch and said, "Okay, guys, can you play me something? Kevin says you have some good songs. I love good songs!"

We had a brand new song called "Baby," a beautiful ballad that never ended up on an album. The first line was "Where did I go? How did I lose my way?" For Chris Robinson to sing that, really soulfully, after everything we'd been through, was undeniably powerful.

When Chris sang those lines, Kalodner exploded.

"OH MY GOD! I FORGOT WHAT A FUCKING GREAT SINGER YOU ARE!"

We immediately stopped playing.

"*Where did you go?!*" he screamed at us. "*Where have you all been?!*"

He was *mad*.

For real. He sounded disgusted.

"You were the new rock 'n' roll band everyone needed! You're the best rock 'n' roll band of the '90s! *What have you been doing?!*"

Nobody could believe it. We had expected Kalodner to be blasé. But he acted like he was our biggest fan, one who felt betrayed that we had wandered from being a kick-ass rock 'n' roll band. As far as he was concerned, we had made two great records, one pretty good record, and he didn't know what the fuck to make of *Three Snakes.* While I can defend the albums Kalodner wasn't high on, he was basically speaking for the world at large at that point. His view was the consensus view of our band.

When we played him "Only a Fool," he hit the roof again.

"This is fucking great! You add horns and you get some singers on the back of it and we have a fucking hit song! Of course only a fool would let you go! I hear that! And I'd be a fool to not work with this band!"

He was so corny and weird . . . and yet so sincere.

As a general rule, we never discussed hit songs. It was forbidden in our cult. Instead, we talked about being a great band and about being able to blow other bands off the stage. We talked about being around for thirty years.

Kalodner was talking about things in a way that should have revolted us, but the truth is we adored him. Because he adored us.

Maybe we still had a shot after all.

On the Friday of our first week in New York, Kevin opened a couple bottles of wine right at six o'clock to celebrate a strong start. We toasted ourselves and then he wished us all a great weekend.

"See you back here Monday at ten!"

We couldn't believe it. We were used to living and breathing our albums while we made them. We *never* took time off. Now we truly were working bankers' hours.

"Wait! Are you serious?" I asked.

"We went over this already," Kevin said. "I'm going home! I'm gonna drink more wine with some friends, I'm gonna see my kid, I'm gonna watch the Formula One race on Sunday. I'm gonna have a good weekend, and I'll be here Monday at ten! See ya!"

And then he left. What the fuck?!

It didn't take me more than five minutes to fully embrace this concept, though. Weekends off? Hell, yes.

On Sunday, Kevin called and invited us over to his place, a spectacular rooftop apartment on the Upper West Side with over a thousand
bottles of wine on hand. He also had a place in the Hamptons with
another three thousand bottles. The Caveman *really* liked wine.

It was a gorgeous sunny day, and we spent the entire afternoon on
his roof drinking $200 bottles of wine like they were light beer. Boom!
Here's another one! Boom! Here's another one. That's how he rolled.
And while we were in New York City, that's how we rolled, too.

The second week was just as productive, if not more so, than the
first. Ten days of tracking, ten songs nearly completed. Everyone was
happy. Seriously. At the apartment I was sharing with Rich and Derrick, we all got along like college roommates. I'd walk down to the
other apartment and the other three guys would be relaxing, listening to music, talking about the new show at MoMA, or watching *The
Three Stooges*. Everyone was enjoying themselves.

The third week started fine, but by Tuesday afternoon some old
familiar tensions were starting to surface. We had clearly reached the
point where Chris had to stick a fork in the socket somehow. He'd
reached his limit for positive productivity.

He picked a fight with Rich, and when I tried to chill him out he
turned on me. And then, for the first time, he turned on Kevin when
he jumped into it. Kevin had dealt with plenty of bullshit in his career,
so he wasn't phased in the slightest. He just said, "Okay, we're done for
the day. Christopher has his ass on his shoulders and this is no way to
work." And he walked out.

On Wednesday, Rich and I walked to the studio together and waited
for everyone else to show up. Chris wasn't there. Neither was Sven.
Nor Ed. Kevin suggested we give them until noon, then give them
a call. We waited, and at noon I called their apartment. No answer. I
called again a few minutes later. Same thing.

Finally, at two o'clock I walked over there. All three of them were
passed out cold. I had to shake Chris awake.

"Yo, man! Let's go! What the fuck?"

I woke up Sven and Ed. I don't know what they had been doing the
night before, but all three of them were fucking out of it. They were
all pissed at me and telling me to shut the fuck up.

I guessed they had all been up doing coke and whatever else they had gotten their hands on. That was bad enough for our productivity, but for Sven it was clearly bad news. He'd been down a very dark road before, and I didn't want to see him walk down it again.

I asked him about it a couple of days later. "Look, man," he told me, "I'm in New York City, in a really nice apartment, I'm making a record in a huge studio, and it's all I can do just to keep it together." It was exactly what I feared. Sven felt immense pressure, and temptation, being in The Black Crowes, and he was reaching a breaking point.

"I haven't wanted to do drugs in a long time, and I'm here and I fucking want to do drugs," he admitted.

But, to his credit, Sven actually did stay clean. For a while, anyway.

As the sessions dragged on, we did rally and finish up with a sense of regained, if not entirely recaptured, momentum. Kevin delivered exactly what he said he would deliver: a loud, fun, energetic rock record. Fans who loved *Three Snakes and One Charm* surely felt whiplash when they first heard *By Your Side*. But we did what we had to do.

Chris later insisted that we, and he specifically, never cared about *By Your Side* while we were making it. That was a lie. And it was a lie that helped to shape perception of the record as a kind of "sellout" move, a step back to our *Shake Your Money Maker* phase as a concession to the record company.

It's a little more complicated than that.

Without *By Your Side*, we would have stagnated forever. That's a fact. We saw one way out, and we took it. It didn't end well, by any means. By the time it was released in January of 1999, it was apparent Columbia wasn't going to do shit for us, and we all did, as a band, eventually check out on it. But *By Your Side* played a crucial role in getting us moving again. No album since our first had as much riding on it. And make no mistake. Without *By Your Side*, the following chapter for the band, which was staggeringly fantastic, wouldn't have been written.

31

The Black Crowes Are Back!
(Even if We Never Left)

We finished *By Your Side* in May, hired a guitarist named Audley Freed to fill out the live lineup, and then launched a club tour in June. At the first venue we played, Toad's Place in New Haven, the promo staff from Columbia put posters and stickers in the club, without our knowledge, that read: "THE BLACK CROWES ARE BACK!" It felt very strange. After all, we had toured the *previous year.* It wasn't as if we'd taken a ten-year hiatus.

But I knew what Columbia meant: the rock 'n' roll band fans loved from the early 1990s was back. It was still a blow to our egos.

Eleven months after the tour cycle for *Three Snakes*, we came back rocking harder and louder than we ever had. It was as if we had traded in weed for speed. Of course, we had also literally traded out band members. The departures of Johnny and Marc were old news to us, but now most of the world was learning about it for the first time.

I was fully anticipating a lot of our fans giving up on us. And there were, in fact, plenty of people who never came back after 1997. Our fan base was gutted. And I *got* that. I still get it.

After a month of dates, Pete let us know there were concerns from the label that we didn't have *that* song, the one that could explode immediately and grab radio by the throat. Kevin Shirley suggested we reconvene after the first leg of the tour to knock out a few more songs and see if anything worked.

232

Once back in the studio, Kalodner made a suggestion. "How about 'It's Only Rock 'n' Roll but I Like It'?"

No one said a word. We were stunned.

Kalodner continued, "Don and the staff think it will be an international hit. An absolute smash. Do this one right, and it'll change everything."

Chris, of all people, said, "Fuck it. Let's give it a shot."

As we started playing through the song, familiarizing ourselves with it, Rich finally pulled the plug.

"I can't do this. This isn't real. 'Hard to Handle' was great because we were just playing a song we loved. This won't work."

And that was the end of that. We all recognized, actually, that Rich was right. So we bailed.

To us, even considering the suggestion indicated we were willing to be team players. To Don Ienner, our passing on the suggestion was a direct snub and indicated we weren't worth another minute of his time.

This turned out to be the final straw, because we'd already made one decision that had pissed him off back in May, and Don didn't give anyone a third chance to spurn him.

Columbia wanted a song from the new album, "Horsehead," for the *Armageddon* soundtrack album. We said "thanks but no thanks" and didn't give it a second thought.

The label begged us to reconsider. *Just give us a song!* But we held firm.

That soundtrack sold twenty million fucking copies worldwide.

After passing on *Armageddon* and then not even recording "Its Only Rock 'n' Roll but I Like It," Don Ienner was done with us. Why lift a finger for a band who doesn't want to play ball?

We went back on the road and stayed there until mid-December, including a month-long run in Europe. Every night, we saw and felt the energy from the crowds. We headed home for the holidays with a real sense of momentum. It spoke to how much of a bubble we were still living in.

Pete's greatest concern, that the mighty Columbia Records would overlook us at the moment of truth, was coming true.

By Your Side was released January 12, 1999. We played a gig at Irving Plaza in New York City to celebrate. Don Ienner and Tommy Mattola came out. They stopped by the dressing room beforehand, we took pictures with them, then they left to find their seats.

"Have a good one! We'll see you guys after! " they promised.

Moments later, we watched out the window of our dressing room as they hopped into their limo and took off. We hadn't played a note. We enjoyed one moment with them that night, however.

Amy Finkle had worked in the business for years, and she had a photo of Ienner from his days as the head of promotion at Arista. I don't remember the context of the photo, I just know it was Don wearing a towel, sitting in a dry sauna, covered in sweat. It was anything but a flattering image.

That night our backstage laminates featured the photo in all its embarrassing glory.

When Ienner and Mattola walked into our dressing room, they'd seen half a dozen people wearing that sweaty photo around their necks. Mattola laughed his ass off. We all did.

Despite Columbia's lack of attention, we were still willing to promote where we felt we could get a result. We even subjected ourselves to a familiar ritual for dysfunctional rock bands everywhere: VH1's *Behind the Music.*

Behind the Music was huge. The series tended to focus on the up and down careers of has-beens from the 1970s and '80s, so we were thrown by their offer to do an episode about The Black Crowes. We might've passed the peak of our popularity, but we were still much younger than anyone else we'd seen on the show. Plus, we'd just released an album and were very much an active band. We had a lot of drama internally, but it wasn't like anyone had died. I didn't think we met the requisite tragedy quota.

"Look, they're actually doing us a favor giving us the exposure right now," Pete explained. We still had a few friends in the industry who were willing to give us a boost, and even we could see the benefit of being a part of the show.

The VH1 people came to my house and I told stories on camera for a few hours. That was my entire involvement. I just tried to keep it light and entertaining, as I knew the brothers would be the focal points.

They asked if we were okay with Johnny and Marc being interviewed. We said it was fine, as we figured it would certainly add to the dramatic narrative. They both declined, however.

In the spring, they sent us the episode with a note that read: "This will be on TV in a month!" We had absolutely no control over it. We watched it together on the bus in Chicago, with a collective "Oh shit!" feeling after putting the VHS tape in the player. It was pretty weird to watch our career condensed to forty-five minutes. But for the most part it rang true, at least in terms of hewing close to our mythology. The thing about being in a band for so long is you pick up the usual talking points without even being aware of it.

The By Your Side tour started with two shows in Milwaukee that February. While the album wasn't exactly blowing up the charts, a lot of our fans seemed to like it. And we were busy again. We had the summer laid out in Europe, both with festivals and our own dates. If nothing else, it was a relief to know we were going to be busy for a while.

Meanwhile, Columbia let the album quietly die. But at least they'd released it, putting us one massive step closer to free agency. We each had our own mixed feelings about the album.

All things considered though, 1999 was an easy year for us. The brothers were rarely if ever at each other's throats, and that made every element of life in The Black Crowes much more tolerable.

Another part of it was having new guys in the band. That kept a lid on the *fucking crazy* for a while, as no one wanted to show their ass in front of the new guys.

Nevertheless, it was undeniable that our album had stiffed pretty much right out of the gate. We put out four singles—"Kickin' My Heart Around," "Only a Fool," "By Your Side," and "Go Faster"—that went nowhere.

Pete did mention once during the year, swearing us all to secrecy, that we were in an option period. The cutoff date wasn't a year from album release, but rather a year from the album being accepted by the label. That meant Columbia had to let us know by September if

they were picking up the next album. We all held on to the slight hope
that history would repeat itself. Just as Def American had let the option pass after *Shake Your Money Maker*, maybe Columbia would do
the same now. If they did, we'd be free agents sooner than expected.
To us, anything would be better than another lap on the track with
Columbia.

32

"Just When i Think i'm Out . . .
Mr. Jimmy Fucking Page"

Immediately following the release of *By Your Side*, we left the country for a two-week whirlwind promotional trip around the world. Toronto, Brussels, Madrid, Paris, Stockholm, Milan, Rome, Tokyo, and then to Miami to play at the Super Bowl. We played TV shows everywhere we went, did lots of interviews, photo shoots, and all other manner of promotion.

We were in Tokyo for four days, our first time there since 1992. I bought a red wrestler's mask upon arrival and wore it for most of those four days, telling everyone it was necessary to ward off evil spirits. It was funny when I first put the mask on, and got funnier with each passing hour. I wore it in restaurants, in bars, to photo shoots. I wore it everywhere. And for those four days, we all had an absolute blast. It worked. That mask was powerful.

In those two weeks it felt like we had as much pure, unadulterated fun as we'd had in the past seven years. Those previous years came into sharp relief once we put together a couple of hilarious weeks in a row, doing the very things we had always claimed to hate: TV shows, interviews, and photo shoots. Without setlists, stage volume, and the many other fighting points that came from playing full gigs, we operated almost entirely without tension.

When I got home, I was really together. So much so that I was able to, for the first time, actually see myself beyond the band. I had literally never thought about life after The Black Crowes with a clear head, or with a contented heart.

237

And now, with both at long last, I felt ready to leave.

I couldn't imagine any kind of a future for The Black Crowes. While I was proud we'd survived, it was clear that the departures of Johnny and Marc were the end of The Black Crowes as a band. Now, instead of a band, we were a group. A damned good one, but still . . . the intangible differences between "band" and "group" were impossible to ignore. It was never again going to be what it once was.

On tour in the States for a few months, The Black Crowes entered no-man's-land. The internal battles for the band's identity that propelled us to both our greatest musical heights and our darkest dysfunctional depths had been replaced by a sad resignation . . . an acceptance that we had blown it. We played solid, workmanlike rock 'n' roll shows throughout the spring, but they were undeniably the most emotionally uninspired of our career. And, oddly enough, we all got along better than we had in years. The price of peace was just too much. We were dead men walking.

And then . . . the phone rang.

Ross Halfin, the photographer, called Pete and unwittingly changed the course of everything in a five-minute chat.

Jimmy Page was putting together a charity gig in London that summer. He had been discussing it with Ross and said he needed a backing band for the night. Ross told him, "The Black Crowes are coming to town at some point with Aerosmith, why don't I ring them to see if they can do it?"

Jimmy said, "Oh, that'd be perfect!"

Pete's answer, before even asking us, was, "Absolutely. We'll move our schedule around if need be."

We didn't have to move anything. It set itself up easily. We were playing Wembley Stadium with Aerosmith and Lenny Kravitz on a Saturday. We had the Friday night before and the Sunday night after open. Rehearsal Friday, gig Sunday. Fucking perfect.

It was just going to be one gig, and a short one at that. We were only going to play forty minutes or so. But that night instantly became the focal point of my life. No matter what else happened in the interim, I was going to play some fucking Zeppelin tunes with Jimmy fucking Page.

Hell. Fucking. Yes.

We opened the tour in Stockholm, with Aerosmith. When we got to the gig, the Aerosmith guys were friendly, warm, and completely hospitable. Night and day from 1990. It was fantastic. They weren't stuck in a sobriety bubble created by some crazy-ass manager, and we weren't idiot kids with stars in our eyes. We got on really well.

After an Aerosmith gig in Cologne, we hopped on the bus for London. The following night, we were going to be in a rehearsal space running down songs with Jimmy. The mood was joyous. We were drinking beer, blasting Zeppelin on the stereo, and feeling pretty full of ourselves. We couldn't stop laughing over how crazy it was.

The tour buses in Europe were double-deckers. There was a lounge/sitting area and a toilet downstairs, and a lounge with a stereo and TV upstairs in the back. The bunks were upstairs toward the front of the bus.

We were all up in the back lounge when Ed rolled out of his bunk. He started to walk toward the back but stopped, put his hand to his side, and went down to his knees. We assumed at first that he was running some sort of schtick.

He stayed down for a few seconds, and when he looked up his face was contorted. He wasn't having fun. Something was wrong.

Amy Finkle, who had joined us on the road a few months earlier, ran to him. She looked back at us and said, "Guys, something's really wrong with Ed."

The music stopped. He was moaning in pain. He had no color in his face. He was a mess. *Holy shit.*

We told the driver we needed to get to a hospital quickly. He pulled over at the next exit, at a truck stop. He ran inside and got the attendant to call an ambulance. He came back out yelling, "Help is on the way, Eddie!"

Ed was getting worse with every passing minute. He was writhing in pain, screaming.

Holy shit, he finally did himself in.

Ed was six foot four and weighed about 150 pounds. He already looked like a skeleton, but now we were all freaked out over how bad he appeared to be. We had no idea what he could have taken, or done to himself. Eddie always operated as a bit of an independent contractor within The Black Crowes. We never kept tabs on him. We knew he was using a wide array of chemicals at any given time, but they never seemed to get in his way.

Only now it seemed we were about to watch him die on our fucking bus in the middle of nowhere on a dark night, thousands of miles from home.

As we heard sirens approaching, Ed looked up and said, "Tell me we're still in Germany, man . . . I don't wanna be in Belgium . . . tell me we're still in Germany!"

I was confused. "What does that matter, Ed?"

"German health care is the best in the world!" he moaned.

Classic Ed. At least his brain was still functioning.

I had no idea where we were, but I said, "Yeah, man, I'm pretty sure we're still in Germany."

As the paramedics walked into the downstairs lounge, they were speaking French. Oh, shit.

"Fuck! Ed, I think we're in Belgium, brother."

"No, man! Go back to Germany! Get me back to Germany, man!"

He had crawled to the staircase and was lying there wearing pants that looked painted onto his skeletal legs. His hair was stringy and dirty, like Shaggy from *Scooby-Doo* after a few years of hard living. He looked terrible.

The paramedics slowly hauled Ed off the bus and into the ambulance, and we followed along for the short drive to the hospital. As we pulled in, Amy and I walked off the bus to get Ed checked in.

They wheeled Ed into a room and the doctor on call was immediately out of his depth. First of all, he wasn't a doctor. He was a nurse. Or a general assistant. Or an actor. Whatever he was, he sure as shit wasn't a medical expert. Second, he didn't speak English. Not a word. And third, he seemed stressed. Really stressed.

Ed was writhing in pain, and from the looks of things, Belgian medical care consisted entirely of frantic hand gestures and repeating phrases in French with steadily increasing volume.

Shit, Ed's a goner for sure.

I was able to figure out some basics—the doctor was actually in another town at the moment, but had been called and would be arriving within two hours. How can the closest doctor be two hours away? Are there only four fucking doctors in the whole country?

Urie, our on-again, off-again band assistant, came in from the bus to see if he could help. He and I sat with Ed while Amy went back to the bus to fill everyone in. Ed was a mess. There was no color in his face, and he was in agonizing pain. I was asking for pain killers, unsuccessfully, and starting to panic.

Urie and I were holding his hands and telling him everything was going to be all right, but we looked at each other with a recognition that we were about to watch our friend die. Ed was crying. It felt like it went on forever.

Thankfully, it was only about thirty minutes before the doctor walked in. She was getting the rundown from the other dude, in French, while she surveyed Ed for the first time. She looked at me and in English said, "What has he had to eat?"

"I don't know," I said. I looked down at Ed. "Ed! The doctor is here, she needs to know what you ate today!"

He just moaned.

She said again, to him, "Ed, tell me . . . what did you eat? What did you drink?"

He looked at her and screamed, "Nothing!"

"Nothing? All day? No food or drink all day?"

Urie and I were almost in tears. I was quite certain that I was about to watch him take his last breath.

The doctor was losing patience. She needed an answer.

"Ed! You *have* to tell me—did you eat anything today? Anything at all?"

Ed stopped moaning, looked up at her and yelled, angrily, "CAFFEINE, CODEINE, AND COCAINE! OKAY? THAT'S IT! CAFFEINE, CODEINE, AND COCAINE!"

And then he went right back to moaning.

Urie and I looked at each other. We both started laughing. I thought, *Okay, we're done here. He'll be fine.*

I knew he was going to be okay. Even in his agony, he was still fucking funny. There's no way "caffeine, codeine, and cocaine!" would be his final words.

The doctor said she needed an X-ray, and thankfully she gave him a sedative. He finally relaxed, and within an hour she had determined that his small intestine was twisted, and he would need laparoscopic surgery. He was going to be fine. Of course he was. Ed was indestructible.

There was nothing for us to do except continue on to London. We left Ed that night and continued our pilgrimage to Valhalla, to rock with Jimmy Page.

Eighteen hours later we were on a totally different planet—inside a small rehearsal room cranking out Zeppelin tunes. There's footage of that rehearsal on YouTube, actually. We worked on songs, shot the shit, and marveled at the fact that four years after he jumped onstage for a spontaneous sit-in during an encore, we were actually working with Jimmy Page. Fucking crazy.

We all went to Nobu for dinner afterward. We sat around a huge table—the band, Rose Mary, Amy, Pete, Jimmy, and Ross—telling stories and feeling like we were on top of the world. Hell, we *were* on top of the world.

We played Wembley Stadium the next day. We met the band Stereophonics, which marked the beginning of a long friendship. And, of course, we played the gig as a five piece. We still set Ed's keyboard rig up, though, and we placed a six foot tall inflatable alien in Ed's place. Chris wrote "E.D. Phone Home" on it, in marker.

The next night, we played the gig with Jimmy. Our set went by in a blur. As we launched into "In My Time Of Dying," I was sweating the fact that in rehearsal, we never got out of the second guitar solo into the turnaround properly. I couldn't really hear Jimmy in that room, and I couldn't figure out what his cues meant. He'd raise the neck of his guitar, or look back and nod, to signal *"eight bars!"* whereas for years I'd been following Rich's cues which always meant *"four bars!"*

As soon as Jimmy started on the solo, I realized I could hear him clear as a bell. Thank God! It was much easier to follow him now than it had been in the rehearsal room. *He's going to hit that high part and then go to the second register for two bars, and then we go.*

We nailed it. It was perfect. Pete was sitting on the stage, right next to my drum tech, laughing and screaming at me as soon as we came through that turnaround.

Oh, baby! Fucking incredible!! You fucking did it! That was amazing, ya rat bastard!

To me, that gig was my payday. My reward for sticking it out. All the fights, all the stress, all the missed opportunities, the shattered expectations . . . no matter how brutal it was just getting there, I got to play "In My Time of Dying" with Jimmy Page.

We picked Ed up on the way through Belgium again about a week later. We had no idea what to expect. Would he be able to stay on the tour? Would he be able to play? Would he have been forced into detox and come out the other side with a new lease on life?

The answers were "Yes," "Yes," and "Absolutely not."

One of the nurses, a dude named Michel, turned out to be a fan. As a going-away present, he gave Ed five hundred Xanax and five hundred Valium. So much for detox. Ed got after those pills like a fucking Wolverine after a rabbit. He was sideways for the rest of the run, babbling incoherently about god only knows what, occasionally making sense when discussing his love of "Marzipan, the royal candy."

Our final show of that European tour was at Shepherd's Bush Empire in London. Noel Gallagher turned up. He hung out in the dressing room after the show for a while. We'd long expected that we'd hate the Oasis guys if we'd ever met them. We couldn't have been farther off base. Within 10 seconds, we recognized a kindred spirit. It was a great night. We were leaving the By Your Side tour on a high note. No limping to the finish line.

It was all good.

A perfect time to jump.

The following day, we flew to Japan for a one-off at the Fuji Rock Festival in Nigata Prefecture. We played a fine set, returned to Tokyo, and then Chris, Ross, his assistant Kazyo, and I went out for ramen. They were the best noodles I'd ever had.

And then, home. Done. *Finis*.

In mid-August, Rose Mary and I were in New York City for a few days and decided to drive up to the Hudson Valley. Just outside of New Paltz, we saw a sign for something called Mohonk Mountain House. We were curious, so we followed the signs and ended up in the mountains at an enormous hotel/spa/getaway from the late nineteenth century. It was a pretty spectacular place.

We hopped in a rowboat and paddled around the giant lake out back, talking about the band. The Black Crowes were finished for the foreseeable future. We had no reason to believe Columbia would let us out of our contract before our final album, and no reason to believe they would lift a finger for us again if we ever did record another album. We had finished the tour in good spirits, but that was surely temporary. Soon enough, something would explode again, knocking us off balance.

I felt great, physically and emotionally.

It was time.

"I'm going to call Pete and tell him I'm out," I said.

"Thank God," she said. "Let's just get on with the rest of our lives. Whatever it's going to be, let's go figure it out."

Right on.

I was completely at peace with the decision, sitting in a rowboat on a beautiful lake with my wife, surrounded by trees and happy vacationing families. It was pretty perfect.

It was August, 17, 1999. My thirty-fourth birthday.

We got back to the room and I picked up the phone.

"Hey, isn't it your birthday?" Pete asked after we exchanged the usual pleasantries.

"Yeah, it is."

"Well, happy birthday."

"Thanks, man. That's not exactly why I'm calling, though."

"Okay, what's up?"

"I'm done, Pete. I'm out," I announced. "I can't do it anymore."

I had done it. I had finally *fucking* done it.

"Okay," Pete said. "I do understand completely. Although, Steve, there is something that I need to tell you." He had a lilt to his voice . . . like he was trying not to laugh.

This wasn't the reaction I had expected. I thought Pete was going to be upset. Or at least launch into all the reasons why it was a mistake.

Nope. He was almost laughing.

"Your buddy Jimmy Page wants to go on tour this fall," Pete said.

Fuck.

"So . . . why don't you take five minutes and then call me back?" Now he actually was laughing.

"Are you fucking kidding me?"

"Nope. Not at all," he replied. "Curbishley [Jimmy's manager] and I spoke last night. We're thinking a handful of shows in New York, maybe a couple in LA. Nothing extreme, but hey, it might be fun! So why don't you hang up and call me back after you think about it for a minute?"

I hung up the phone to the sound of Pete's laughter. He knew how much it meant to me to play with Jimmy.

I looked over at Rose Mary. I was speechless.

"What?" she asked. "What the hell was that?"

"Jimmy Page wants to go on tour with us."

"No way!"

I looked out the window for a minute. I went straight into *Godfather III* mode: "Just when I think I'm out, they pull me back in!"

I called Pete again.

"Hello?"

"Hey, Pete, it's Steve."

"Hey, Steve, what's up?"

"Nothing, man. What's going on?"

"Hey, isn't it your birthday?"

"Yes."

"Well, happy birthday."

"Thanks."

"Anything else going on?"

"Nope. Me and Rose Mary are in New York, just chilling. What's going on with you?"

"Hey, guess what? Jimmy Page wants to tour."

"Really? That's great. How many shows?"

"Just a few. Maybe five or six. It's gonna be great!"

"That's cool! Lemme know when you figure it out!"

I hung up, again to the sound of Pete laughing.

The bad news was that I was still stuck with the Robinson brothers.

The good news was that my reward for hanging in there all those years had just been gloriously upgraded from a one-off in London with Jimmy Page to a *fucking tour* with Jimmy Page!

Holy shit!

We were going to work up a complete set!

We were going to play full shows!

We'd probably make good money in the process!

This was the perfect ending to my run with The Black Crowes.

Pete's plan was to play six shows in October: three at the Roseland Ballroom in New York City, one at the Worcester Centrum Centre outside of Boston, and two at the Greek Theatre in Los Angeles. We had the entire month of September to get ready.

Sven and I got together and jammed a few times, making sure we had the arrangements down. We were laughing through the entire process. He got to be John Paul Jones, I got to be Bonham. It was a dream come true that neither of us had ever even thought to dream.

We didn't all get in a room together until about a week before the first gig. Everyone flew into Atlanta for a couple of days' rehearsal, and then we were off to New York City.

The weekend before the gigs with Jimmy, we played a giant multi-city charity festival gig at Giants Stadium called NetAid along with Bono, Puff Daddy, Sheryl Crow, and some other giant pop acts. Jimmy was on the bill as well, playing with just a rhythm section as a three-piece.

Ed and I were hanging outside our dressing room, which was a trailer in the parking lot. As Ed was having a smoke, Sting came walking by. Or, more accurately, Sting, his wife, and an entourage of thirty people walked by. Sting's vibe struck me as that of a king surveying his land, fully expecting to be greeted with respect and adoration. As he passed, he looked over at Ed.

Cigarette in his mouth, coffee cup in his hand, Ed raised the cup and said, "All right, man . . ." as a way of greeting. Sting held his gaze for a moment and turned away without a nod.

Ed said to me, loudly enough to be heard by the entire group, "Who does that guy think he is, Sting?"

We both fell out laughing.

Less than two minutes later, the whole entourage, with Sting leading the way, came walking past us in the other direction. Again, Sting turned to steal a quick glance at Ed.

Ed said to him, with genuine concern, "Oh, man . . . what happened? Did they close catering already?"

Sting turned away from Ed again, this time with a mild look of distaste. Ed and I just sat there laughing for ten minutes.

Ed was the fucking best.

Rehearsals with Jimmy started the next day, and we were all bouncing off the walls. We had done a lot of work ahead of time, and he was noticeably appreciative of the effort.

I kept thinking about how close I had come to missing out on this whole thing. *If Pete and Curbishley had spoken a week later, or even a day later . . . fuck it. Let it go. No one else knew how close I came to leaving.*

All that mattered was that I *was* there, and I was fucking excited.

Beyond everyone having the time of our lives, this run of six shows was exactly what The Black Crowes needed at that point. The buzz for the tour was huge. All six shows sold out immediately, even though no one even knew what we were going to be playing. They bought all those tickets on the strength of our names.

It was such a shot in the arm for us. We had just tried to play ball with Columbia and it hadn't worked. *By Your Side* was our worst-selling album yet. We didn't want to stay with them, but who was going to be interested in us now? We thought our situation with Columbia was unwinnable when we started, and it was by that point somehow worse.

But now . . . there was hope. We had an endorsement from Jimmy Page. This was clearly going to put us in a different context. There was excitement around the band again. Even I felt that.

In rehearsals, Pete pulled me aside and said cryptically, "Don't make any decisions this week. Or next. Let's just get these shows done and see where we are."

I knew that meant something, and I knew Pete well enough to understand it was in my best interest to listen.

I said, "I got ya, man. Thanks."

I was back in. For now.

Jimmy was always easy to work with. He struck me as being like an English country gentleman, very soft spoken and gentle. I'm sure he could be domineering and strong willed, but we never saw that side of him. And in this situation there was no pressure.

Jimmy didn't try to make us sound like Led Zeppelin, or Page/Plant. "You're already a band," he told us. "I'm joining *your* band."

Jimmy was only fifty-five at the time. Hell, I'm close to that age as I write this. He'd been up and rocking again with Robert in Page/Plant for a few years, and then Robert pulled the plug, just like that. Then we showed up, a fucking proper world-class rock band in our own right, totally energized and up for whatever he wanted to do. He couldn't have put together a band in 1999 that could touch The Black Crowes. For him, it was simply *add water and boom!*

Jimmy wasn't precious about the songs. It was obvious when we did that one-off in London that he didn't give two flying fucks if there was an occasional flub. He only cared about the vibe, about whether it felt right. When he got excited in rehearsals he'd say, "Yes! That's the spirit, innit?"

When it felt right to him onstage, his blood would really start flowing. We'd all feel it right away. It was as if a Superman cape emerged a few songs into every set, and he'd just take off. When he launched, I held on for dear life and knew that if I didn't keep up, I was gonna look silly. I loved it. It felt like I was playing basketball with a bunch of dudes in the NBA. I raised my game. I never played better. I never had more fun.

We only rehearsed with Jimmy, I think, for four or five days, but they were long days. They were more involved than any Black Crowes rehearsals had ever been, I can guarantee that.

It was spectacular. Jimmy always complimented my playing. He complimented everyone's playing. And he absolutely loved playing off of Chris. Even in rehearsals, he was bouncing around, working that classic singer-guitarist act like it was 1968 and he was trying to prove himself. He was a fucking geyser of inspiration for me.

I was thrilled. Had he offered me a job to go off and play with him after this little tour, I'd have been on the first flight to London. I'd have been Jimmy Page's drummer, no questions asked.

33

Asleep at the Greek

The three nights at the Roseland Ballroom were all riotous. Every friend we'd ever made in the Northeast just happened to be in town. Go figure. I hadn't had that many ticket requests since *Southern Harmony*. It seemed we were suddenly the most popular band in America again. Thanks, Jimmy!

Even Columbia Records was excited. A whole crew of those fuckers came down for the first night. We welcomed them with open arms. The truth is we were so excited to be playing with Jimmy, and to shove it in their faces, that we didn't mind them being there. The more the merrier.

An hour before the first gig, I sat down in a lounge chair in our dressing room and fell asleep. That was standard operating procedure. I could fall asleep anywhere, and usually did. A twenty- or thirty-minute power nap and I'd wake up completely focused and recharged. That's the kind of thing you learn to do when you're playing for a few hours a night and still feel hung over from the night before.

When I woke up, Jimmy was staring at me in disbelief. He thought I'd nodded off. The look on his face was total shock, as I hadn't struck him as being a junkie.

I heard Chris say, laughing, "No, man, he's just asleep. He does that."

Jimmy was blown away. "How can you do that?" he asked. He was fascinated.

"It's just how it is. Gotta power down for a bit," I said.

I was very comfortable around Jimmy by then, but still, it felt a little weird to wake up and find Jimmy Page peering at me.

Jimmy was a live wire before the gig. He paced the hallway, a ball of nervous excitement. This wasn't like that London charity show a few months earlier. This was a full gig. We were going to play for two and a half hours.

As we stood off to the side of the stage just before the lights went down, Jimmy started riling us up.

"Let's go do this!" he said, like a coach revving up the team. "Are you ready? Are we going to do it? *Let's give it to them! Let's give it to them, yeah?!?*"

I was about to jump out of my skin.

Holy shit. He's SO excited.

The lights went down and we walked onstage. The cheer from the room was deafening. The audience was packed in tight, and it was obvious: whatever we were about to do, they were ready for it.

Jimmy gave us all the look. "Ready?"

Chris said, "Play that fucking thing!" And Jimmy took off.

We opened with "Celebration Day." It took the audience about two seconds to get a clue as to what was happening. From the kit, it felt like every single person in the room was screaming. I had goose bumps.

Then Chris sang the first lines of the song: "Her face is cracked from smiling / All the fears that she's been hiding / And it seems that pretty soon, everybody's gonna know."

As the band came in on the first full downbeat, I swear to God that the roof of the Roseland Ballroom blew off the joint.

From that moment on we could do no wrong. When "Celebration Day" ended, I realized I hadn't taken a breath in three and a half minutes. My chest was heaving. *Okay, settle down . . . breathe. It's all good. We're on our way.*

We played "Custard Pie" next. You could feel the anticipation in the crowd between every song. *Oh my God, what are they going to play next?* Hell, I had a setlist and even I felt that excitement.

Holy shit, "Sick Again!"

Between songs, those of us who weren't English guitar gods exchanged mile-wide smiles all night long. We had some rough moments, a few real train wrecks, but it didn't matter at all. The excitement in the room was incredible. For Black Crowes fans, it was like pouring gas on a raging fire. For Jimmy Page fans, they were thrilled to see their man onstage with a banger of a band, having the time of his life.

Jimmy hadn't been that happy onstage with Page/Plant in years, if ever. He was pumping his fists in between songs, making faces with members of the audience. He was like a kid in a candy shop. When we'd catch a good groove, he'd come back and give me a look like, *Yeah, motherfucker!* and I'd give him my best *Yeah, motherfucker!* look right back at him. We were locked in. It was fucking joyous.

We closed with "Whole Lotta Love," complete with Jimmy's theremin solo in the middle section. Sitting at that drum kit, watching and listening to Jimmy manipulate that thing . . . it was just too much.

As we walked offstage together, there were hugs all around.

"Well done, boys, bloody well done!" Jimmy was beaming. We were like that little tugboat in *Dunkirk*. We made it back, man! We survived the war!

Rose Mary, who grew up a Led Zeppelin fanatic, couldn't even speak. My brother Jim was backstage and all he could say was "Damn, you boys *got it done* up there tonight!"

From the soundboard that first night, Pete watched the gig and was blown away. Not just by the gig itself, but by the vibe both in the crowd and onstage. He'd never seen us so happy. He'd never seen us playing with such selfless joy. And Jimmy? Shit . . . Pete was a lifelong Zeppelin fan. He grew up on those records, and held Jimmy in the highest possible esteem. To see *Jimmy Page* having that much fun? Pete's wheels were spinning. Hard. He knew magic when he saw it.

This moment had to be captured. It needed to be shared with the world.

He turned to Kevin Shirley and said, "We need a mobile truck studio in LA. We *have* to record those gigs. This needs to be a live album."

After a few beers in the dressing room, I walked down the hallway past the production office. I looked inside to see Pete standing with Bill Curbishley and Ron Delsener, the legendary New York concert promoter. They were standing in a tight circle, deep in conversation.

Holy shit, this thing ain't ending anytime soon.

Twenty minutes later, I grabbed Pete and pulled him aside.

"You wanna tell me what the fuck you guys were talking about?" I asked, grinning.

"Next summer," he said.

Fuck yes. Bingo. Holy shit. We're just getting started.

I had never been more deeply committed to The Black Crowes than I was at that moment.

We played much better the second night at Roseland, and then the third night was *way* better. We just straight-up murdered that third gig.

We left the venue and all met up at the Whiskey Park. The band, everybody's wives or girlfriends, our crew, and a million friends packed that place. We had a late night, and it was raging. In the space of three days, our world had transformed from "this should be a lot of fun" to "we're going out next year and it'll be fucking massive." We didn't know what shape the tour would take, or how many shows it would be, or where we would play . . . we didn't know anything. But we didn't care. Jimmy wanted to continue, and we were all the way on board.

God, it could be like this all the time, if we could just allow ourselves to enjoy it and admit that we want to be a huge fucking band.

"Fucking three more, man. Let's go," Chris said. "I got this shit figured out, now. I'm going to fucking kill it in Boston."

The planet stopped spinning for a moment. Chris gave us a pep talk!?!

This felt like what I'd always imagined it should feel like. We could never allow ourselves to feel happy about being The Black Crowes. But being Jimmy Page and The Black Crowes? That was different. We were going to have some fucking fun for once.

The fourth gig was at the Centrum in Worcester, about forty minutes outside of Boston. It was the lone arena show of the run. The room was about three times bigger than Roseland, and the response from the crowd followed suit. Joe Perry came out and sat in on "You Shook Me," and of course the fans ate it up. Chris was right—he had figured that shit out, and he was tremendous. When he felt like it, he was still a bona fide fucking arena rock frontman.

We were staying overnight in Boston, so we hopped in a couple vans to head back after the gig. Rose Mary, Chris, Sven, Jimmy, and I all piled into one, and as our driver pulled onto the highway, he turned on a local rock station. The DJ was raving about the show we had just played. "I'm getting reports that it was the best rock show in town for a long time, man. . . . They killed it! So here's a little Zeppelin for those of you heading home from the concert!"

Then "Nobody's Fault but Mine" came on. We'd just played it ourselves an hour or so earlier. And now I was sitting in a van next to Jimmy Page, listening to the recorded version as we blasted back to Boston. That kind of shit never got old.

"Turn that up!" Jimmy said.

The driver cranked it and we all started rocking out. I looked over at Rose Mary, who could barely process what she was seeing. Her favorite musician of all time is Jimmy Page. Her first concert was Led Zeppelin in 1977, when she was twelve. And now we were in a van, all playing air-guitar and air-drums with the man himself.

It was pretty much the coolest thing of all time.

The second-coolest thing of all time had gone down in New York City one day earlier.

Pete was summoned to Don Ienner's office following our three-night run at Roseland. Don welcomed Pete like a long-lost friend. He'd heard all about the shows, and he was fired up.

"The band's on fire, Pete! It's all anyone is talking about! *This* is what we needed!"

Pete nodded and confirmed that everything Don had heard was true. The shows were really special. The energy, the vibe in the room, the musicianship on the stage . . . it was magic.

Don asked what our plans were. More shows? An international tour? New music?

Pete said, "Well, Don, we are in fact looking ahead to next year, but we have two shows in LA this week, and the plan is to record both with a mobile truck studio for a live album."

Don exploded. *"Now that's what I'm talking about!* What's the status of Jimmy's contract with Atlantic? Hell, I don't care what his contract says, we'll make it work! This will be fucking huge!"

Pete Angelus had waited a year for this very moment.

Four days before he walked into Ienner's office, The Black Crowes had been an afterthought at Columbia Records, with one optional album remaining on their contract. Columbia would never let us leave, and they would never allow us to make a record anything close to what we would have wanted. We could only imagine what they'd demand for our next album. My guess was not one song, but an entire album of Rolling Stones covers. Or they might literally ask us to rerecord *Shake Your Money Maker* with guest vocals from Mick Jagger.

Three days later, thanks to the gigs with Jimmy, we were the toast of the town, and we were very much the toast of Columbia. Don smelled blood in the water and he wanted some of it. Badly.

Pete said, "I'm sure everything can be worked out with Jimmy. This is very exciting, Don. So . . . are you offering us a deal?"

"What are you talking about?" Ienner said. "You still owe us an album."

"No, actually, we don't."

"Yes, actually, you do!" Don was annoyed.

"No, Don. Actually, *you* missed the option," Pete said. "We're no longer signed to American Recordings, or to Columbia. We're free. We're totally unattached. But, of course, I'd be happy to talk about a new deal right now."

Lightning had indeed struck twice for The Black Crowes. For the second time in seven years, Pete was able to inform someone who had us by the balls that actually, as it turned out, they didn't have us by the balls. If anything, *we had them* by the balls. That shit never happens. And that shit *absolutely never* happens twice.

Ienner freaked out. He picked up his phone and screamed at someone from the legal department: "Get that fucking Black Crowes contract in here right now!"

Pete stood up and said, "Well, Don, it looks like you have a few things to go over . . ."

Ienner cut him off. "What the fuck?! This is bullshit! Why didn't you fucking mention this before?!"

"Well, Don," Pete said calmly, "it seemed fairly obvious that the label wasn't really interested in The Black Crowes, so what would have been the point?"

As Pete left Don's office, some poor dude from the legal department ran in, and Don was in his face right away. "Did you miss their option? Did you fucking miss their option?"

Pete could hear the screaming halfway down the hallway as two other label people ran past him into Don's office.

"Somebody fucking get him back in here!!!" Ienner screamed as Pete entered the elevator.

Pete walked out of that building on Madison Avenue with a master plan already coming into clear focus.

We were back. We were in control.

And the best part of all? It was real. It was genuine. It was organic. Jimmy loved our band, and we loved Jimmy. Everyone was having the time of their lives. It was infectious, and it was powerful. And this time around, nothing was going to stop us.

At that very moment, as Pete strolled to the hotel savoring the good news he was about to share, it seemed incomprehensible that anyone could knock this freight train off the tracks.

But then again, we were The Black Crowes.

We did have one small problem: Jimmy had no interest in making a live album. Why ruin a good thing? Why fuck with something that's purely fun by adding pressure?

Pete laid it out very simply to Jimmy. "We'll record both nights. Kevin will mix them. You won't see the mobile truck, you won't see a crew, there will be no distractions. The recordings will be your property. We'll cover the costs, but you'll have the tapes. If you don't like what you hear, it'll never see the light of day. If you do like them, then we'll move forward, together, and figure how to release it and with whom. It will be your call, and your call alone."

Jimmy was clearly intrigued, but hesitant.

Pete kept going. "If you don't like it—no, if you don't love it—I'll carry the tapes into the parking lot myself and we'll fucking burn them." Pete pulled a Zippo lighter out of his pocket and held it out to Jimmy. "It'll be the greatest backstage bonfire the music business has ever not seen!"

"Okay, sounds good to me, mate," Jimmy said, laughing. What else could he say? Pete had offered him a no-lose situation.

Before the first night at the Greek in LA, we sound checked forever. We were all still bouncing around like ping-pong balls, but Jimmy seemed a little . . . off. He was still drinking then, and we thought maybe he'd tied one on last night. All we knew was that he wasn't his usual buoyant self. Not that anyone gave it much thought. By the time the gig rolled around, we assumed he'd be jacked up like always.

But he wasn't. The vibe from sound check carried over to the show. He was rattled and had an off night. He couldn't relax, and we all felt it throughout the whole gig. The audience had a great time, of course. They were as fired up as any LA crowd I'd ever seen. But onstage it was a bit of a battle.

Apparently—and this came as a shock—Jimmy Page actually was human.

Afterward, Jimmy went into his dressing room alone. Then he took off a few minutes later for the hotel. Shit.

Kevin came in from the mobile truck and confirmed that it had been an off night. "Man, there were a lot of clunkers up there," he said.

At that moment, we felt like ditching the live album immediately. It hardly seemed worth it, especially if it was going to screw up our vibe. We still had a good night. The dressing room was full of friends and we carried on back at the Sunset Marquis Whisky Bar until they threw us out. But it was a bit of a drag to know that Jimmy wasn't happy.

The next day, we again had a lengthy sound check. This one felt totally different, though. Jimmy was back to the guy we'd done the first four shows with. He was totally relaxed, laughing easily. Everyone fell into lockstep. We knew we were going to have a good night.

Jimmy asked if we could all talk in the dressing room afterward. As we gathered around, his personal assistant walked in with a large box. Jimmy opened it up and said, "I got a little something for all of us." Then he began handing out tour jackets he'd ordered. Black fleece zip-ups that had the "Jimmy Page and The Black Crowes" logo stitched on the left side of the chest. We had made jackets in the past for our own tours, but it had honestly not occurred to any of us to memorialize this short run. We were so touched.

"They do look good, don't they?" Jimmy said proudly as we tried them on. We took a group photo, everyone in their jackets, and proudly basked in the glow of Jimmy's kindness.

And, for the record, it really was a quality jacket. I still have mine.

We had a few hours to kill before the gig, and Jimmy was standing in the doorway to his dressing room. As I walked down the hall toward him, he flagged me. "I was thinking about taking a nap. Are you going to take one today?"

I laughed. "Yeah, of course."

"Well, look in here," he said, "my dressing room has two sofas. I thought we could take a nap together."

I was caught between thinking this was the single weirdest, most unexpected moment in my life and feeling like it was the most natural thing in the world.

I focused on the latter. "I'm always up for that. Let's go."

I think Jimmy just loved feeling like he was in a band again. I was clearly loving every minute of playing with him, and we had developed a nice little bond over the past week. He also had an absurdist sense of humor, and the double nap idea clearly tickled him.

The sofas were set up at a right angle in the corner of the dressing room, with a small table separating the tops of our heads. We both lay down on our backs and started chatting about the shows and how well received they'd been. I'd had a late night, and my sound-check adrenaline quickly faded. Within three minutes, I was knocked out.

I slept for a little over an hour. Finally, I sat up and looked over at Jimmy, and he was sound asleep.

I stayed there for a minute or two, amused by the moment but also genuinely touched by his friendship, and appreciative of all that had transpired. It was perfectly still in the room. I was filled with gratitude.

Jimmy suddenly woke up. He looked over at me and sat up. He had been out cold, which was unusual for him.

"Well, we'll see how that worked out soon enough, I guess," he said sleepily.

"It'll be great. It'll set you free, my man," I said, standing up.

I opened the dressing room door as Chris and Rich were walking past. They both gave me a surprised look. Jimmy routinely popped into our dressing room, but none of us had ever hung out in his.

I said, "Oh, hey . . . just woke up."

They were in shock. "You went into Jimmy's room and fell asleep?" Chris asked.

"No, we just took a nap together," I explained.

The three of us fell out laughing

We all had a lot to learn from Jimmy. I soaked up everything he had to offer like a sponge. Jimmy Page taught me all I would ever need to know about the importance of finding the vibe, or the "spirit" as he called it. He told me one night that if you're not nervous before a show, it means you're not going to do anything new . . . and then what's the point?

Meanwhile, I taught Jimmy Page how to take a nap before a gig. I'd say we're even.

Jimmy Page and The Black Crowes' *Live at The Greek* was taken entirely from the second night. Chris had to recut a couple of vocal passes. He couldn't hear himself onstage very well, as he was singing over the three loudest guitars on planet earth, so some of the originals were just too far out. But the drums, bass, keys, and all guitar parts were nailed down in the moment.

I had a great night, even though a few of the tunes were flying. Some of that shit feels like the tempo is twice as fast as the original. But the communal energy onstage and in the house dictated the spirit, and we just rode the wave.

Between the set and the encore, as we took our five-minute break, I saw Mike Mills from R.E.M. at the side of the stage. I dropped out of college and chased this whole crazy thing in the first place because of how much R.E.M. inspired me. I'd never met him before. And now there he was. It was a fucking fantastic full-circle moment for me.

I walked up to say hi, and before I could say a word, Mills yelled, "What a fucking blast!" Jimmy was standing at his side.

"Hey, Mike," I said. "That's Jimmy Page right there. Be cool."

He laughed and said, "Yeah, I know. He's pretty good!"

We shared big smiles and then I walked back to the kit.

Anyone who walked into those gigs with any reservations forgot all about them within three songs. We just killed it. We were confident, we were prepared, and we were fucking excited. Kinda hard to beat that combination.

For Sven and me in particular, we were flexing muscles in a way we never were able to as The Black Crowes. We just hit long balls, one after the other. We had to live up to the legacy of that music. We couldn't phone it in.

Jimmy and I walked offstage together that night, arm in arm. He was pumped. And, also, he was relieved. He'd crushed it, and he knew he'd crushed it.

Ross Halfin, who'd been at every show shooting photos and barely raising an eyebrow all week as we constantly impressed ourselves, walked over and said, "That one was really good, wasn't it? That was the one!" Hell, even Ross was smiling. I don't think he'd ever paid us a sincere compliment before. It was unsettling. Thankfully, it was a one-off. He's never done it again.

Kevin Shirley came bouncing into the dressing room a few minutes later from the recording truck, with a large dose of Caveman excitement. "This album is going to be awesome, trust me!" he enthused. "Well done, everybody!"

Pete burst in yelling, "Is this the dressing room for the baddest motherfuckers in rock 'n' roll?!"

In just over a week, through six shows in three cities, The Black Crowes had done the unthinkable. We suddenly had a clean slate with a wide-open future.

I wasn't going anywhere.

34

Sven Pipien, Over and Out

We flew home with no firm plans in place. We had a commitment from Jimmy to tour the following summer, but that's all we knew. My own plan was to find a place to live in Brooklyn, hopefully before the end of the year, and otherwise relax and enjoy some downtime.

Chris finally left Los Angeles. He got an apartment in New York City, in Chelsea. Rich had already relocated to Connecticut. I casually mentioned to them that I was going to be making a few trips to the city over the next couple of months to find my own apartment. I thought maybe we'd get to a Knicks game together.

I shouldn't have said anything. We were still the band that didn't know how to take time off. Within days, we were making plans to start working on new material, and by the first week of December, the brothers, Sven, and I were back together in New York.

We didn't have a label yet, but we knew we were going to work with Kevin Shirley again. He had a great feel for the band by this point, and he was as excited as we were at the prospect of working together without Columbia looking over our shoulders.

He suggested we build a studio at his house in the Hamptons. We loved that idea, as it would allow us a looser schedule, an ability to keep the budget in check by all living there, and we could establish and maintain a vibe that was more our speed. We hoped to find the perfect middle ground between the *Three Snakes* experience and the *By Your Side* experience—a house to live and work in, but with both harder-rocking songs *and* a very decisive captain at the controls.

261

We shipped all of our gear from Atlanta to SST, a storage/rehearsal facility in Weehawken, right next to Hoboken. It was literally a couple of hundred yards from the mouth of the Lincoln Tunnel. As soon as I found a place to live, with the three of us in the area, The Black Crowes would essentially be a New York–based band.

We planned to spend a couple of weeks working on new songs at SST. Sven and I moved into a little corporate short-term rental apartment in Koreatown. It was cheaper than a hotel, gave us way more space, and there was great Korean food on the block. If I had to be away from home, at least that all made it easier.

We started, as per usual, with a burst of momentum and efficiency. Rich was full of ideas. He had tons of great parts, and more often than not there was a very clear Zeppelin influence on display. He wasn't aping anything. He was simply infused with Zeppelin, and it came out in his ideas. He'd clearly been soaking up inspiration, both consciously and subconsciously, from Jimmy, and it showed. To me, his playing and his writing were the best they'd ever been. It carried over to my playing as well, which was more bombastic than ever before.

A few new tunes came together immediately. "I'm on My Way" leaned heavily toward an "Over the Hills and Far Away" vibe in its earliest stages. Ultimately, it shape-shifted and became "Soul Singing," one of the more popular songs from the album *Lions* that was released in the spring of 2001.

A leftover from the *By Your Side* sessions, "Old Man and the Midnight Sea" was reworked dramatically over the next year and finally wound up as "Young Man, Old Man," also on *Lions*. There was one more, "Bled to Death," that we had played live a few times on the By Your Side tour. It was long considered to be an anchor track for whatever came next, but was ultimately never even recorded by the time we were making an album.

After a week, we were noticeably slowing down. It was mid-December, and there was finally an entire day where literally nothing new was accomplished. The following day Chris rolled into SST at three in the afternoon, drunk off his ass. I don't think he'd been to bed from the night before. He rolled in, curled up on the couch, and passed out. Rich, Sven, and I jammed for a bit, loudly, but he didn't budge. It was a wash.

I wasn't upset. On the whole, we'd had a productive week.

"All right, I'm going home," I finally said.

"Okay, what time tomorrow is good?" Rich asked.

"No, I'm going *home*. This is nonsense."

I half expected a message from Chris bitching at me when I got back to Atlanta that night, but no one ever even mentioned it. That was the first time I noticed a very clear side effect of working with Jimmy. The eternal, intrinsic power structure in The Black Crowes—the brothers *über alles*—had been disrupted. In Jimmy Page and The Black Crowes, I was as integral as anyone onstage not named Jimmy Page. And everyone knew it.

In January, Rose Mary and I found a great place in Park Slope and made plans to be there by the end of March. We were thrilled to be right across the street from Prospect Park. We had a huge dog, and we were about to have a baby . . . we were going to be in that park a lot.

The tour with Jimmy was falling into place as well. And it was way, way beyond what I had initially hoped for. For the US dates, we were going to be touring with The Who. The bands wouldn't play on the same night, but rather on consecutive nights in the same venue, while sharing production. Same lights, same sound, same crew for both. One load in per city, one load out per city. A show every other day. We'd all save money on production costs, and fans could choose to buy tickets to one or both shows, with a discount if they chose both. It was brilliant.

We had five tour legs scheduled: three legs in North America with The Who and then one leg on our own in Europe and Japan. Fifty-five gigs in all. The big capper for the US tour was two nights at Madison Square Garden, offered as a pay-per-view event on TV, with each band doing a set. *The Garden with Jimmy Page? And The Who on the same bill?* You gotta be fucking kidding me!

It was going to be our biggest-ever year financially. It was *absurd* money, especially considering that I would have done it for free.

Rehearsals with Jimmy weren't set to start until June. We were still putting new tunes together for about a week each month, and Sven and I stayed in the same apartment each time.

The songs were shaping up well, but in early March I could no longer deny that something was needling me. Sven was acting a little erratically.

I woke up one morning early, around six o'clock, and heard Sven come in through the front door. I startled him when I walked into the front room to see what was going on.

"I decided to take a walk down to the World Trade Center!" he said, unprompted.

"Um . . . that's like eighty fucking blocks away," I replied.

"Yeah, it was really good to get some fresh air!" he half yelled as he walked past me and into his room.

At SST that afternoon, I told Chris and Rich about it. If he was using again—and by then I'd been around enough chemicals to recognize that he was—we had to put a stop to it right away. I hated the thought of him being in that hole again.

There was also the fact that we had a long, busy year ahead of us. Sven would have to have his shit together to get through it.

Chris was concerned, but the fact is that he was a mess, too. He was in an on-again, off-again relationship with a straight-up nightmare of a woman. He was embarrassed about it and tried to hide the fact that they were still seeing each other, but we all knew. He was miserable. He'd been drinking hard and doing coke again pretty regularly since December.

We booked a gig for April, in Charleston, South Carolina. It was a big outdoor show at a AAA baseball stadium for a rock station that had switched formats to alternative but was still playing The Black Crowes. We were second on the bill, with the band Filter set to headline. I only remember that because when I saw the offer, my first question was "Who's Filter?"

We traveled to Charleston on two flights, as there wasn't enough availability to get everyone down there together. Chris, Rich, Amy, and I arrived midday, and the other guys had flown in an hour or two earlier. We checked into our hotel, and had a few hours to kill.

We got the message to everyone to meet up for lunch at a place around the corner. Everyone turned up except Sven.

Amy had heard from him. He was meeting up with our old friend Clint Steele, who'd driven over from Atlanta for the gig. Those two had done a lot of drugs together in the past. We all felt a sense of dread.

At three o'clock that afternoon, we met in the lobby to head to the gig. As we loaded into the van, Amy told us that Sven was going to meet us at the stadium with Clint.

Uh-oh.

Chris and I immediately protested.

"He's already gone," Amy told us. "I gave them directions to the ballpark, Sven already has his backstage laminate and a parking pass, and he has the schedule for the day."

"Why did you let him go on his own with Clint?" I asked.

"What did you want me to do, physically restrain him? He's an adult in his midthirties," she replied. While that was undeniably a valid point, it was not reassuring in the slightest.

Our set time was eight o'clock. At five, Sven still hadn't turned up at the ballpark. Amy called his cell phone every fifteen minutes. He never answered. She had Clint's number, too. No answer there as well.

The crowd was swelling in the stadium, and we were hearing about the length of the lines to get in and all kinds of logistical problems throughout the day. The longer it took for those guys to get to the venue, the harder it was going to be for them to get backstage.

By six o'clock, with Sven still nowhere in sight, we were all at DEF-CON 1.

Through all of the bullshit that had gone down with The Black Crowes over the years, no one had ever missed a gig. Ever. That was the overriding rule of Rock 101: YOU FUCKING SHOW UP. I was really upset. I was scared for Sven, and I was sad that he was risking everything.

Of course, those emotions didn't present themselves as such, as I was still a few years away from successfully processing my actual feelings in an honest manner in real time.

Instead of sympathetic concern, I was fucking furious. I was going to kill him.

At six thirty, there was still no word. It was time for plan B.

We couldn't play the gig without bass. And we were not going to fucking cancel. Could Audley play bass? Or Rich? Could that possibly not sound horrible?

Robert Kearns, Audley's old bassist from Cry of Love, walked into the dressing room. I am sure he was flummoxed by the intensity of the response with which his presence was received.

"Hey, man! Great to see you! Do you know any of our songs?"

"Yeah, of course. Hell, at the very least just tell me what key they're in and I'll play quarter notes or something," he said, shrugging.

Audley started charting out the songs. He and Robert had played for years together, so they communicated efficiently. Within minutes, Robert was studying the charts and they were cramming for the impromptu test we'd thrown at him.

I appreciated Robert for his willingness to put himself on the line for us, but my fury at Sven overwhelmed that sense of gratitude. *Thank God for Robert . . . but fuck you, Sven.*

At 7:55 P.M., we left the dressing room to walk to the stage. We were about to perform a forty-five-minute set in front of about eight thousand people with a bassist we'd never played a note with.

Fuck it. Nothing left to do but make the most of it. Looks like Robert Kearns is about to audition for The Black Crowes. Let's see what he's got.

On the stage, a local DJ was on Chris's mic to introduce us: "These guys are one of the best rock bands on the planet today . . ." I looked over to Robert. He was wearing Sven's bass, holding his charts, deep in thought. I smiled at him. He smiled back.

Here we go.

We were at the bottom of the stairs, seconds away from walking up onto the stage, when we saw a commotion in the crowd. Security had just helped someone through one of the gates off to stage left, near our location, and now he was running toward us.

"Hey, guys, sorry! I can't believe it," Sven said breathlessly. "The security were being total assholes."

Chris looked at me. "What do we do?"

"We're fine, Sven, we got it," Rich said tersely.

"I'm fine! I'm here! I'm ready!" Sven barked, his words a frantic jumble. "Let's go. Let's do this, sorry."

Sven looked over at Robert and immediately apologized. "Oh Jesus, man. You're probably freaking out right now. I'm sorry I put you through that, man."

Fucking Sven. High as a kite, his gig on the line, and he takes a moment to consider what Robert was going through. Always a gentleman.

I stepped forward and pulled Sven aside.

"Look, man, I'm really sorry," he stammered. "I just want to—"

"Sven, shut the fuck up. I don't give a shit right now why you're late. Are you okay?"

"Yes, yes."

"Can you play the show?"

"Yes, what do you mean?"

"Are you too high to play? Yes or no? You better fucking tell me the truth."

"I'm fine, man. I am totally fine."

"All right."

Sven flashed me a wounded look.

"Don't you fucking look at me like that," I yelled. "Don't you fucking talk to me. Just play the fucking gig. Let's go."

And with that, we walked right up the stairs to start the show. Within ten seconds, I was slamming the ride cymbal to start "No Speak No Slave."

Chris had already written a fucking barn burner of a setlist. Just rock song after rock song. We played a brand new one, "Come On," and I've long held the belief that it was the greatest performance of that song, ever. We should have discarded it immediately afterward.

It was an absolutely furious show. But it did little to burn off the anger we were all feeling.

Walking back to the dressing room, Sven tried to apologize again.

"Get the fuck away from me," Chris screamed at Sven. "No one has ever missed a fucking gig in this band."

"I didn't miss the gig," Sven said meekly.

"Did you fucking hear me? Get the fuck away from me! You couldn't make it to the dressing room before the gig, so you sure as shit ain't gonna go back there now!"

Sven turned and walked off, which was the smart play. He was, truly, risking a beatdown.

Darius Rucker was backstage. He's always a great hang. He invited us back to his house for the night. There was a Final Four game on, he had a great stereo, a rooftop deck, and a fridge full of beer. *Yeah, man. We need that.*

We stayed at his place for hours, smoking pot, drinking beer, watching hoops, and talking about Sven. *What the fuck are we going to do now?* We didn't have any good options. We were either going to stick it out with a guy we no longer trusted on any level to be reliable, or hire someone else and risk pissing off Jimmy.

Actually, I was the only one raising that particular alarm. The brothers didn't think Jimmy would give a shit. I wasn't in the mood to argue the point that night, but I knew he would. He had given Sven's playing way too much love for it not to be an issue.

The following morning, with no clear solution in sight, Sven didn't show for van call to the airport. It was the crack of dawn. Everybody was on the first flight out to their various hometowns.

"He's driving back to Atlanta with Clint," Amy told us.

"Shit . . . high as they are, they're probably halfway to Dallas by now," I said.

We all laughed, but it wasn't funny.

Rich and I talked to Pete the following afternoon. Nobody wanted to replace Sven, if we could avoid it. We decided to have a call with him, and simply say, in a sense, *Let's not dwell on what happened. It was a mistake. We're willing to move on, but you have to get clean.*

Pete left Sven a voicemail saying we'd have the call at 5 P.M. Eastern Time the following day.

Chris tapped out. He had tickets to the Mets season opener that day. That was fine with us, as it would probably be easier without him.

Sven called me a few minutes before five. He said, "I don't want to have this call. I know what's going to happen. I'm sorry, man, I'm so sorry! But I can't talk to everyone!" He was frantic.

I reassured him, saying, "Sven, you're NOT being fired. When Pete calls, PLEASE answer it and talk to us. It'll be okay, I promise. But you have to listen to what he's going to say. Please!"

Pete called Sven several times before he finally picked up.

"I know what you're going to say," Sven said before Pete uttered a single word.

"Well, actually, Sven, I doubt very seriously you know what I'm going to say," Pete replied. "It's apparent to us now that you've gotten into trouble again with drugs. When you joined the band, it was a pretty specific stipulation that you wouldn't do this. You're in violation of the deal you signed. I'd like to offer you another deal. Let's look at it as if we're starting over. It's going to have the same stipulation, and there will be no more wiggle room. You have to get clean. If you commit to that, we'll move on."

"Yeah, yeah," Sven said. "Well, you're not my friend, Pete. You're not. I know that. You've never been my friend!"

He was completely rattled, even worse than he'd been with me a few minutes earlier.

"Sven, listen to me."

"You're not my friend, Pete," Sven said again.

"That's true, I'm not," Pete said. "I'm the manager of The Black Crowes, and my job is to protect the band."

"You don't have to tell me shit, man," Sven said. "None of you guys care about me. None of you ever did, you're not my friends."

"Sven, hang on, man," I interjected.

But Sven was on a roll. He whirled himself up. And up. He was losing control emotionally. He repeated, several times, that none of us were his friends. And then he hung up.

"Should we call him back?" Pete asked.

"No," Rich said. "Fuck him."

"Maybe I should call him," I offered. "Maybe I should go see him."

"I wouldn't go see him, but if you feel like calling him, go ahead," Pete countered. "Do you think he can even make sense of what we're saying?"

"If you want to call him, go ahead," Rich said. "I'm not talking to him again. Fuck that."

After a few seconds, Pete said, "Give him a call, Steve. But let me say one thing: rehab isn't like, two weeks. If he's gonna be clean by June, we need to get him somewhere right now."

I called Sven back. He didn't answer, so I left him a voicemail. I told him again that we weren't letting him go. I begged him to call me back. He called me back later that night, when I wasn't home. His message was hard to listen to.

"I know what you're trying to do, you're trying to help me, man. I know you always had my back. You were always my friend. But I know

I'm out. I know I'm fired." He rambled on and on. And that was it. Message over. Sven Pipien, over and out.

I called Pete immediately after I played the message. "He's fucking gone," I said, sighing.

It was terrible. Thankfully, I guess, I'd seen enough terrible things by then to not let it completely derail me. I had too much shit to do. I was moving to Brooklyn in two days. I had a baby on the way. Sorry, Sven, I gotta move on.

Later, we'd laugh about how disjointed Sven sounded. I even saved the voicemail and played it for everyone, which disgusts me looking back.

Make no mistake, we didn't actually think it was funny. It was horrible and everyone, even Chris, genuinely felt bad for Sven. But we couldn't express it. If we suddenly showed empathy and concern for each other, the whole fucking thing would probably unravel. It's too bad we were so stunted emotionally, as it should have been patently clear by then that a little unraveling would have done us some real good.

Despite my resolve to maintain focus, I actually was pretty rattled. Sven and I lived in the same neighborhood. My final two days as an Atlanta resident were spent looking over my shoulder.

On my last night in town, I stopped to get gas. As I filled my tank, Clint Steele pulled in on the other side of the pump. I couldn't believe it. Was this a coincidence? Was he following me? We just took each other in without saying a word.

He looked beaten down. He needed a shower. He was in a bad way. I was as healthy as I'd been in years. I was moving to New York the next morning. I was touring the world with Jimmy Page in a few months. I was happily married with a baby on the way.

We couldn't have been on more divergent trajectories.

Thirteen years had passed since I'd moved to Atlanta for us to start a band together. Those thirteen years suddenly felt like a flash.

Clint, Sven, and me.

We were young, we were strong, we were hopeful.

And now?

I was flying in a stratosphere none of us could have even imagined back then, and from the look of things, their future prospects had pretty much disappeared into a fucking haze of crystal meth.

I clearly saw and deeply felt all of that, silently pumping gas on the corner of Monroe and Ponce, on April 4, 2000, five feet away from the guy who, in 1986, had made the most important phone call of my life.

It broke my heart.

35

Trouble Brewing
in Valhalla

There was yet another development swirling through the spring of 2000. Against all odds, we landed an incredibly lucrative record deal, at what turned out to be the last moment such a thing was even possible in the record industry . . . at least for a rock band like The Black Crowes.

We had become, suddenly, a very hot item and there were several labels making pitches to sign us. The tapes from the final Greek Theatre show had indeed turned into a live album. On February 29, 2000, *Jimmy Page and The Black Crowes Live at The Greek* was released on TVT Records as a one-off, with no obligation for future recordings.

It was a very innovative approach at the time. Fans could go to a website, pick as many as they wanted of the twenty-five tracks we offered, and then receive a corresponding CD in the mail to their home within a week. You only paid for the tracks you wanted. This was years before Spotify or even iTunes. And it was a huge success. *Live at The Greek* sold well all around the world, actually going gold in the United States, which was our best sales result since *Amorica*.

Pete took many calls, ultimately setting up a few meetings for the four of us to take in person. The first was with our old friend Steve Balcom, who at the time was running Mammoth Records.

Steve respected us, and was a straight shooter. But during the meeting, things went a little sideways after Steve offhandedly mentioned he would serve as our A&R guy. Steve felt uniquely qualified, knowing us as well as he did, to insert himself into the creative process.

He brought positivity, enthusiasm, and genuine love to the meeting. He was the exact opposite of Don Ienner. But, still, Chris shut him out the second he heard "A&R."

We left the meeting subjected to Chris's rants. "I can't believe Steve thinks he can tell us how to write songs!"

By the time we were back on the street looking for a taxi, I had eliminated Mammoth as a contender. If there was one thing I knew implicitly, it was that working with Steve Balcom would ruin our friendship.

Fuck that, let's go find some strangers to alienate.

Next we met with V2 Records, the label Richard Branson founded five years after selling his first label, Virgin Records, to EMI.

"I love you guys," the dude from the label told us as we sat down. "I think with *By Your Side* you were just at the wrong place. It was obvious they didn't lift a finger for you."

He was certainly off to a strong start, and continued saying all the right things. Assigning blame elsewhere for our long, continuing downward streak in album sales was music to Chris's ears.

V2 seemed like a pretty hip place to be. They had a small but exciting roster of young bands, including Stereophonics, the Welsh band we'd all become very friendly with, and The White Stripes from Detroit who, unbeknownst to us at the time, were about to take over the world.

"We are building a roster with great new artists, but we need some tent poles," he continued. "You're a mainstay, a truly great American rock band, and we want to be your home."

It was ultimately an incredible sales pitch. If anything, it sounded almost too incredible. Surely reality would bite us on the ass when they made the official offer.

Or not. The offer came in the next day: five albums for $1 million each.

Are you fucking kidding me?

We were expecting, at most, 150 grand for one record with an option.

We couldn't believe it—$5 million! That was insane.

The offer spoke to several things, including our status as a really good live band that still (potentially) had a bright future. But, truthfully, it took playing with Jimmy Page to remind everybody of that fact. That offer from V2 ultimately spoke to the eternal power of Led Zeppelin and their music, twenty years after they'd disbanded.

When Pete shared the news, we didn't even exchange glances before all saying, "Let's do it!" He hadn't said a word about A&R, or a recording/release schedule, or promotional commitments. We heard that number and jumped without a second thought.

After a few minutes, I pulled Pete aside to register my disbelief. "I'm really never getting out of this band, am I?"

"Sign the deal," Pete advised, smiling. "You're going to do the Jimmy tour. You're going to do the first record for V2. Then, you see what happens . . . see how you feel. Same as always. You're not stuck."

It was pretty clear that 2000 was shaping up to be a great year.

When we rolled into rehearsals at the Congress Theater in Chicago that June, all of the shows on the first leg of the tour were either sold out or nearly sold out.

I was unsurprised to find out that Jimmy was very disappointed about Sven. As easygoing as he'd always been with us, Jimmy was a man very much used to being in control of his musical environment. He didn't blame us for Sven flaming out, but he was dismayed that the rhythm section he'd grown so fond of wasn't waiting for him when he got to town.

Beyond that, Jimmy was pretty particular about who he opened up around. At that point he'd been *Jimmy Page* for over thirty years, which can be draining to say the least. He was slow to warm up to new faces. I don't think he had more than a few moments of passing small talk with Greg Rzab, our new bassist, during rehearsals, and that quickly shut down entirely after Rzab tried to bend his ear at the hotel bar one night. Jimmy instructed his assistant to keep "the new guy" away from him.

Rehearsals proceeded more or less as they always had. Everyone was in great spirits, and we added some new songs for the new year: "Misty Mountain Hop," "In the Light," "Hots on for Nowhere," and a few more.

The gigs in the summer of 2000 were a little different than they'd been in the fall of 1999. This time around, we didn't have that wondrous, spontaneous vibe to lean on. There were real expectations. Could we be better this time around? How could we top the live album?

The new songs were one element, but more than that we made a conscious effort to rein the tempos back a bit. We wanted to groove more.

We started that leg in the Midwest, slowly making our way to the Northeast. The shows, without exception, were all a blast. Jimmy was in fine spirits and we all felt a tremendous sense of momentum building. We looked forward to the arena shows in Europe and the multi-night run at the Budokan in Tokyo. Led Zeppelin were truly gods in Japan. That was gonna be nuts.

We added a side gig at a festival in Milwaukee between Pittsburgh and Holmdel, New Jersey. It was a fly-in, fly-out opportunity on what would have otherwise been a night off while The Who played New Jersey. Gov't Mule played right before us. It was Jimmy's first time seeing them, and while he loved Warren Haynes's guitar work, he was especially fond of Allen Woody, the bassist in the Mule.

"That guy's fantastic!" he said over and over.

I remember thinking, *We might have to borrow Woody for the fall legs . . . sorry, Warren.*

Tragically, Woody died less than two months after that show. He was a fucking freight train of a bass player and an absolutely wonderful, warm-hearted man. It was a huge loss, not just for Gov't Mule, but for everyone who knew and loved him.

The tour was going really well, but other than the few hours on-stage each night, I was preoccupied with what was happening back home. Which is to say, I was constantly checking in with Rose Mary, now very pregnant, and doing my best to fight down the fear that she would go into labor prematurely and I wouldn't be there for the baby's birth. We had, in fact, scheduled a four-week break to wrap perfectly around her due date, but still . . .

At the gig outside of Boston, I called home after sound check. Rose Mary was having a rough day. A million tiny little things had piled up and I could hear it in her voice. She was struggling.

I asked Jimmy's assistant, Wilf, if there was a chance I could hitch a ride on Jimmy's plane after the show, as I knew he was going back to New York right after the gig. He had a sweet little six-seater he came in and out on throughout the tour.

Wilf said he'd check and get back to me. A few minutes later, Jimmy bounded over.

"So, I understand we're traveling together tonight!" he said, excitedly.

"Yeah, if that's cool, thanks!" I said.

"We'll be moving right from the stage, so be sure to stay with me after, okay? We'll hop right into a van with no time to waste," he explained.

I had to laugh—Jimmy was tour managing my egress for the evening. It was awesome.

We played, we rocked, and Boston was *having it*. We left the stage to thunderous applause. It might have been the best night of the run. We all felt it throughout the whole gig. Really special.

As we waved our goodbyes, Jimmy caught my eye. He was grinning. We walked off together and he said, "Let's keep moving, we don't want to get caught up in the traffic!" As if I'd forgotten the plan. *Hell, how could I forget? I was gonna fly outta there with Jimmy Page on his plane, for fuck's sakes.*

We climbed into the van. Me, Jimmy, and Wilf. There were six cop cars surrounding us. The audience was still screaming for another encore when we started rolling. It was a bit of a flashback to The Rolling Stones experience in 1995.

We both had towels and were wiping the sweat from our heads.

"That was a really good one, wasn't it?" he said. "That first down-beat on 'Sick Again' wasn't quite right, we have to get that timing together, but I really felt great. 'Nobody's Fault' *really* got them, didn't it?"

We talked about the show, very excitedly. He was, as always, a complete live wire after the gig. In the moment it felt totally natural. Just two guys talking about the gig they'd played. My only thought beyond what we were actually talking about was that he clearly loved having me there. He would have loved having any of us, I think. Usually, he flew with his assistant and his tour manager, but with me he was able to actually talk about the gig we'd played. I think he felt like he was in a band again.

The van pulled into a tiny airport outside the Providence, Rhode Island, airport within about twenty minutes. We got out of the van, stepped immediately onto the plane, and were airborne in less than two minutes. We landed at Teterboro Airport in New Jersey about twenty minutes after that. I had a car waiting there to take me to Brooklyn.

I'd walked offstage outside of Boston at 11 P.M. and I walked into my apartment in Brooklyn at 12:40 A.M. That's a pretty fucking great way to roll. Jimmy was thirty years into that life. I had one day of it under my belt. I understood at that moment what someone had told me once about flying private: *It's not about luxury . . . it's a fucking time machine.*

No shit.

I walked into my apartment feeling like the luckiest man on earth. Just ahead of my thirty-fifth birthday, we had boundless possibilities. We were working for the rest of the year, playing shows that I absolutely loved. We had yet another chance with a new label to take full advantage of all our momentum to reestablish The Black Crowes. Assuming we didn't fuck this thing up, we were already well on our way to, as Jimmy had said, *taking back our seat at the table.*

But it didn't go down that way.

We were already well on our way to fucking this thing up.

After the gig in Detroit, on the short bus trip from the venue to the hotel, Chris, sitting in the front lounge, said out of the blue, "You know, I'm getting kinda tired of all the 'baby, baby, baby' and *Lord of the Rings* shit."

He'd decided, apparently, that he was bored singing Led Zeppelin songs for tens of thousands of adoring and grateful fans. "I'm starting to feel like I'm in a fucking cover band."

I let that one go.

He started again, two nights later, after our gig in Pittsburgh. But this time Rich, who *never* agreed with Chris about anything, chimed in, too.

"I can't wait to play my own fucking music," Rich said.

I couldn't believe my ears. I was livid.

"Seriously? Fuck you both. Jesus Christ, you're both fucking useless," I said, sighing. I wasn't screaming. I was speaking very matter-of-factly, as one does when one is entirely right. "This is one year of your life, *one year*, to reset and reboot the entire rest of our career. Correct me if I'm wrong, but the last time we played our own music no one gave a flying fuck!"

"You don't understand, man," Chris replied. "I didn't get into this just to be a jukebox."

"Are you fucking serious? Do I actually have to remind you of what an honor it is for the band to play with Jimmy? Or of what this fucking tour means to your future?" Pete chimed in.

We were both suddenly on high alert. We couldn't believe this shit. Chris was a hundred percent committed to Jimmy Page and The Black Crowes when he could feel how much we needed it. But, hey, now that V2 had come in with that contract, fuck it! We're back, baby! We don't need this anymore.

Pete and I gave each other a look that said, *We have to stop this right here and right now.* We both geared up instantly for a battle.

But, shockingly, it ended as quickly as it began. Chris backed down completely and kept his mouth shut about it, for the most part, from that moment on. Pete didn't have to lay out the ten most significant benefits to our career by touring with Jimmy. I didn't have to threaten to murder him with my bare hands if he kept running his fucking mouth.

Neither one of us said another word.

All that happened was this: Kate gave him a stern look and said, "Babe, don't be ridiculous. This tour is the best thing that ever happened to you guys."

Kate was Kate Hudson.

She'd been around for the past few months. Or, rather, we'd been around for the past few months, depending on your point of view. Chris and Kate had met earlier that spring at a *Kids in the Hall* show in New York. He called me the next morning, at nine. I saw his name on the caller ID and assumed he hadn't gone to bed yet. I expected him to be wasted. It took one second to hear that wasn't the case. He was lucid and excited.

He said, "I met Goldie Hawn's daughter last night."

I didn't know Goldie Hawn had a daughter. I *did* know that Chris had a lifelong thing for Goldie.

"Goldie Hawn has a daughter that's old enough for you to be running around with?"

Almost Famous, the Cameron Crowe film about 1970s rock that made Kate a star, wasn't in theaters yet. So I, along with most of the world, didn't know who Kate was.

Three days later, Chris called again to say they hadn't been apart since he'd last called. By the time the summer tour started, they were a couple. They were an item. *A thing.*

And in the eyes of everyone associated with The Black Crowes, it was fucking glorious. Kate laid down the law right away. *If you're doing cocaine, we're not going to be together.* He hadn't done a bump since. He was madly in love with Kate, and she wanted him to straighten his shit up. God bless her, she gave it a hell of an effort.

That night in Pittsburgh, Chris looked at Kate and laughed. That's all he did. All the hot air that had been building up inside him simply evaporated like an eight ball of coke in the wind.

36

"Which One of Those Two Stupid Motherfuckers Did This?"

The first leg of the tour ended with a gig at the Jones Beach amphitheater on Long Island. We had a great night with a ton of friends and family. We'd had so many stressful gigs over the years in New York, but now they all seemed a thing of the past. With Jimmy, we were four for four in New York City.

There hadn't been any more hiccups since Pittsburgh from either brother about not enjoying the shows. I guess there's something about playing to over ten thousand screaming, overjoyed people a night that tends to make even the most hardened of cynical hearts warm up a bit.

We played "Your Time Is Gonna Come" on *Late Night with Conan O'Brien* the following night, and then had a month off. After the tune, Jimmy, Chris, and Rich sat on the couch with Conan for a few minutes. Chris was in media mode and had some funny moments. The rapport he and Jimmy shared was very much on display.

To celebrate the end of the first leg, we all went to dinner in the West Village. Many toasts, stories told, and laughs later we said farewell for a month, in the best of spirits.

Rose Mary and I went home to Brooklyn and waited for the big day. Her due date was still a week off, but our son had other plans and waited an extra week to make an appearance. Conall was born on July 24, 2000.

Two weeks later, we started the second leg in Albuquerque. I spent the time between sound check and the gig showing pictures of the baby to everyone I crossed paths with, whether they were interested or not. It had been tough leaving home the day before. I had said bye-bye to a two-week-old baby . . . who would be five weeks old the next time I saw him.

After the gig, Pete, Amy, Chris, Rich, and I took a private plane to Los Angeles for some reason. Maybe we were investigating the logistics of upgrading to a plane for the rest of the tour. We landed at the Santa Barbara airport, or maybe Van Nuys, and hopped in a van to the Sunset Marquis for a day off.

I woke up the next morning with a message to call Pete. I ordered some coffee, got myself set up at the little garden table outside my villa, and gave him a buzz. He told me that Jimmy's back had acted up during his flight to LA the night before, and he was in a lot of pain. We'd been told that Jimmy had a wonky back, but I hadn't really given it much thought. He always seemed fine to me.

Pete knew a back specialist/witch doctor in Arizona he swore by. By the time Pete was updating me, this guy was already on a flight to LA. He got to the hotel around noon and went right to Jimmy's room. I felt a little trepidation, but told myself I really had no reason to worry. Jimmy had been bouncing around onstage the night before. He was gonna be fine.

A few hours later, I walked down to the lobby to meet Ross Halfin for a walk up to a bookstore, and Jimmy was standing by the pool. He was wearing shorts and a T-shirt, holding a large bottle of Evian. When he saw me he pumped his fist, smiling.

"Hey, Steve! How are ya?" he said.

"I'm good, Jim . . . how are *you*? I hear your back is fucked up. Any better?"

"I feel great, thanks!" He was beaming.

"Did you see Pete's guy?"

"Oh God, yes. He's a miracle worker. He was incredible."

"That's great to hear," I said. "What did he do?"

"Well," Jimmy began, "he spent some time stretching me all out, and eventually got up on top of me and started to manipulate this and that . . . it took a bit but he must have found the trouble because everything fell back into place! And now he's got me drinking water! I hate drinking water but I'm going to do whatever this guy says!"

He must have really been in a lot of pain for a while, because he was like a new man. I could see it in his eyes that he felt like a million bucks.

"Oh, that's awesome, Jim, I'm so happy to hear it!"

"I'm gonna stay in, get my rest. I'll see you tomorrow," Jimmy said, giving me a little hug.

The next day, Monday, we played *The Tonight Show with Jay Leno*, over in Burbank. We got to the studio precisely in time to sound check. Well, The Black Crowes did, anyway.

Jimmy hadn't shown yet. We went ahead and sound checked without him. He didn't arrive until we were doing the blocking for the cameras, in fact. But nothing seemed amiss. He said hi to everyone like it was any other day, then took his place as we ran through the song.

After the camera blocking, Jimmy went directly to his dressing room. TV shows are so tedious. Even when you trim it down as much as possible, there are still a few hours of waiting around. It's unavoidable.

Once the show began, we still had almost an hour to wait, as the musical performances are always last on *The Tonight Show*. A production assistant finally turned up to escort us to the stage. When we got there I was surprised to see Jimmy already in place, ready to go. He must have gone down a few minutes ahead of us. It occurred to me that I actually hadn't seen him since camera blocking. That was unlike him. He usually popped his head in to see what everyone was up to. *Whatever.*

They came out of a commercial break, I heard Jay Leno introducing us, and Jimmy turned back and gave me the *Are you ready? Okay, let's do it!* look.

I counted in "The Wanton Song" from *Physical Graffiti*, and away we went. It felt good. Actually, it felt *really* good for a TV show.

Jay came over to shake hands with everyone after the performance, friendly as ever, and we walked back up to the greenroom. I was thinking about the night ahead. I was gonna head back to the hotel and take it easy. I wanted to catch up on some sleep and make sure I had my guest list figured out for the next night's gig at Irvine Meadows in Orange County. I walked into the greenroom, opened a beer, and sat down.

Suddenly, Pete walked in and shut the door. He had something on his mind.

"What's up?" I asked.

Before he could answer, the door burst open again as Audley and Ed walked in. Pete motioned for me to follow him into the hallway.

We were alone out there.

"Jimmy is going home," Pete said.

"Okay, cool. Is your guy gonna work on him again?" I asked.

"No," Pete said. "Not to the hotel. Jimmy is going *home*. The tour is over."

I looked at him blankly. Pete never joked about this kind of shit.

"What do you mean?"

"He's leaving. He's *already* gone, in fact. He walked right out to his car and he's already on his way to the airport. They pulled the plug on the tour. No make up dates. It's all done. It's finished."

"Is it his back?" I asked, trying to process the shocking news.

"Well, yeah, that's what he says."

"I saw him yesterday afternoon by the pool, right after your guy worked on him. He felt great . . . he was drinking water and laughing . . . holy shit . . ."

It was all hitting me like a slow-moving wave.

"I saw him a few hours later, around six, and he was in a great mood. He looked like a new man," Pete said. "I didn't hear anything after that or at any time today about his back flaring up again, which is odd because I told Jimmy I was keeping the back doctor in town in case he wanted to see him again. What the fuck could have happened since then?"

"He was fine on the show. He was *just* rocking out down there. He didn't look like anything was wrong and that was ten fucking minutes ago." I couldn't make sense of it.

We were both stunned. The tour had been going so well. Jimmy was clearly on the mend. We were asking each other questions that neither of us could answer.

"Well, Amy's booking flights for everyone. You'll be out of here tomorrow," Pete said finally.

We heard a big laugh from down the hallway. We looked over to see Chris and Rich about thirty feet away, talking and cracking up about something.

"Well, they're obviously fucking broken up about it," I said, pissed at them for not giving a shit.

"No, they don't even know. I haven't told anyone else yet."

I stared at the two of them, laughing without a care in the world. My mind was completely blank. I couldn't formulate a linear thought. I was so sad, and I was so confused. Nothing was adding up.

"Which one of those two stupid motherfuckers did this?" I finally blurted out to Pete.

"I don't know," Pete said quietly, "but I'll fucking guarantee you I'm going to find out."

Pete called Chris and Rich over and told them the news. The color drained from Rich's face, but he didn't say a word. Chris took it in for a few seconds, sighed, and said, "Well, fuck . . . I'm ready to just be The Black Crowes again, anyway."

And that was that.

We had played eleven of our fifty-five scheduled gigs. We disappointed hundreds of thousands of fans. We saw European and Japanese arena shows vanish into thin air. We didn't play with Jimmy and The Who at Madison Square Garden. And I was never going to get to play Zeppelin songs with Jimmy Page again.

I landed at JFK, got a car to Brooklyn, walked into my apartment, and sincerely didn't look back. I'd missed three days with my baby boy. I wasn't going to miss any more for a while. All good. Two days after I got home was my thirty-fifth birthday. A year earlier to the day, I had called Pete to quit the band. It had been *one hell* of a year.

Within a few weeks, our thoughts and focus turned to a new album. V2 had not only committed an extraordinary amount of money to the band, but they also had never assigned anyone to work as A&R. They pretty much said, *Here's a bunch of cash. Turn in something when you're ready.*

We'd had a loose plan all along to head out to the Hamptons with Kevin Shirley and make a record at some point. Now, as "some point" was approaching, Chris and Kate spent a weekend out there with Kevin and some other friends. I never heard a satisfactory explanation of what happened, but something sure as hell went down because when Chris and Kate got back to the city, Kevin was out. No debate. We were *not* working with Kevin Shirley again.

Chris had long wanted to work with Don Was. They'd met in the early 1990s when Don was working with The Stones, and they had always kept in touch. Back in '97, Chris sent Don a copy of *Band* to gauge his interest in producing us. Don told him, "There's nothing to do. This is the album. All I could do is mess it up." That had stuck in all our brains. For what it was worth, Don Was apparently heard everything in *Band* that the rest of us had.

We set up shop at Montana rehearsal studios in midtown and began to plow through the many songs and ideas we had compiled in the past two years. It was just the brothers, me, and Don initially. Rich and I would track a tune, he'd throw on a bass line, and we'd move on. We had a lot of demos put together very quickly. Ed came in after a bit and we fleshed out the demos even more.

We'd decided to move down to a studio on the Lower East Side when it came time to actually track the album, but we were really productive at Montana. The vibe was relaxed and the brothers were actually getting along really well.

We were listening back to a tune called "Losing My Mind" and Don turned to me, saying, "Am I crazy, or should we think about just staying here to make the record? This stuff all feels great."

I'd had the same thought. Much like the *Band* sessions, there was a vibe that was so natural and so organic. We asked the brothers what they thought, and they agreed. The stuff we were cooking up really sounded great.

But we'd already booked the studio, Theater 99, a converted vaudeville theater. It was a cool space, and we really did want to get down there. We had our hearts set on it. So, with just a hint of second-guessing ourselves, we pulled up stakes and moved downtown as planned. It was autumn in New York City, which is about as good as life gets. Chris, Rich, Ed, and I were on hand throughout. Rich played bass on everything except for one or two tracks that Don handled. Rich didn't want Audley around, and was in fact lobbying to replace him before the album came out and we hit the road again.

Don ran a loose ship, but I wasn't complaining. I was really enjoying myself, actually. I really liked a lot of the songs, and Chris and Rich still, somehow, were getting along better than I had ever seen.

Our new "everybody gets along now" reality was in no small part thanks to Kate. She had no time for the brothers' fights and reminded Chris regularly and quite vociferously that nothing should come before family. It was mind-boggling to see her shut him down. Whenever he'd start to whip up into a frenzy over Rich, she'd just shoot him a look, and it'd be done.

When the band split in 2002, there was a narrative within the fan base, and music media in general, that Kate was the Yoko One of The Black Crowes, sowing division by telling Chris he should leave the band. That was way off base. Kate wanted the band to succeed, she wanted the brothers to get along, and she was, generally speaking, a source of positive energy at all times.

The studio setup in the theater was pretty unconventional. We were playing on the stage and the control room was at the back of the seating area, in what would be the projection room if it were a cinema. The basic tracks had no separation. We were playing loud as hell, so the drums and guitar bled into each other throughout. Anybody in the theater had to be absolutely quiet during takes. Any sound at all would find its way onto the tape.

Craig Ross, Lenny Kravitz's lead guitarist, came by and added a guitar solo to "Greasy Grass River," another basic track we brought downtown from Montana. Ed had been talking up The White Stripes for a while. He'd known them from Detroit for years, and Jack and Meg White came by one day as well. We had friends around all the time. It was a spectacularly relaxed environment.

We recorded the sounds of elementary-school children during their playground recess across the street one day, and their laughing and screaming wound up in the middle section of "Midnight from the Inside Out." Rose Mary brought Conall to the studio one afternoon.

We recorded him crying for a few seconds, and that ended up on the song "Cosmic Friend."

Chris essentially took his hand off of the reins this time around. For whatever reason, he gave Rich an enormous amount of creative control, and that played a large part in keeping their tension at bay. Chris was too happy with Kate, or too tired of her chastising him, to fight about anything concerning the record, for the most part.

So we all got along. Which was nice. We *did* struggle, however, to get the songs *just right*. We had a whole lot of "almost ready" tunes. Had we been working with Kevin Shirley, I don't doubt we'd have spent more time tightening down all the writing screws. Don had a very different approach, though. Truth be told, I wasn't entirely sure what his approach was at the time. All I could be certain of was that he wasn't in good shape. He would say the same thing now. He's been sober for more than a decade, thankfully, but he was anything but in 2000.

I got coffee with Don a few years ago and he said, "I really don't even remember working with you guys."

I wasn't surprised. He told me that back in those days, his approach when working with artists was simply to do whatever drugs they were doing at the time. He was a human mood enhancer, in a sense.

I love Don. We all enjoyed his company, but I can't look back and remember any specific arrangement or songwriting tips he came up with. I'm sure he provided both, but I was enjoying life as a new dad and not giving any thought whatsoever to the production details of the album as we made it.

"Soul Singing" was a tough song to figure out. It was originally an acoustic tune with very little percussion underneath. We kept tinkering and tinkering but never quite found the right direction. Only after we had finished recording did Rich finally combine elements from two very different approaches to come up with the finished version. We ultimately found that tune on the road, once we played it a few dozen times.

I always viewed *Lions* as the ultimate testament to Rich's ability to come up with fantastic riffs and parts, and our inability to utilize them to their fullest potential. His time with Jimmy opened up a whole new creative portal at precisely the time that Chris was becoming less and less able to contribute. He'd turn up occasionally and shove some non-sense like "Ozone Mama" down our throats, but it was an entirely uninspired time for him, ultimately.

On *Lions*, we started strong and we finished weak.

We were still The Black Crowes.

In late September, just before we started recording the album, Chris and Kate announced not only their engagement, but also their wedding details: New Year's Eve, in Aspen.

Rose Mary and I were at their apartment one night and they shared the news, a few days before letting everyone else know. We were happy for them, if not also wondering what the fucking rush was. They'd just met in March or April, and Kate was only twenty-one.

"Knocked up?" I asked.

They both laughed. Nope. Just ready to get married.

I asked Amy to look into flights. I was fine to get out there a few days early, but my family and I had to be on the first flight out on January 1 so we could get down to our own vacation in the Caribbean, which we had booked months earlier. But finding flights in and out of Aspen over the holidays with such short notice was impossible.

Rich was in the same boat, of course. Amy talked to us together at the studio one night. "Look, I've done a ton of work with this. I think your best bet is to fly private in and out of White Plains. You can fly out the twenty-eighth or twenty-ninth, and then get outta there on the first. It's expensive, but there's no guesswork on the roads or anything like there would be if you flew into Denver."

How much?

"Thirty grand."

The cost of travel alone for Chris and Kate's wedding had already exceeded the *entire* cost of my own wedding, which included two weeks in a villa on St. John.

That said, it was worth every penny. If the opportunity were to arise again, ever, to attend a social event hosted by Goldie Hawn and Kurt Russell, I'd be there with fucking bells on.

They really know how to put on a show. We arrived in Aspen on the evening of the twenty-eighth, left four days later, and every minute we spent there was remarkable. Rose Mary and I stayed with Chris and Kate in the guest house at the family ranch, just outside of town. The setting was beyond picturesque, and Kate's entire family was wonderful to us.

The rehearsal dinner, on the thirtieth, was in a restaurant atop one of the Rockies. It was accessible by either horse-drawn sleigh or cross-country skis. We chose the open sleigh pulled by giant Clydesdale horses, as there was schnapps on board and, honestly, who the hell wants to strap on ski gear to go tie one on?

The sun had just set, the sleigh bells were ringing loudly as the horses pulled us through the woods, and snow was lightly falling. As we approached the restaurant, which was really an old, spectacularly appointed cabin, smoke was pouring out of the chimney, candlelight was flickering through the windows, and the aroma coming from the kitchen was overwhelming.

It hardly seemed real.

The wedding itself took place at the ranch, in the yard between the main and guest houses. Despite the subfreezing temperatures and what felt like a triple-digit crosswind blowing, the ceremony itself was beautiful. At least it certainly seemed that way. Between Chris and Kate continually choking with emotion, and the steady sound of the locomotive-strength gale-force wind, it was hard to actually make out any of the words. But still, it was lovely.

BR549 was on hand as both the wedding and reception band. They had played a few tunes before the ceremony started, and now they were standing just off to the side, their hands stuck, literally frozen to the vintage and brittle wooden instruments with which they made a living. Chuck Mead, one of the two singer-guitarists, turned to us and said, "Well, now I know what those musicians on the deck of the *Titanic* felt like."

Both for the moment at hand and as an overview of Chris and Kate's future together, it was the quote of the day.

A fleet of giant SUVs carried everybody to a lodge for the reception. The word "lodge" doesn't really do the place justice. It was, like everything else that weekend, simply gorgeous beyond words. As we were having cocktails before dinner, the schtick was running pretty thick. The over/under on the length of marriage was set at three and a half years.

I mentioned it to Kurt Russell and he said, "Well, I love Kate to death, but hell, gimme twenty bucks on the under!"

It was that kind of weekend. Nothing heavy, just a lot of fun. Everyone at the reception was buzzing. A really fun, long night was ahead of us.

There was, however, one dark cloud in the room, and that was the fact that the best man, Rich, was incapable of even pretending to be happy for his brother.

They'd gotten along pretty well while making the record, but that clearly wasn't translating to the big event at hand. When it was time for a toast, it was obvious Rich hadn't prepared one. He wasn't the most comfortable public speaker to begin with, so some preparation would have served him well. It occurred to me watching him struggle with his words that he hadn't realized he would be called upon. I don't think he'd thought, for even a passing moment, about what to say until he was standing there.

Has he never been to a wedding before? Or seen a fucking movie about a wedding? Does he actually not realize the best man gives a fucking toast?

He'd had a hard time throughout the whole trip, apparently, not that I was aware of it at the time. Rose Mary and I were having a blast, and as Rich had stayed in town at a hotel, we only saw him the night of the rehearsal dinner, and then at the wedding and reception.

He and his wife, Emma, left the reception just as the party was gearing up.

BR549 hadn't even started playing yet.

I tried to stop him.

"Stay for the reception," I insisted. "If you don't want to dance, don't dance. But you have to be here. You're the best man."

"Oh, that doesn't matter," Rich grumbled. "Emma doesn't feel good, and we have a long travel day tomorrow."

Chris was really upset about it. He couldn't believe that his brother, the best man, was the first guy out the door. He was trying his best to shake it off, but it really hurt him. We were talking with Kate about it when Goldie came over.

Kate mentioned it to her, and Goldie said, "Oh, honey, it's a hard thing for Rich."

Kate said, "Why? How can it be hard to see your own brother so happy?"

"Because Chris won. I mean, it's just that simple."

Ouch. But she was exactly right.

The band started up and got everybody dancing. It was a hell of a party. I went over to Kate at one point and said, "You know you have your fucking hands full, right?"

She laughed and said, "I got this."

Chris came over and we hugged each other. We said that we loved each other and I told him I was so happy to see him so happy.

I also said, "Seriously, man, don't fuck this up."

I got a little choked up, actually. I was drunk, of course. But I just wanted this to work out for him.

"Are you crying?" Kate asked.

"Well, I could cry, if I really wanted to push the moment," I joked. "This is a beautiful night and it's a beautiful start to something. I want the best for both of you guys."

Drunk or not, I meant it.

BR549 said they'd happily play until sunrise. That sounded like a great idea, and I for one assumed the party would literally roll all night, but that turned out to be too ambitious. By three in the morning it was winding down pretty quickly.

Rose Mary and I were trying to figure out who could drive us back to the ranch when Kate told us to jump in with her and Chris.

I said, "It's your wedding night, you guys need to be alone." She laughed and said, "We're going back to the same house, you idiot, get in."

Fair point.

We climbed into their SUV for the drive back. Chris had rebounded during the party, but now that we were heading home he got upset again. He was truly crushed about Rich having left early. Kate consoled him, telling him not to worry about it.

From the backseat, hammered, I shouted, "Fuck him . . . didn't you just marry a fucking movie star for fuck's sake . . . why don't you focus on what makes you happy instead of your stupid fucking brother?"

I might as well have suggested that he sprout wings and fly.

We were driving home from the most beautiful wedding day I'd ever seen. Miserable.

We were walking in a figure-eight in a field of grass in 1987 after a successful gig. Miserable.

We were leaving London after a hugely successful first tour. Miserable.

With every moment of triumph there was a corresponding crash.

Chris was a control freak. A control freak without linear thoughts, or contemplation, or a set goal at any given moment . . . but, still, a control freak.

Chris had a burning, *raging* need to control the emotional charge of any positive moment. When things got too good, he always had to bring them crashing back down to earth.

Somewhere in the most fundamental building blocks of his psyche, somewhere very early in the development of his worldview, a number had been improperly inserted into the code. Therefore, his formula was forever off, and nothing was ever going to add up properly.

The result was a complete lack of faith in positivity.

An inability to trust in others.

A certainty that the good times wouldn't last, that they couldn't last, and therefore must be destroyed.

And thus, controlled. Poor guy. He was flying blind. Always had been. Always would be.

37

At Long Last . . . Out

Our flight left Aspen the morning after the wedding. By the time we finally checked into our villa in the Caribbean the following afternoon, we were completely fried. We extended our trip so we could still have a full ten days.

One day at the bar by the resort pool, I saw Robert Plant. He was renting a shack in the woods on the other, far more remote side of the island. (Of course he was.) He had come to the bar with his girlfriend to have a few frozen cocktails.

We chatted for a while. He fussed over the baby, and we talked about Jimmy. He said, "I thought he played better with you lot than he had with me in years." He told a few stories about their many battles and differences of principle, and I said that he and Jimmy were like an old married couple. He said, "I don't know if I should slap you or thank you for that."

I told him that I was thinking pretty seriously about leaving the band, and that in fact I had tried once before but Jimmy got in the way.

He laughed and told me he completely understood. "Bands are hard work," he said. "You boys have always been special, but things change. You can't be afraid to move on. If you stick with something out of fear, you're wasting everybody's time, not just yours. You'll be fine. You're a smart fella and a good drummer. Don't waste your time. Ever."

Uncle Bob.

Always the best.

We got back to New York as another snowstorm rolled in. It was gonna be a while before it warmed up. Welcome back to reality, indeed.

In February, we played an "album completion" gig in New York City. A video retrospective played on a big screen before our set. We were eleven years in, but that video made it feel like fifty. So many ups and downs. So many reboots. So many fucking people. Our new bassist, Andy Hess, was the eleventh man to claim a spot in The Black Crowes. He would hardly be the last.

A week later we played a private corporate party in Las Vegas. We had turned down offers for years and finally gave in. We flew out, drove directly to a casino ballroom, had a meet and greet with about fifty people, and then played a sixty-minute set. It was easy, and Chris was fine with it. Things really were shifting radically.

Pete gathered us after the set to finalize our summer touring plans for Europe. There were two wildly different possibilities.

Plan A: Open for Neil Young and Crazy Horse for about ten shows in arenas. Good money, helps grease the wheels for our own headlining dates and other festivals. Not to mention, it's fucking Neil Young and Crazy Horse.

Plan B: Open for Bon Jovi for about ten shows in stadiums. GREAT money, STUPID money, goes way beyond simply greasing the wheels for our own dates and festivals. Puts a ton of bank in our pockets. Flies completely counter to everything we've ever said we stood for.

Rich and I shot that down before Pete could even finish telling us what the offer was. No fucking way.

Chris said, "Hang on . . . how much are we talking about?"

Pete told him the number, which was mind boggling, and followed that up with, "Look, I'm just letting you know that the offer is there. But I don't think it's truly worth considering, especially with an offer from Neil right next to it. We might have been forced to consider it two years ago, but we've worked past that. Crazy Horse is the play here."

"Fuck it, man," Chris countered. "We're in Vegas playing a corporate for money. Let's just do the Bon Jovi dates and make a ton more."

What? Seriously? Is this a fucking joke?

Rich said, "You go right ahead. There is *no* way I'm doing that."

I said, "I can't believe you're saying this. You'd rather do that than spend a couple weeks with Crazy Horse?"

This was the same guy who, three years earlier, had walked onstage in sandals, cargo shorts, and a Lakers jersey. And who, six months after that, literally renounced his Grateful Dead T-shirt collection and started wearing a denim jacket with a giant AC/DC patch on the back. And who, a year after that, went on *Jay Leno* wearing leather pants, a giant felt hat with feathers, and a black tank top with the word "pimp" on the front. He was a fucking boomerang. He saw the world in complete extremes. In or out. For or against. Black or white. Always.

We'd just made an album with zero label interference. V2 gave Pete complete control of our promotion. And, suddenly, because of one private gig we were Goldman fucking Sachs?

"Look, I'm just saying that all anyone really wants around here is to make money, so let's just take the fucking money," he countered.

There it was. Chris officially launched his "all they care about is money" campaign in Las Vegas that day in February of 2000. Last I checked, he's still deep in the trenches of that particular skirmish.

"Who's saying anything about *just* wanting to make money? Pete's not. Steve's not. I'm not. It's Pete's job to tell us what's out there. It's just information!" Rich said. He was really flustered. "If we did those shows, you'd freak out on us for being greedy, and *you're* the only one suggesting it. There's no fucking way I'm doing those gigs!"

"Okay fine, but don't bitch at me if you two are out of money one month after the tour ends," he said.

Projection, thy name is Chris Robinson.

Chris, Rich, and I flew to Europe for a two-week promotional tour in mid-March. Dozens of interviews in a different city each day. We were all getting on fine. No tension, no nonsense.

Chris flew home early, leaving Scandinavia to Rich and me. We filled the energy void from Chris's absence without any conscious effort. It's classic group dynamic stuff. During interviews, we were far more animated than we'd have been if Chris were still there.

Rich and I had long talks about what V2 could deliver both short and long term. We both wanted to fully recommit internationally. It was time to invest in South America and the rest of Asia. Not only did we recognize that we had a profound opportunity with V2, but also that without success, it would surely be the last of its kind.

With every new chapter, I had more perspective on the band but more importantly, on myself. I had imprisoned myself in the band's turmoil for years. My personal fears, insecurities, and codependency allowed those walls to close in. It was unquestionably a volatile environment, but I had, most assuredly, walked myself into those dark corners. It had been impossible to admit that, right up until the moment I actually admitted it. And then it was as plain as day. So, for the past few years I'd been walking myself back out.

I wasn't thinking about leaving the band on a day-to-day basis. Far from it. I was actually enjoying myself, and very much hoping the best for the album and tour. I saw myself as a guy who had packed a parachute, knew it was ready to go, but hadn't stepped on the plane yet. That plane might take off at the end of the year, or it might take off in ten years. The point was that I was ready to jump whenever the time came.

Lions was released on May 7, 2001. It didn't set the world on fire, debuting at number twenty on the *Billboard* chart. That was better than *By Your Side* but well below the albums we put out in the early 1990s. The reviews were mixed, but then again, the reviews were always mixed with us.

As we were setting up a promotion plan with V2 early in the spring of 2000, Pete was plotting out our year on the road. We had some spring festival offers that would take us to the album release and just beyond. We had a European run from mid-June through July, with a few shows in Japan after that. We had theaters back in the United States for the autumn.

We had a month to fill in our tour schedule from mid-May to mid-June. Pete was brainstorming ideas. We needed a band to tour with . . . someone to co-headline with. But with The Black Crowes playing last each night.

Then it hit him, definitively, like a lightning bolt: Oasis.

That band centered around two brothers who fought all the time. Their biggest commercial success (at least in the US) was behind them. Their ability to sell tickets across the United States had steadily declined. They could use a tour, just as The Black Crowes could, in sheds where they didn't have to worry about assuming all the risk. It would certainly be a very easy pitch to promoters. Pete even had the perfect name: The Tour of Brotherly Love.

He pitched it to us, fully anticipating a negative response. Instead, we immediately went for it. *Hell yeah! Do you really think they'd do it?*

Oasis agreed immediately. And, in spite of the bands' respective reputations, The Tour of Brotherly Love turned out to be just that. We all got on like a house on fire. It was a veritable love fest. And it was a far cry from what I would have believed possible the first time we ever saw Oasis, back in 1995 at Glastonbury Festival.

The Black Crowes had originally headlined Glastonbury in 1993. Two years later, we found ourselves second on the bill to an upstart English band that had quite literally taken the United Kingdom, if not the world, by storm. Of course, we didn't care about that shit. Our attitude was, *Who the fuck is Oasis?*

During our set that night, I saw Noel Gallagher at the side of the stage, checking us out. *That's one of those Oasis guys. Hope you feel good about following this, motherfucker. Your band can't touch us.*

As Oasis took the stage, there was no denying that the playing order that night was appropriate. The crowd lost their fucking minds.

I watched a few songs and thought, *Yeah, they're okay, I guess.* Nothing about their playing blew me away. There was never a real groove. And the singer was useless to me. But they definitely had some songs. They struck me as a classic "great songs, good band" kind of band, whereas I thought that The Black Crowes were often a "great band, good songs" kind of band. The history of rock music shows quite clearly that the former succeeds far more than the latter.

I came around to a begrudging respect. The singer, Liam Gallagher, won me over by simply never doing much of anything. He barely moved, he glared at the crowd, and he could hardly be bothered to even really sing for fuck's sakes. After a while, I had to hand it to him. It was kinda punk rock. Whatever it was, it was definitely working. The place was going apeshit.

And then I heard Liam say between songs, "It's nice to get that silly southern shit out of the way so you can hear some real music."

I couldn't believe it. I was standing with Pete. I looked at him and said, "Did that motherfucker just say what I think he said?"

Pete nodded. "He sure did."

That fucking kid is about to learn more than he ever wanted to about silly southern shit.

I grabbed a bottle of Jack Daniels and walked into the Oasis trailer. I took a seat, started slowly working through the bottle, and waited. I was going to kick the living shit out of that kid when he showed up.

After a few minutes, a member of their crew walked in. He was startled to see me. "Sorry, mate, think you might be in the wrong trailer?" he said quite pleasantly.

"No, this is my trailer."

"Um . . . no, mate, this is Oasis's trailer. I think yours is just across the way."

"This IS my trailer!" I said again. "You tell those motherfuckers onstage they are welcome to come in here and try to take it from me."

He walked out quickly. I could see the inherent humor in the situation, and I could imagine the English press going crazy with it. *No-name drummer from Black Crowes beats up Oasis singer.* But it didn't slow me down. This was business. It had to be done.

I guess word got out that I was in there, as Mark Botting finally came in.

"Hey, you know, mate, we have to make that ferry to get across the channel."

"I'll fly tomorrow," I said. "I have to kill this kid."

It's safe to say that I wasn't a little drunk—I was *really* drunk.

Mark said, "Well, mate, I would love to help you out, you know that, but I can't let that happen. We've got to get moving."

"Sorry, Mark, I gotta do what I gotta do."

He walked out and came back a moment later with Chris. "Dude, we gotta go. Kick his ass some other time," Chris said.

I couldn't believe it. This was the first—and last—time I ever decided to start some shit myself and no one would jump in with me? What kind of bullshit was this?

"Get Johnny over here!" I demanded.

Now they were both laughing at me. Even in my state of mind, I knew what that meant. Game over. This wasn't going the way I hoped.

Okay, fine. Fuck it. I got on the bus and eventually passed out, still foaming at the mouth over that asshole saying that shit and no one else doing anything about it.

Six years later, on The Tour of Brotherly Love, The Black Crowes and Oasis had a fucking blast together. Both bands later said, for years, that they'd never enjoyed a tour with another band as much as they did that month. There was a clear recognition of similar strengths and weaknesses in both bands, clearly, because we fell into a groove right away and simply had fun together.

The third gig of the tour was at the Greek in LA. We were all hanging together in the dressing room afterward and Chris said, "Hey, did you guys know that Steve almost killed all of you at Glastonbury?"

They had no idea what Chris was talking about. So I gave them the whole rundown. They were all laughing hysterically. "There's no fucking way Liam ever said that," Noel insisted.

"I heard him!" I said.

"I promise you—that kid had never even *heard of* The Black Crowes in 1995. And there's no way in hell he would've slagged you off. We watched your set and we all thought, 'Holy fucking shit, that band's amazing.'"

Liam came into the room at that precise moment. Noel yelled to him, "When did you first hear of The Black Crowes?"

"Glastonbury in '95."

"What did you think?"

"Fucking tight, man."

"Did you fucking slag us off from the stage?" I asked.

Liam gave me a confused look. "What? No! I thought it was a proper fucking rock band."

Oh, okay. Well, never mind then.

The Gallagher brothers clearly have their own issues, but to me they had a better sense of humor about themselves, and about everything surrounding life in a rock band, than the Robinson brothers ever did.

That spring while we were in London doing promotion, both for *Lions* and for the forthcoming tour with Oasis, Chris and Liam did a series of interviews together. Liam was married to the actress Patsy Kensit, and of course Chris was married to Kate. A journalist asked them,

"What is it about rock singers and famous actresses?" Chris hated those kinds of questions. He would bristle at the notion that his relationship with Kate was anything other than a pure and abiding love.

Liam? Not so much. "Shagging famous women is better than regular ones," he said.

I fucking fell out of my chair. Liam was hilarious *and* authentic.

On our European tour, which included those dates with Neil Young, we waffled between nights onstage when we were arguably the best rock band on earth and nights when we were five musicians with their token stark-raving-mad basket case. The rest of us regularly walked to the stage without a clue as to what was about to happen. In the middle of a great show, Chris would turn on the audience and accuse them of wasting our time. In the middle of a lifeless gig, he'd be cutting jokes and laughing between songs. Amazingly, he reached a whole new level of unpredictability.

Six Japanese gigs marked the end of our summer abroad. Rose Mary and Conall met up with me in London and they did the Japanese trip as well. Conall celebrated his first birthday in Tokyo, in fact. We had a fantastic time, taking full advantage of every moment, knowing full well by the time we got there that it was my last tour with The Black Crowes. For real this time. Jimmy Page wasn't about to call and ask us to tour again. I was done.

Pete flew over to Tokyo, as long planned, so we could have a meeting to discuss any and all plans for 2002. I had already decided I wouldn't be back, but of course I kept that to myself. We had a day off and scheduled the meeting for two in the afternoon in Pete's room. Rich and I showed up exactly on time. Chris wasn't there. He wasn't there thirty minutes later. Or an hour. Or two hours.

He didn't turn up until much later that night, and when Pete angrily asked him where he'd been, Chris said simply, "Kate and I were shopping and we just stayed out. What's the fucking big deal?"

Pete said, "I flew over here, at your insistence, because you're going on vacation next week, and you said you wouldn't be able to speak for a while, and we agreed to meet today, *in fucking Japan*, to map out next year!"

Chris said, "Oh, there's nothing to map out. There's no Black Crowes next year. I'm gonna start working on my solo career."

Pete was stunned. "Chris, hang on a second. You're welcome to do something else, but you can't just put the entire band on hold. V2 is expecting another album by the end of next year. Or the deal goes away."

"I don't care," Chris replied. "I really don't think I'm coming back anyway. If my own record does well, I won't be back no matter what."

Pete said, "No, no, no. You committed to deliver five albums to the label. They committed five million dollars to the band. Lemme help you with the math—you have delivered one, so you owe four more. Those four albums get the band to a twenty-year-career . . . you're gonna throw that away because you can't make your own record and a Black Crowes record *over the course of a full year?* If we lose the V2 deal, and then a year later you decide to get The Black Crowes back together, what then?"

Chris laughed. "You'll just find us a million dollars for a new record somewhere else."

And that was it. Done. He had nothing left to say. He walked out, barely acknowledging that Rich and I were also in the room.

Pete looked at us. "Well, who wouldn't enjoy flying five thousand fucking miles for that bullshit?"

I was hyper aware, as we started the final leg of the *Lions* tour, that I'd be seeing a lot of these cities and venues for the last time, at least as a member of The Black Crowes. And I really enjoyed it. I felt like I'd been truly forged in fire, and now I was the strongest I'd ever been. Even more than I'd been just a few months earlier. That scene in Japan had clinched it. I was free. And for eleven gigs, it was a lot of fun.

We had a day off in Los Angeles on September 10, 2001. We were at the Sunset Marquis, of course, and I spent the whole day doing as little as possible. My cousin Jeffrey had moved to LA and we met for nine holes at a pitch and putt course in Studio City, but that was it. We made a plan to do the same thing the following morning at nine.

My phone rang just after six that morning.

"Wake up, wake up, wake up!" Rose Mary said frantically. "We're under attack."

I was wide awake in one second. I turned on the TV and saw both towers of the World Trade Center engulfed in fire and smoke.

My first thought was to head straight to LAX and get home. I was three thousand miles away from the scene, whereas my wife and son were three miles away from the scene. I was panicked, to say the very least. For an hour we sat on the phone, both flipping channels, updating each other with every new bit of information we could find. We barely said anything for minutes at a time. All I knew was that I couldn't hang up.

After the first tower fell, I snapped out of my shock.

"Babe, you need to get out of the city," I pleaded.

"Everybody in New York is trying to get out of the city right now," she said. "If I'm trying to leave, everyone is trying to leave."

At some point, Pete called to confirm the obvious. We'd cancelled that night's gig at the Greek Theatre. I couldn't imagine playing any more shows, truth be told. I wanted to get home and stay there. But that wasn't going to happen. No one was getting into New York City anytime soon.

We had a gig scheduled at the University of Arizona for the following night, and the promoter there called to ask that we not cancel if at all possible. He made the entirely reasonable point that the students probably needed a show more than ever. Anything to distract them from the nightmares in New York, DC, and Pennsylvania.

So at midnight we set off for Tucson. We hadn't decided whether or not to play, but it was in the right direction, anyway. We just wanted to start moving east as soon as possible.

We all loaded up into the bus. CNN was on the TV in the front lounge. Nobody slept the whole ride to Tucson. We couldn't look away from the television.

By the afternoon of the twelfth, we had decided to play the gig that night. We barely sound checked. We were just as shell-shocked as everyone else in the country, of course. At 9 P.M., we walked onto the stage, and it was dead silent in the room. The kids were all in there, waiting. It was sold out. It was just . . . so quiet. It felt odd that nobody cheered as we walked out, but not as odd as it would have felt if they *had* cheered.

"We're kind of feeling shaken up and weirded out like everybody else," Chris said. "So, if it's all right with you we'd like to start off a little slower than usual, and then we'll get some good vibes going and we'll work our way into it."

We opened with "Ballad in Urgency" and "Wiser Time." Some guy down front started a fight after a few songs, and Chris stopped the show to call him out. One guy in the house was causing trouble and, as always, Chris fixated on him, but this time we all agreed with it. *Who could fight on a night like this? Stop that shit.*

Throughout the night, I saw kids in the crowd crying as they sang along. The show was a huge release for them, and for us. There were a few spontaneous "USA!" chants in between songs. There had never been a time more suited for that, to be sure.

The next three shows after that were a blur. I was solely fixated on getting home to my family. After our gig in Dallas at the Bronco Bowl on the seventeenth, Amy hooked up a private plane for her, Rich, and me to fly back to New York City a few days ahead of our Beacon shows. Chris and Kate were on their own bus, so they were content to stay on the ground for a long drive back.

Throughout the Dallas gig, all I could think about was getting home. I was dying to leave. But as we were leaving the dressing room to head to the airport, I was surprised when everybody had a huge release of emotion. We were separating for the first time since Tuesday, and everyone was suddenly teary eyed as the three of us said our goodbyes. There were hugs all around. Everyone fell apart a little bit, and we wished each other well on our respective trips home.

Three hours later, our plane flew past ground zero on its way into Teterboro in New Jersey. All three of us were crying as we stared out of the windows down into that hole in the ground, still smoldering and smoking, one week after the whole world changed.

The Beacon shows that week were unbelievable. As heavy as the gigs in Arizona, New Mexico, and Texas had been, they couldn't compare. Nothing could have. The intensity in that room for those three nights was indescribable. We were playing for an audience who had witnessed the devastation firsthand. There were even workers from ground zero standing at the side of the stage.

Chris wrote in our biggest hits each night. "She Talks to Angels," "Hard to Handle," "Jealous Again," and "Remedy" all reappeared in the setlists. We played an epic version of "My Morning Song" the first night, and it felt like the whole house was crying as we finished.

Chris knew, always, what people really wanted. He simply preferred to do what he wanted most of the time. But those nights at the Beacon were the exception, thankfully. We couldn't possibly rock hard enough for those crowds, but we tried our best. They needed it. We needed it, too.

As we walked offstage the second night, eight or nine firemen were standing in the wings. They were covered in black ash from ground zero. They'd come uptown to take in the show. I walked up to the first one I saw and gave him a hug. He started crying on my shoulder.

"Thank you guys so much!" he said.

This hero was thanking *me* for playing a rock show. I cried right along with him.

"Thank *you*," I choked out.

I hugged all those guys. They were all filthy and within seconds I was filthy, too. The rest of the band, as they walked by, all did the same. Nobody said anything profound or memorable. What was there to say? It was just an amazing moment, being there with those guys after being there *for* those guys when they really needed a lift.

A couple of years earlier, I thought that playing a one-off with Jimmy Page would be my going-away present. Now, I *knew* that the privilege of playing for those firemen was actually my going-away present. I could always feel proud of those three nights, regardless of anything else. It was an amazing thing to be able to do. And I was pleased to see that everyone else in the band felt the exact same way.

The Lions tour ended on Halloween night at the Orpheum Theatre in Boston.

I knew it was my last show, and I was ready to get on with my life. It seemed like a perfectly good time to shave my head.

Our production manager traveled with clippers like Johnny had back in the day, as he kept his hair very short. I told him after sound check, "Hey, man, I need some help tonight. I wanna shave my head between the set and the encores. Can you hook me up?"

"Are you being serious?" he asked. I'm sure my request didn't make much sense, as I had really long hair at the time.

"I'm dead serious. Find a room where we can do this. I don't want anyone else to know about it. You can't tell anybody. This is gonna be my Halloween costume."

The dressing rooms at the Orpheum are tiny, and they are scattered over the second, third, and fourth floors. My man set himself up on the third floor. As we walked off after the set, the rest of the band hit the dressing room on level two and I continued up to level three. He put a towel over my shoulders right away and started to work. My hair was really thick and full of sweat. The clippers couldn't do the job.

"Shit! You got any scissors?" I yelled.

"Hang on," he said, grabbing a pair he'd brought along just in case. He was grabbing big clumps of my hair and cutting as fast as he could. After he'd cut 90 percent of my hair off, he went back to the electric clippers to finish the job.

There was one tiny little swoop up front that dangled down my forehead. I said, "Leave it!" and ran down the stairs to the stage.

The rest of the band had already gone back on. They clearly hadn't done a head count and were surprised to realize I wasn't there. Rich had already started the intro to "Miracle to Me," which didn't have any drums for the first verse. As I was walking out to the stage, Chris said, laughing, into the mic, "Anybody have any idea where our drummer is?"

I stepped up to the kit and took my seat. The crowd were all chanting my name.

As the band looked back, one after another, to see my bald head, they all fell out.

Shaving my head was worth it just for the looks on everyone's faces. Chris was dying, doubled over laughing. Rich stared at me like, *What the fuck?* I was completely deadpan. *We doing the song? What's going on?*

The whole place was going apeshit once the lights came up and they could all see me. The audience *loved* it. But I never cracked.

The last song we played was "Stare It Cold" from *Shake Your Money Maker*. The sense of finality was overwhelming.

At the end, I walked around the kit to wave goodbye to the audience. As the rest of the band moved along, heading to the dressing room, I lingered for a few extra seconds, all alone. I was applauding back to the crowd, thanking them from the bottom of my heart for the past eleven years. I made eye contact with just about everyone in the front row, and said thank you to them all.

I probably stood there for a grand total of fifteen seconds, but it felt like an hour, as I had *never* done anything like that before. I wasn't crying, or even sad. I was fucking elated. It was time to go the fuck home.

I walked into the dressing room and everyone exploded with laughter. I was the toast of the night. Every member of the crew came up to laugh with us. It was the perfect way to end the tour, the year, the band.

"Let's all hit the hotel bar!" Chris insisted.

"Sounds good!" I said, having absolutely no intention of going to the hotel bar.

The second that gig ended, in my mind I was the former drummer for The Black Crowes. All that was left to do was dot some i's and cross some t's.

Chris, of course, had no clue. It would have never occurred to him that I would quit. But Rich knew something was up. I had told him, several times, in fact. I had told him in Stockholm, in Osaka, and then again in Atlanta just a week or so earlier.

He wouldn't stop staring at me in the dressing room. He was the only one not laughing at my bald head. Finally, he pulled me aside.

"You're quitting, aren't you?" he asked.

"I've already told you that," I said.

"I know, but it's real, isn't it? You're done. You're not coming back."

"I don't think so, no."

Dammit. I almost got choked up for a second. He looked like he'd had the wind knocked out of him.

I spoke to Pete often after that. He knew where my head was, but he also knew it was in my best interest not to quit. He tried several times to convince me to wait out the planned hiatus. Do whatever I wanted, but don't cut the cord. Let Chris go out on his own, fail miserably, and he'll be back.

I agreed that was most likely going to be what happened. But I'd simply had enough. I didn't want to spend another minute living in two realities. I was ready to go, and it was time.

He made his final pitch to me on the morning of December 20.

I thanked him profusely and sincerely, but told him it was time. I sent him a note from my attorney and asked him to send it to the brothers. I was officially withdrawing from The Black Crowes partnership, and from The Black Crowes, Inc.

Rose Mary and I were in a grocery store in Brooklyn Heights at sunset when he called to tell me he'd sent them both the note. It was over.

Later that night, after we put Conall to sleep, we called Pete to talk about it. Within minutes, we found ourselves laughing hysterically at so much of the insanity we'd endured. The realization that everything I'd ever suggested, and pretty much most of what Pete had ever suggested, had been ignored. For years. We imagined all of the things we *would have* said had we known from day one that would be the case.

It was cathartic. And then some.

I slept like a baby that night.

For real.

The next morning, I called Johnny Colt in Atlanta.

"Hey, man," I said. "You said to call when I was comfortable. Well . . . I'm comfortable."

38

The Poison Pill

Rose Mary and I flew to Los Angeles in January of 2002 to look for a place to live. We had a toddler and another baby on the way and figured, if nothing else, let's go somewhere for a few years with great weather. Babies and winter clothes had already proven to be more than we could handle.

We drove straight from LAX to see the first house on our list. We met our realtor, a friend of Pete's, at the front door. As we were greeting each other in person for the first time, she said, "Oh, before I forget—I was just showing Slash a house and I told him I was meeting with you. He said to give you his number and ask you to call him."

I thought, *Well, that's pretty good for my first hour in town,* and put his number in my pocket. The door to the house opened and the owner said, "Sorry, I'm still here but just leaving. Take a look around, hope you like it." It was Gilby Clarke. I laughed to myself. What were the odds? I called Slash the next day, and within a couple of months after I'd settled we were jamming regularly. He was working through some new song ideas and looking for a fresh start on things. We had a great time. In his book years later, he described that as the beginning of Velvet Revolver, which was of course news to me.

We didn't buy Gilby's house, but to our surprise we actually did find a house we loved almost immediately. We had flown out to begin a preliminary search thinking we'd at least narrow it down to a few neighborhoods, and a week later we flew back to Brooklyn with an accepted offer on a home.

Stereophonics played that week in LA, at the House of Blues on Sunset. I went to the gig with a friend, and as we caught up with them in the dressing room before the set, Kelly Jones, the singer, said, "I hear Chris is coming out tonight. Will that be weird?"

"Maybe for him. I think I'll be okay," I said, laughing.

I saw Chris and Kate right as the show ended. They came over to me and Kate gave me a hug. Chris extended his hand and said, "What's up, toughs?"

I just said, "Hey, man."

That was it.

I knew that if Kate hadn't been there, he wouldn't have come near me. That was entirely her, insisting he be cordial.

We flew back to Brooklyn and began making plans to head west in a month. But before the move to LA, I had a trip to London planned. That month, Roger Daltrey was hosting his annual series of gigs at the Royal Albert Hall to raise money and awareness for the Teenage Cancer Trust. Robert Plant, Oasis, and Jimmy Page were all going to be playing shows. That sounded to me like a fun trip.

I called Ross Halfin to ask if Jimmy was going to have any free time. He said he would ask Jimmy and get back to me. He called back within ten minutes.

"Yeah, he'd love to see you. He's playing on the Saturday of that week, and he suggested you come down early for sound check and then he'd have some time after."

Excellent. I was looking forward to catching up.

I had a great few days, hanging with Oasis the night they played, with Kelly and a few other friends in town. I had an all-access pass for the whole week, so I could just come and go to the Royal Albert Hall every day. Each time I walked into the building, I had a Pavlovian response. I'd start pacing a bit, feeling distracted immediately. I had to remind myself a few times that I wasn't playing a gig that night and just to relax and have fun.

On Saturday afternoon, I got down there around three o'clock. I walked right up to the stage where Jimmy was playing with a rhythm section. I hadn't seen him since he'd abruptly left from *The Tonight*

Show eighteen months earlier. Ross told me Jimmy stopped drinking shortly after our tour, and I could see it in his face. He was lean, and also his hair had grown out some and he'd stopped dyeing it black. He looked great. He actually looked younger than he had a year and a half earlier, despite now being totally gray.

He finished playing and came right over to me.

"Hey, Jim," I said.

"Hey, big fella, I'm so happy to see you!" Jimmy exclaimed. "This is great!"

He led me to his dressing room. As we walked in I said, "This was our dressing room in '95, the night you came to see us with Robert."

"Yes, I remember that! So it was . . . and now look at us." He was in great spirits. We sat down in a couple of chairs that were facing each other with a tiny table in between.

"Ross tells me you've left the band?"

"Yeah, it was time. I hung in for as long as I could, but I need to do something else," I told him. "When we all got back together without you, I thought, 'Well shit, our best guitarist isn't here, what's the fucking point?'"

He laughed at that.

"Is the band done, too, do you think?"

"Yeah, I think so. I mean, who knows? Chris is going solo and he killed the band's record deal with V2."

The mood was actually light. We weren't sad or angry as we bemoaned the loss of The Black Crowes. I was so happy to see him, and it reminded me right away that we'd grown pretty close when playing together.

"Listen, man, I really wanted to see you because I never got the chance to tell you just how much it meant to me to play with you," I said. "I really loved every minute of it, and I got so much from it, too. I realized how far off track I'd gone from simply loving to play music. It was really tough for me to maintain that in the Crowes, but you brought that back. And I just wanted to say thank you."

"Well, that means so much to hear that," Jimmy beamed. "Thank you so much."

"I'm happy that I can tell you this now," I added, "instead of at the end of a yearlong tour, drunk and crying."

He laughed again and said, "I really wish we could've finished those dates. But, you know, my back was a real problem. It was very painful. I had surgery not long after, in fact."

Jimmy paused.

"Now," he said finally, and a little mischievously, "do you want me to tell you what else happened?"

My heart sank. *Oh shit. He's really going there.*

"Yeah, actually, I do," I said with a fake laugh.

Jimmy leaned forward. "Well, if you remember, my back was really acting up in Los Angeles. And Pete's guy came in from Phoenix, I think, and he really did an incredible job on me. I felt like I was all better."

Yes, I remember all of that exactly.

"So that night, at the hotel, I was thinking about you guys," he said, "and about your new record deal with Branson. You'd already been through a lot, and it was important that you get your next record *right*."

Well, that's awfully fucking nice of you, Jimmy fucking Page of Led fucking Zeppelin, to take the time to contemplate our future and the importance of our next steps.

"I had spoken with Pete about all that in New York before, and he'd suggested that when the time came to make your next record, it'd be great for me to contribute something—a guitar solo, or a tune, or maybe even produce a track."

Yeah, I knew that. Pete told Chris, Rich, and me he'd offered that to you and we all agreed it'd be awesome to have you on our next record. And?

"So I was thinking about all of that I and thought I'd go see Rich to talk about it."

As those words left his mouth, my stomach turned. I honestly could have thrown up right on the spot.

"I went to see him up at his villa," Jimmy continued. "He was with his wife and kids, and I asked if he had a minute so we could talk. I told him all those things I just told you—how much I loved the band and since the world was paying attention to you again, it was important to get it right. Now was the time to make a really great record. And I told him I could easily put a guitar solo on a song, especially if it were to be the first single, or I could even produce a track. I didn't think producing the whole album made sense, but either way I wanted to start thinking about how best to use my name on the next go-round."

Jimmy Page offered to help us out with our next studio record? He was willing to happily extend himself like that? Sounds good. Why am I filled with dread?

"Rich didn't say much, at first," Jimmy added. "But I'd had another idea and I thought this was the best one. I'd been working on some riffs for Page/Plant, but Robert never wanted to work on them. So I said, 'Why don't you and I sit down with Chris, let's flesh them out, finish the songs. We'll put all three of our names on them as a co-write.' I thought they could fit very well with the band, if you guys liked them. I was excited about that, I thought it would be fun. I said I would be happy to promote it as well. Do TV shows and the like . . .'"

We were sitting just a few feet apart from each other. It was totally quiet in the room, other than his voice.

"You know what he said to me?" Jimmy asked, still genuinely mystified by what he was about to share.

Here it comes. I don't know if I actually want to hear this.

"'No thanks! We're good! All the new songs that Chris and I are writing are great. They're the best we've ever had, really, and there's a lot of them. We don't need more songs.' That's all he said."

I think my heart actually stopped beating for a few moments. I felt like I had just grabbed a live wire and taken a few million volts of electricity. I knew for certain I had never conjured anything approaching the level of embarrassment, coupled with rage, flowing unchecked up and down my spine all of a sudden.

I felt physically unmoored from my own brain.

"Now, I know who I am," Jimmy said, growing animated. "I know my value here, to a younger rock band. And I was stunned. I couldn't believe it . . . I mean, I didn't know what to say. I'd walked over to his room, thinking I could really be of service beyond the tour, and I was offering him several suggestions. And he just said no . . . and that was it! He just said *no!*"

He laughed a little. Eighteen months later and he was still blown away by the whole thing.

Jimmy continued. "So I said, 'Well, okay then.' I walked back to my room thinking, *What am I doing here? Why am I even working with this guy? He mopes onstage every night, so he's not even having fun, anyway.* I knew I would need back surgery eventually, and there I was delaying it, putting it off, and in a lot of pain . . . and for what? I was insulted. I really was. I knew how much it had helped the band to do the live album. I knew Branson wouldn't have given you all that kind of a deal without *Live at The Greek.* I thought, *I should have talked to Chris anyway, but actually I'm glad I talked to Rich. This is ridiculous.*

"And, Steve, I don't know how long I could have carried on, to be honest. I had been in so much pain. And when I got home, I did have to get the surgery, right away. But, you know, I'd been willing to give it a real go, and then I realized I just couldn't do that anymore for some-one who didn't appreciate me."

It was impossible to process.

Jimmy loved playing with us.

We loved playing with him.

And Rich took that away.

"I honestly don't know what to say," I said. "I mean . . . um . . . I can't apologize for Rich, because, um . . . because well . . . fuck him. I won't apologize for that fucking idiot. All I can say is I'm sorry that happened. He never told anyone about that. I don't think anyone had any idea. We were always wondering . . ."

I thought back to that moment in the hallway at *The Tonight Show* when Pete told the brothers Jimmy had split. And Rich—that fucking imbecile, that stupid cocksucker, that raging grease fire of a fucking human being—didn't say a word.

He knew what he had done.

He fucking knew it.

And now, eighteen months later, I was sitting face to face with Jimmy as he very calmly and matter-of-factly laid it all out for me.

I was beyond angry.

"Look, I never held that against you or Chris. I loved playing with you guys, you know that. I was really sad that it had to end that way."

I needed to get out of the black hole I'd stepped into.

"Well, I appreciate you telling me, as much as it hurts to hear that," I said. "Hell, if nothing else, it certainly confirms that I made the right decision getting the fuck out of that band."

He laughed at that.

I said, "If you ever have anything going on, I hope you know I'd drop anything in a second to come over and play with you again."

"Well, I'm really glad you said that," Jimmy said, smiling. "I'd love to play with you again."

"I'm serious. Just lemme know. I'm on the first flight anytime."

Jimmy laughed. "Yes, something will pop up," he said. "You always pulled me back so well. You would get behind the beat a bit. Nobody since Bonzo does that like you would. It always felt so good to play with you."

Okay, we're done here. We've peaked. Nothing is going to top that.

I said I had to run out to meet some friends, but I'd be back for the show in a few hours.

He wished Rose Mary and the baby well, and asked that I pass his regards along to Pete.

I walked outside to a February afternoon in London. I was glad we'd reconnected and happy to know we were on good terms.

And yet . . . there was also the matter of my murderous rage.

I crossed Kensington Road, turned left on the sidewalk, and walked toward the southwest corner of Hyde Park. I was shaking with anger, gesturing wildly with my arms, screaming aloud at Rich, who was of course three thousand miles away. Any one walking, cycling, or driving past must have thought I was completely out of my mind.

"You said NO to Jimmy Page? *Jimmy fucking Page* came to your door to offer help and you said *NO* because you and Chris had a great batch of new songs? Really? *Really*, Rich? You did? What songs? What songs did you have?

"'Lickin'? 'Greasy Grass fucking River'"? Those are better than something Page had up his sleeve? Are you out of your fucking mind? How is it even remotely possible that you could think to say, 'Nope, I don't want to hear some BRAND NEW FUCKING RIFFS FROM JIMMY FUCKING PAGE'?!?

"What other guitarist on planet earth would think that?!? What other *musician* on earth would think that?!? Jesus Christ!!! If Yo-Yo Ma were asked, 'Wanna hear some ideas Jimmy Page is kicking around?' . . . Do you know what he'd say? He'd say, 'YES OF COURSE I DO, THANKS!'

"And even if you don't want to hear his songs . . . WHAT KIND OF FUCKING IDIOT WHOSE CAREER WAS JUST SAVED BY FUCK-ING JIMMY PAGE DOESN'T HAVE THE FUCKING SENSE TO SAY YES?!?

"Pete already told us he and Jimmy had talked about it . . . Pete opened that door to Jimmy, and Jimmy walked up to it, and you SLAMMED IT SHUT! So you made Pete look like a fucking idiot, too! What the fuck is wrong with you?!?"

I was, um, kinda out of my mind.

I came upon one of those red English phone booths and stepped inside to call Pete.

"Pete, it's Steve," I said. My voice was shaking.

"Hey! What's up? Aren't you in England?" he asked.

"Yes, I am in England. And, well, I just spent about a half hour with Jimmy backstage at the Royal Albert Hall."

"Oh, well isn't that nice? And how's Mr. Jimmy Page doing?"

Pete was relaxed and clearly anticipating a funny anecdote.

"He's great, he said to give you his best. Um . . . he let me in on a little something you might wanna hear. Are you sitting down?"

Pete was very serious all of a sudden.

"Did he tell you what happened?"

I laid it all out. I told him the entire story. He didn't say a word for about fifteen seconds after I finished.

"Pete, can you hear me?"

Pete's mind was racing down all the same roads mine had, and then some. He and Amy had worked tirelessly for months putting that en-tire tour together. Budgets, travel, lodging, venue selection, market selection, merchandise decisions, the pay-per-view plan. They spent every waking minute from the end of our first run with Jimmy in Oc-tober of 1999 until August of 2000, when he left the tour, consumed with making sure no details were overlooked. But, more importantly, he was the one who had personally extended the offer to Jimmy to work on our next record. He loved and respected Jimmy, and I could tell from his silence that he was completely fucking devastated.

"Ahh, I appreciate you calling but I need a minute to collect my thoughts here, Steve." Pete finally said.

"I'm flying back tomorrow. I land at JFK at five in the afternoon. I'm driving to Connecticut, and I'm going to kill Rich in his home. I hope he's alone."

"Don't do that," Pete said wearily.

"It's not that I want to, Pete. I *have* to. I should have fucking killed him the first time, when he took the fucking bus! This kind of slight cannot go unpunished."

"I agree, but can we talk when you land?"

"Okay, fine. I probably don't need to kill anybody. But seriously—what the fuck do I do? How do I just sit on this?"

Pete said, "I don't know, Steve. Jesus, I don't know what to say."

I hung up.

There really wasn't much else to say. I couldn't quit the band, as I'd already done that.

At least I knew one thing for sure. Under no circumstances would I ever play music with, or even associate with, Rich Robinson again.

39

Me, Hunter S. Thompson, and Bruce Springsteen Walk into a Bar . . .

Shortly after quitting The Black Crowes in December 2001, I got the shingles.

I was in pain for three weeks. It was hell. But it was also my penance. I'd quit a street gang and therefore I had to "walk the line," getting the shit stomped out of me before being truly free.

I said that if the band ever did reunite, I'd never go back, solely because I couldn't bear the thought of walking the line again when the whole thing inevitably blew up for the second time.

Pete always found that schtick amusing. But it didn't prevent him from calling me a few years later in the summer of 2004 to let me know he'd just had a meeting with the Robinson brothers.

"No!" I said preemptively.

"Hang on," Pete insisted.

"Not interested."

"Just listen to me. They want to put the band back together. They want to tour next year. We had a very long talk. They are very aware that they made a lot of mistakes. They would like you to come back to The Black Crowes."

"I am not interested."

"Let me finish."

I really didn't need to hear the rest of the pitch. I was happy, healthy, and I'd been pretty busy playing sessions since 2002. George Drakoulias hired me for all sorts of things and introduced me to a lot of producers in town, in a sense giving me a career for the second time. I wasn't playing live very often, which was fine with me. After so many years doing my own thing in my own band, gigging with new people didn't hold a lot of allure. But I loved studio work—show up, learn the tunes, track them, have some laughs, go home. No bullshit.

Just before Pete called to talk about the band reuniting, Rose Mary and I had moved to Nashville. Not unlike my first day in Los Angeles, I immediately found something to do. I ran into a producer at a coffee shop who'd just had a drummer drop out of a session. He asked if there was any way I could be at his studio the following day, and from that day forward I was working.

It didn't take long to realize there were only a handful of drummers in town doing steady session work. As the new guy in town, and having made my bones in a band that many musicians respected, I was in demand almost immediately.

I hooked up with Jeff Cease, too. We hadn't seen each other in years, but we picked up where we always had, with an easygoing friendship. My first live gig in Nashville was with him, in fact. He was backing up a songwriter buddy of his and asked me along. When I pulled up to the club, drum kit in the back of my car, he said, laughing, "When's the last time you set your own kit up for a gig?"

"I don't know," I said, "but I'm pretty sure you were at that one, too."

Over the fall of 2004 Pete and I talked regularly, and he would occasionally mention the reunion the brothers were planning. He kept me abreast of developments, despite my insistence that I wasn't interested. I knew what he was doing: mentioning details in an offhand manner and planting seeds in my head.

I did have one question: "Are they going to call Johnny and Marc?"

"Those guys are off the table," Pete maintained.

"Okay, that's all I need to know."

The brothers still didn't get it. The Black Crowes at its best was a hell of a lot more than just the two of them with some interchangeable side parts.

Pete cut right to the chase. "If they move on and put a band together without you, they are not going to come back and ask you to join again."

"I totally understand that," I replied. "I'm not playing a game, Pete. I really don't want to do it. And, the truth is, it's probably going to work better without me, because there is just too much baggage between us."

I really meant that.

I said as much to Johnny Colt when I got together with him for a few days in Atlanta. And then, to my surprise, he turned it around on me, making me question whether I was being completely honest with myself.

"Look, The Black Crowes really is the three of you guys," Johnny said. "You need to really think about the reality of that band going on without you."

He pointed out that he and I talked about the band. A lot.

"Well, yeah," I said. "I don't bring it up, but if someone else mentions it, I don't *refuse* to talk about it."

"Here's the thing, man. If somebody mentions The Black Crowes to me, I say I don't want to talk about it. Because I really don't. Do you ever say that?"

"Sometimes," I said, slowly.

"Your connection to that band is much, much deeper than mine ever was," Johnny argued. "Just don't fuck yourself here. If they hit the road, and they somehow *do* make it without you, how are you going to feel?"

Johnny's words really gave me pause. Was he right? Had I overlooked my own desire because I was trying to protect myself somehow? I didn't think so, but I owed it to myself to give it some real thought. I drove back to Nashville that night with a lot on my mind, all of a sudden.

Pete called soon after to say they were actually jamming with drummers, but hadn't found the right guy yet.

Well, yeah. Good luck.

"Looks like Neal Casal is playing guitar," he added.

Neal had played with Beachwood Sparks, our opening band back in 2001, and then went on to play with Ryan Adams for years before ultimately joining Chris's band, the Chris Robinson Brotherhood, in 2010. But in 2005, he had no prior direct connection to The Black Crowes.

"I get it that Johnny and Marc might not work," I said. "But it's ridiculous that they won't even try to get them back. Putting the band back together with all new people is sad."

"Well, they did get ahold of Sven, and he's back now," Pete said.

"Sven?!" I exclaimed. I hadn't heard a single thing from or about him since he flamed out in early 2000.

"Apparently he's clean. He went to a rehab in Germany, I think, and he's sober now," Pete claimed. "They had a good conversation with him."

Jesus, Sven is walking right back into the frying pan.

"Well, I'm glad to hear he's okay," I said, quite sincerely. But that was still not moving the needle for me.

Not long after, I heard through the grapevine that Marc Ford had suddenly bailed out on a tour that he'd committed to with Blue Floyd, a Gov't Mule side project playing bluesy versions of Pink Floyd tunes.

I called Pete.

"You got Marc back?" I asked.

"What are you talking about?"

"Marc Ford just left a tour without any notice and I gotta think the only reason he'd fuck Warren Haynes over was if he was rejoining The Black Crowes."

Pete sighed. "Okay, I'm not gonna lie. Marc's coming back. But I really need that to stay between us."

Apparently, Neal had told someone not only about his involvement with the shows in New York but of an entire tour pending, and it ended up being printed in an article.

Pete was furious. He prided himself on keeping band business confidential. He called the brothers and insisted on firing Casal and calling Marc Ford.

Both Chris and Rich argued against it.

Pete ignored them.

He called Marc that same day. They spoke for a few minutes and it was done. Marc Ford was coming back. He was sober, committed to staying sober, and very much wanted to play a part in rewriting the story of the band.

Pete called the brothers and told them, "Marc's back. End of story."

"Look," Pete said, once again dusting off his sales pitch, "Sven's sober and Marc's sober. Even Ed is clean."

"Hold on," I said. "Ed's not clean. Ed is *never* clean."

"Well, that depends on what our definition of clean is," Pete countered. "Look, no one is asking you to commit to anything beyond a tour this year. And Chris will be on his own bus with Kate. You don't have to see him except onstage. The setlist will include songs the audience wants to hear. *Every night.* There is a real commitment to doing this thing the right way. The whole idea is that we get on the road, play the gigs, and at every step along the way, make mutually agreeable decisions that all lead to a common goal: to reestablish The Black Crowes as a great live band with a future and, in my opinion, that is not possible without you."

Marc's return changed the entire dynamic for me. I knew Johnny was an impossibility, but now, if nothing else, the brothers had admitted that Marc mattered. Pete had to drag them to that point, but still, there they were. And Sven coming back, and God willing staying clean, was also attractive to me.

For the first time in the entire process, I told Pete that I might be interested in doing it.

But I also said that if I were to return, it would have to be as a partner. No way was I coming back as a hired sideman. I was in the exact place Pete warned me about in 2001 when he tried to keep me from quitting. *Don't ever give up your piece, or your leverage.* At the time, my sanity and peace of mind were far more important.

That was still the case in 2005, although I could certainly see his point far more clearly.

"I'll talk to them, but I don't think that's possible," Pete said.

"Look, if you want me to come and meet with these guys, it's all or nothing," I demanded.

"At this late date—"

"Pete, there is no 'late date.' You are two months from playing a show. The band is more valuable with me as a full partner."

"I agree with you, a hundred percent," Pete said. "But the shows are already sold out and your name is not attached. If we had done this three months ago, it was probably a different conversation."

He was right. The brothers immediately rejected cutting me back in. They offered a good salary with a percentage of the back end. It wasn't bad, but it wasn't equal. And I couldn't accept that.

And that's how it ended. At the moment of truth, with the shows fast approaching, they stuck to their guns. Pete called to say we'd missed out. He was genuinely upset about it.

I told him not to worry. I knew he'd call me back soon.

"Pete, whoever this new drummer is . . . he's about to get crucified. The brothers don't fully understand what I did. And they won't understand until they're on a stage in front of an audience."

Pete said, "Well, for what it's worth, I think Rich does know that. He's been very adamant that they need you back. Anytime we discuss this musically, he makes it very clear that he knows the band needs you in order to really be The Black Crowes."

I soon learned that Pete was indeed telling the truth about Rich. He did fully understand my value to the band.

The materialistic, car- and gear-obsessed compulsive spender agreed that I should be given back my equal share.

It was Chris, the hippie free spirit, who refused to even entertain giving up any ground that he had gained.

Of course it was.

They booked a few warm-up club gigs before the run at the Hammerstein in upstate New York and New England. The word that filtered back to me from those gigs was essentially *The Black Crowes are back and one drummer short of where they need to be.* Chris was berating the new drummer onstage nightly, and Rich was constantly giving him direction with little or no effect.

Nevertheless, as a full tour had been announced in the interim, they carried on. The Black Crowes were off and running again. And it seemed I couldn't *not* hear about it.

Friends were emailing and calling. Anybody who caught one of the gigs felt the need to let me know their thoughts. It was always the same thing: "Everyone is in good spirits, they really talk a lot about appreciating a second chance to do it right, and it's just not the same without you."

And I always thought the same thing: *Yeah, I knew that. Too bad no one else did.*

I'd be lying if I said I wasn't enjoying the knowledge that they were unhappy onstage. I could see all the looks Chris and Rich were exchanging. I could hear all their frustrations boiling over on the bus after the gigs. I knew exactly what was happening in that world. And I thought it was hilarious.

I called Pete in early May to let him know I was coming to LA in June for a weeklong session. I was hoping he'd have time to get dinner.

He ignored that entirely and dove right in.

"Look, I'm just going to be totally straight with you," he said. "The crowds are great. The band is happy. But they're going to kill this guy playing the drums."

I laughed. "Yeah, that's a no-win for that kid. Poor guy."

"They've decided to replace him. They have hired a new drummer, and he's apparently very good."

"Yeah, I know," I replied. "It's Jeff Sipe."

"How *the fuck* do you know that?"

"We have a mutual friend, and he called yesterday to ask if I would talk to Sipe about some of his concerns."

"Are you fucking kidding me?" Pete yelled.

I laughed, knowing how much Pete hated information leaks.

Jeff Sipe is a tremendous drummer. Technically speaking, he blows me out of the water. Hell, in just about any musical situation, Jeff Sipe would make more sense than me. But not in The Black Crowes.

Onstage, he didn't have the requisite power. He hadn't learned to play the drums sitting next to Rich, blasting a Marshall half-stack in tiny clubs. He'd never been in a band with a frontman like Chris, who could spend half a gig frantically imploring him to give more and more as the intensity built throughout a set. Offstage, Jeff Sipe is a well-adjusted guy. A thoughtful and gentle soul. An adult. He would have lasted about thirty minutes in that fucking cauldron.

"Steve, seriously—let's end these fucking conversations. Just come back to the band and give me an opportunity to make things right, when the time presents itself."

Two completely unrelated events happened that spring that subconsciously played a large part in my general softening to the idea of returning to The Black Crowes.

The first was the fact that Hunter S. Thompson killed himself. I was crushed when I heard the news. And my first thought was to call Chris. It was a reflex. I couldn't believe it. *I want to talk to . . . Chris?* We were both huge Hunter devotees. I knew I could get more out of a postmortem conversation in ten minutes with Chris than six hours with anybody else. It was the first time, at all, for even a moment, that I missed Chris Robinson.

And of course Hunter just had to blow his fucking head off on February 20, the anniversary of my moving to Atlanta. A day that every year, without fail, still leaps off the calendar.

Then, a few weeks later, I watched Bruce Springsteen give the induction speech for U2 as they entered the Rock & Roll Hall of Fame. U2 had been one of my favorite bands for years. I took actual inspiration from them. They didn't simply make records I liked—their records from the 1980s had made me want to be in a band, too.

Bruce's speech was beautifully written, and perfectly delivered. He spoke at length about what a band is supposed to be, and why the relationships between musicians are so meaningful. It was fantastic. And it bummed me out for three days.

Fuck. We blew it. We were supposed to be a band like that.

Now, six weeks later, I told Pete that I would think about it. For real. I wasn't just putting him off. We hung up and I did exactly that. For ten minutes. Then he called me back.

"Steve, come to Atlanta this week and rejoin," he implored. "If nothing else, just have a better ending. One we can both feel good about."

What Pete was offering, along with better compensation, was closure. I definitely liked the idea of touring for six or eight months, and shaking hands at the end. The Black Crowes in 2001 had felt like a balloon slowly releasing its air. I wanted to rewrite that ending.

Oh fuck. I'm actually interested in this.

"Steve, we play in Atlanta all weekend," Pete said. "The first show is the day after tomorrow. If you come back in Atlanta, the band's hometown, this Thursday night, and nobody knows you're going to be there . . . that's going to be a fucking incredible moment when you walk out and take the stage! Don't fuck around! Get back to me."

I hung up the phone.

Rose Mary and I sat and talked for a few minutes. At this point I was just putting off making a final decision.

"Forget your pride," she finally told me. "Just be honest. In your heart of hearts, what do you want?"

"I want The Black Crowes to get back everything we fucked away. I want to be a great band again and I want to do that with Pete calling the shots," I admitted.

I was still living the dream I'd had. For me, apparently, it still wasn't over.

The next afternoon Pete called again. I missed his call, but he left a message saying he'd try me back in a few minutes.

The phone rang about five minutes later.

It was Chris.

"Hey, man," he said.

"Yeah?"

"Look, I know you've been talking to Pete."

"Obviously."

"Look, dude, we really want to do this right. Marc's clean. Sven's clean. Ed is as clean as he's ever going to be. We really need you and we really want you back. I know you want it to be like it was before. I'm just going to tell you, it can't be at first."

It was all very coded language, to keep him from committing to anything.

"Come on, man, just do it," he begged. "We will make every decision as a group. We're voting on everything. We have to do everything as a band. We just fucked it all up before. We want to do it right this time."

"All right, man," I said. "I'll let you know."

"Dude, the gig in Atlanta is tomorrow."

"I know," I said, "I'll let you know."

"All right. Well, thank you for thinking about it."

I hung up with Chris and called Amy. I said, "Amy, I need you to be honest with me. I know you always are, but please don't sugarcoat anything. I need you to be completely straight with me."

"Of course."

"Is Sven clean?"

"Yes."

"Is Marc clean?"

"Yes. In fact, Marc and Ed are both submitting to drug testing. That's part of their agreements."

No one had told me that yet.

"Are you serious?"

"Yes."

"Okay, so Ed isn't drinking?"

"Ed's sober," she said. "But I will tell you, last week he slipped. He got drunk on a day off in New Orleans. No one freaked out on him. He apologized, and he's been on the straight and narrow otherwise."

"How weird is it going to be, if I come back?" I asked.

"Well, you know how it is," Amy replied. "If you come back, I'll cry. Sven will cry. Marc and Ed will high-five you. Chris will do a dance, and Rich will be really weird because that's how he is."

Well, I couldn't argue with that.

"Look, Chris and Rich went out and did nothing on their own," Amy said. "They just died, careerwise. And they know it. They know that they need The Black Crowes. They know that they have to get along. And they also know that if you come back, everything the band ever should have been, and could have been, can still happen. I know your deal isn't exactly what you want, but give it a chance. I really believe it's different now."

Amy and I talked for an hour. We hung up at eight, which was nine in Atlanta, on Wednesday night, exactly twenty-four hours before the start of the next night's gig.

Finally, I called Pete.

"All right, man. I'll do it."

40

The Long Goodbye

Between 2005 and 2013, The Black Crowes toured relentlessly and released three studio albums: 2008's *Warpaint*, 2009's *Before the Frost . . . Until the Freeze*, and 2010's *Croweology*, along with several live albums. It was a productive time by any measure. And, initially, the band was as good as it had ever been. In 2005, we walked offstage many nights saying, "Man . . . that was the shit right there." In many ways, it really was a new band. Marc Ford was indeed sober, and he was playing better than ever. And Sven was without question in the best shape I'd ever seen him, and his playing, as always, was fantastic. He wasn't about to fuck this one up. He'd been through God only knows what kind of hell, but he'd clearly not lost one iota of his humanity.

Ed, meanwhile, was struggling. The many years of drug and alcohol abuse had surely taken a very real toll. He was still playing really well for the most part, but it felt like an inevitability that he was going to fall eventually, and fall hard.

We made it through to Halloween in one piece. We played a couple of warm-up club gigs in late December and then played Madison Square Garden on New Year's Eve, which was supposed to be the icing on the comeback cake, a strong and unified statement of resolve, resilience, and hope for a long future.

It wasn't.

It was a flat night, actually.

The main problem was that we'd played a gig the night before in Providence at a club called Lupo's. We were on fire. It was a scorcher.

It was whatever word you use to describe the best fucking gig you've ever seen.

Only The Black Crowes would be transcendent at Lupo's and then flat in the Garden.

And on New Year's Eve, no less.

We played a corporate gig in Florida in January of 2006. Ed turned up to sound check drunk. So much so that he couldn't play. We had to send him home.

In March, we flew to Europe for a few shows in London and Amsterdam. The crowds were fantastic, and for a week or so they really buoyed us as some red flags were appearing on the horizon. By the summer, while we were on a package tour with the Drive-By Truckers and Robert Randolph and the Family Band, the wheels completely fell off. Marc and Ed were using again. Thankfully, Sven steered clear this time.

We took a break for a month in mid-August, with eight more weeks of dates scheduled for the fall, and the shit really hit the fan.

The Black Crowes quit on Ed.

Kate quit on Chris.

Marc Ford quit on The Black Crowes.

That was one hell of a break.

Marc Ford faxed in his resignation two days before the first gig of the fall leg. Paul Stacey, an English producer and world-class guitarist, had just been working with Chris and Rich on some new tunes, as he was set to produce the next Black Crowes album sometime in 2007. Paul flew home to London from New York, and landed to hear a voicemail from Amy saying, "Hey, we need you to turn right around and fly back today so you can fill in for Marc for the next eight weeks. The tour starts tomorrow."

To Paul's eternal credit, he did just that. He played wonderfully, but was unfortunately never a serious consideration to join the band full time. He'd been Chris's friend originally, and in fact had played with Chris during the hiatus for a couple of years. So Rich wasn't about to accept that.

Ultimately, Luther Dickinson joined the band and gave everyone a real shot in the arm. Stylistically, he was unlike anyone else we'd ever had, and his presence played a large part in the natural progression of the band's musical direction. Luther's father, Jim, was an iconic musician and producer who'd worked with The Rolling Stones, Bob Dylan, Big Star, and The Replacements—all of our biggest heroes. Luther was virtually royalty to us.

He stayed with the band through 2010. By Luther's final tour, The Black Crowes were undeniably a special band again. It had taken a few years to truly find itself, but there were nights that year when we reached as high as we ever had.

Ed was initially replaced by Rob Clores, a rock-solid player who came fully prepared for the gig. He knew the songs backwards and forwards from the jump. But Chris didn't like him. I don't know why. It didn't matter why. He clearly wasn't going to be around long.

We'd first met Adam MacDougall in the winter of 1997, when he played in the band that opened for us in Europe. He was a great player. Ed, in fact, was the one who pointed that out to us. He'd say, "Man, that kid has it." Chris ran into him all those years later and asked him to come out to jam. Ed's endorsement still carried weight. Adam joined in 2007.

He was the sixteenth person to play onstage as a member of The Black Crowes. In a perfect world, that would have been ten more than necessary.

It took the Robinsons several years to bring me back to equal standing financially.

Years later, whenever Chris complained about the other members of The Black Crowes "only caring about money," I'd laugh to myself. *Oh really? I came back for less and stayed for less.*

Far more galling than anything concerning my personal status within the band was the intensity, and depth, of the abject hatred unleashed between the brothers. It reached levels of unprecedented hostility between 2007 and 2010.

There had been a brief period of time when everyone in the band voted on all manner of decisions. But that ended swiftly once a few votes didn't go the way Chris wanted. As things started to go awry in 2006, Chris responded by rejecting all other input and took total control, again, and Rich responded with all the fury and resistance he could muster.

And for once, I couldn't really blame Rich. Not one bit.

By 2009, Chris had fully committed to his narrative that *he* was The Black Crowes.

He ranted endlessly. "I write the setlist every night. I oversee the artwork. I design the laminates. I oversee the merchandise designs. I'm the one that keeps the crowd going. I am the only one performing! I do everything. You guys don't do shit. All you do is get paid."

The band did, in a sense, become "Chris Robinson and the No-Names," but that was all on him. I came back encouraged by the thought of "doing things the right way." But ultimately that didn't happen, because Chris destroyed the kinship in The Black Crowes.

By the time it was all said and done, Chris's greatest talent was clear to see. He was a fucking genius at surrounding himself with other people filled with real talent, dedication, and humanity and dragging them all down into the muck and filth and disorder of his own existence. And when they wobbled, or struggled, or fell . . . he moved on without them, kicking them out the door. And for that he wanted more. More credit, more control, and more money. Always more.

I never looked at The Black Crowes as "my band" after 2006. The Black Crowes was my job. And in that context, I could see it was a pretty damned good job. I was earning a good living playing music. That alone put me in a rare category among musicians. I didn't take it for granted. But whatever the band had once been at its greatest, was gone.

I accepted that. I said the right things, I played the part of the good company man, and I played my ass off. I still really enjoyed the gigs. I appreciated the great ones probably more than ever, oddly enough. That's not how I wanted it. And that's not what I ever would have signed up for again.

But that's where I was.

I rarely put myself in the middle of Chris's and Rich's battles. It was clearly pointless. There was no middle ground, or third option. There were only Chris's ideas and Rich's ideas and Pete in the middle trying to guide us to the best decisions.

Every moment of the band's existence had become a sheer test of brotherly will. They couldn't agree on anything. Ever.

Somehow, it just got worse and worse. From the *Warpaint* sessions in the summer of 2007 until the end of the tour in 2010, everyone in the band and crew of The Black Crowes *not* named Robinson conducted a master class in professionalism, duty, and resilience while the brothers crashed and burned around us continually.

There were fistfights on the bus. There were insults lobbed at wives. There were threats given and received with staggering regularity. It never ended, so it never began anew. It was constant. And every night, through all of that, a few things happened that neither Chris nor Rich could be bothered to notice or acknowledge:

Amy and the crew had the touring machine running like a fucking Swiss watch.

Pete fought with every ounce of energy he had to try to get them to see the light, and to try to bring them together not only for the sake of the band, but for each other's sakes.

And Luther, Sven, Adam, and I got onstage and played like the badass motherfuckers we are.

All for naught.

We finished 2010 with a run of dates at The Fillmore in San Francisco. Everyone assumed it would be the end of the band. For real, this time. It wasn't dramatic. It was just inevitable. The shows were really good, of course, because we were The Black Crowes.

Give us a head start and a full tank of gas, and we'll drive right into the fucking ditch. We'll fight about who caused the crash, and we'll fight about who's gonna fix it, and we'll fight about who is gonna get credit for fixing it, but then somehow, against all odds, at the last possible second, we'll get back on the track and almost win that fucking race. Almost.

In the fall of 2012, The Black Crowes were yet again, somehow, gearing up for another tour. Our mission was simple. We were going to play a lot of shows in 2013, always including our most well-known tunes, in order to set the table for a huge tour in 2015, the Shake Your Money Maker twenty-fifth anniversary / farewell (for real this time) tour.

We had a couple of major issues to address. The first was that Luther Dickinson bailed. He called me in September and said, "Man, I hate to say it, but I can't do the tour. I just can't go out and play that music right now."

I got it, of course. No sweat, man. God speed.

We hired Jackie Greene for the tour. He became the seventeenth person to perform onstage as a member of The Black Crowes.

The second major issue was dicier.

Chris decided, despite our contractual agreement stipulating a three-way split, that he should make more money than Rich and me. Chris demanded that we each give him 5 percent of our net touring and merchandise income. He refused to tour otherwise.

We were furious about Chris's demand, but Pete saw a pragmatic solution that would result in a more favorable financial outcome. He proposed that we accept Chris's terms with the added caveat that Chris, in turn, would participate in band VIP meet and greets before every show. If he agreed, the added income from the meet and greets would mean our year-end net was actually higher than it would have been under the existing agreement.

To me, it was a no-brainer.

There wasn't a principled stand to make. Hell, the band clearly *had no principles*. If "Mr. All About the Music" needs to take a few points out of my pocket in order to feel special, let him.

But Rich was a harder sell.

"Fuck him. No way. If we give him 5 percent this year, he'll want 10 percent next time."

In hindsight, I gotta give Rich credit for that one. I mean, he grossly underestimated Chris's greed, but he nailed the general concept.

We went back and forth for days, finally signing off on an agreement that stipulated the new terms remain intact for any and all future Black Crowes tours.

Financially, we had a solution. But in all other aspects the insult and injury were irreparable. And with that taste in our mouths, we were set to tour again.

By the time the tour started in March, we were already making plans to record some new tunes for release in celebration of our twenty-fifth anniversary. We even discussed, at length, making a documentary about the band.

In July, we started a leg of dates with Tedeschi Trucks Band, and things really took off. The vibe between both bands was extraordinary. They inspired us to really bring it every night, and within a week we were talking about plans to do this again every few years. It was a total love fest. Shocking but true. We rolled into August with a head of steam.

We were drawn even closer together that fall when Stan Robinson passed away in September.

Rich had been managing his father's care for the past couple of years. He basically moved back to Atlanta to take care of Stan. Chris had been out of the picture—he and Stan had been estranged for a few years. But, thankfully, on a break during the previous month, Chris visited and they buried the hatchet.

Now, as Stan neared the end of his life, he had both of his sons by his side. And they were united, and very open and tender with each other. There was nothing, in my opinion, that Stan would have wanted more.

Not unlike the Mr. Crowe's Garden days, I found myself a part of the Robinson family at the very end. We had a day off in Atlanta, and I spent a few hours that afternoon in Stan's apartment with Chris, Rich, and Nancy. I thanked Stan for all he'd done for the band and, by extension, for me. He treated me like another son from the first time I ever went to their house. I don't know if he was aware I was there, but I told him everything I wanted to, and having the opportunity to say those things to him, and to share in that hard time with the family, meant an awful lot to me.

The next morning, Rich called. "I think Dad's about to pass. Can you come back over?"

I raced over to the apartment. The four of us—Nancy, the brothers, and me—sat with Stan for a few hours.

He passed that afternoon. There was a very real stillness as he released his last breath. He'd had a very tough run, and he was finally at peace.

We were all crying. We hugged and held each other for several long minutes. I was honored to be there with them.

After everything we had been through together, there was still room for genuine, real-life emotion. All that other nonsense seemed so insignificant. The entire band seemed insignificant. I just felt good that the brothers were able to see each other as, well, brothers for once.

Before long, it was time to address logistics. Rich oversaw the paperwork with the funeral home, just as he'd taken the lead with Stan's health care. Chris thanked him repeatedly for taking such good care of Stan.

I gave Rich a long hug and told him I was proud of him. He'd really stepped up, and he'd done a great thing for his dad over the past couple of years. He could feel good about that, both as a son and as a father. He'd given his own sons a wonderful life lesson, too.

Chris turned to me after a while and said, "Man, I need to get back to the hotel. Can you take me?"

Stan lived right across the street from Jalisco, the Mexican joint we went to on my first night in town all those years earlier. I looked over as we drove by.

Chris was still crying, trying to pull himself together. He held my hand for a few seconds and said, "I'm so glad you were there. Thank you so much."

I said, "Of course. I got you, man. We're good."

"Okay, this is going to sound crazy but I'm fucking starving," he said. "I have to eat something."

We pulled into Houston's restaurant on Peachtree Road. Chris ordered martinis for both of us in Stan's honor.

We sat in a booth, working our drinks, and Chris looked across the street.

"That's your old building, isn't it?" Chris asked.

We were right across the street from the building where I bought my first condo, right after the Shake Your Money Maker tour.

"Yeah, my condo that you never came to."

"No, I came over there. Didn't I?"

"Nope. Not once." I said, "You never saw that condo, you never saw the house in Virginia Highland, and you never came to my apartment in Brooklyn."

"I saw your house in the Highlands!"

"No, you saw my house in midtown. You never saw the one in the Highlands."

Chris just looked at me. "God, why not? Why didn't I ever come over? Did Rich?"

I laughed. "Yeah, Rich saw every place I ever lived. You hate going to other people's houses. You are always worried that someone's place will be cooler than yours."

"That's really what it is, isn't it? God, I'm such an asshole."

"Yes, you are, my friend. And as we used to say back in the day at Atkins Park when you were in the bathroom—'He's an asshole, but he's our asshole.'"

"You used to say that?"

"All the fucking time."

We were both laughing.

We went back to the hotel. We were scheduled to play in Birmingham that night. We weren't going to make it, obviously, but we were able to reschedule for the following night instead.

At that Alabama gig, word had clearly gotten around. The air was a little extra heavy that night. You could feel it in the room.

For all of us, it was obviously a very emotional night. Chris never addressed Stan's death directly, but at one point he and Rich shared a long hug onstage. The brothers never thought about canceling. Stan wouldn't have approved.

We left Birmingham that night for a twenty-four-hour drive to Telluride, Colorado. We sat in the back lounge together as we hit the road. Chris was holding court a bit, telling stories we'd all heard a hundred times, but of course no one was bothered that night. Chris was tripping, and asked if everyone would do some mushrooms with him.

Rich passed, but everyone else said, "Sure."

It was a really mellow drive, and Chris let everyone else pick music to listen to. That had never happened before. It was a great trip, all things considered.

It was also the beginning of the end of any semblance of unity and friendship in The Black Crowes.

In October, we took a ten-day break. Chris flew home feeling very connected to his brother and to The Black Crowes.

A week and a half later, that feeling was gone.

His eyes were black again that first night back onstage. Any and all trace of the old Chris, the guy who had reappeared during those vulnerable days after his father passed, was gone.

Rich and I both saw that in the aftermath of Stan's death, something seemed to have died inside of Chris. Perhaps it was the final, flickering embers of The Black Crowes. Without Stan around anymore, what was Rich to Chris now? Certainly not a brother. Just a guy who played too loud, I guess.

Whatever it was, the 2013 tour shifted very quickly from a successful campaign full of emotionally charged, authentic moments of tenderness and compassion, to a death march . . . a funeral procession not just for Stan but also for the band itself, which dragged through the holidays and finally ran aground in the new year.

Chris retreated fully back into his own world. He punched the clock until it was over. His hostile attitude made everything difficult for the rest of us. By the time the tour ended, we were all ready for it to end. Again.

In early 2014, The Black Crowes played a few private events, including one for Fox Sports the night before the Super Bowl, in New York City.

A month before that gig, Pete had brought us another offer for the same week. Howard Stern was turning sixty, and two nights before our Fox Sports gig, there was going to be a massive party in New York to celebrate his birthday.

We'd been asked to be the house band for the night. The hope was that we'd play a few of Howard's favorite Black Crowes songs, and then back up other singers who were also appearing. Howard had long championed the band, and his producers knew he'd love to have The Black Crowes there.

Pete was thrilled. In his mind, there was no better way to thank Howard for his love and support through the years. Howard wore a Black Crowes shirt on the Letterman show shortly after *Shake Your Money Maker* had been released, in 1990. He had played our music on his show religiously since then.

Playing this party would be our pleasure, not to mention an honor. Rich, Pete, and I thought it was fantastic. We could arrive in the city one day earlier than planned, and have a fun night showing our appreciation for arguably the biggest radio superstar in history.

Chris had one question: "How much?"

Pete said, "How much what?"

"How much are they paying us?"

"Are you serious? They're not paying us anything. We're doing this as a show of respect."

"What? You think I'm playing for fucking Howard Stern for nothing? Who does he think he fucking is, asking us to play for free?"

Pete said, "Well first of all, Howard isn't asking. His producer, Gary, is because he knows what it would mean to Howard. You know they love the band. This is an enormous opportunity to show our appreciation for years of support and—"

Chris cut him off. "Fuck Howard Stern. I don't owe that motherfucker anything! The last time you made me do his show, I told you I would never fucking go back!"

Pete was insistent. "Chris, for fuck's sakes! Howard loves The Black Crowes! He has shown it repeatedly for years! And what about his listeners? What about The Black Crowes fans that listen to him every morning? You don't think they might enjoy hearing him talk about The Black Crowes playing at the party?"

"Nobody I fucking care about listens to him."

"Chris! What does that even mean? Do you *actually think* that Black Crowes fans don't listen to Howard Stern? And you don't think showing our appreciation and respect to Howard is the right thing to do?! You can't be fucking serious!"

"One hundred fifty thousand dollars."

"Is that what you think we should be paid for playing Howard's party?" Pete asked, astonished.

"No, that's what I should be paid. I don't give a shit what the rest of the band makes. He wants me at his party, I'll do it if I make a hundred fifty thousand dollars."

We were silent. It was astounding, but true, that after all those years Chris could still render us speechless.

Rich suggested that the rest of the band could still go to the party and back up the other performers.

Chris truly went ballistic at that. *"No fucking way are you doing that! No one from this band is doing shit for Howard fucking Stern!"*

I don't know why Chris hates Howard so much. I don't want to know. It wouldn't make sense anyway. What I *do* know is that when Chris was invited to appear as a guest on Howard's show a few years later, as his solo career was inevitably circling the drain, he jumped at the chance.

He dusted off his long-forgotten rock star mask, slapped it into place, and fake-laughed at Howard's jokes, telling stories about Jimmy Page and the good old rock 'n' roll days as he yapped and jumped through hoops for Howard like a sad, stoned circus animal.

Chris has spent years projecting himself as a care-free, hippie-dippie guy. And there are certainly some people out there who still buy into that. But it's not real.

The real Chris Robinson is the angriest person I've ever known.

He's also the most judgmental person I've ever known.

I called him a lot of names over the years. I don't do that anymore. Now that it's been years since I've spent time with him, it's much easier to see him for what he is.

He's an addict.

He's a narcissist.

And both of those conditions have progressed unabated for years.

I doubt he'll ever get help. I don't think he could ever face himself, the careers he's damaged, the promises he's broken, the lives he's shattered . . . I don't think he could live with it. It's just too much. So he continues to self-medicate, always dodging reality, never looking back.

On *Lions*, there's a song called "Lay It All on Me." Chris writes about achieving the dream of his life, and then throwing it away. "Now you wish you hadn't blown it," the song goes. "Well, lay it all on me."

I remember reading those lyrics in the studio. I was moved, and I told him I was really surprised he had expressed that.

He said, "Yeah, I'm just picturing someone like, you know, my dad. Sitting there thinking, 'Shit, I blew it.'"

I said, "Your dad? What are you talking about? You're writing this to yourself."

He looked at the lyrics again, thought about it for a few seconds, and said, "Oh, yeah . . . maybe."

Yeah. Maybe.

In February of 2014, Chris's wife sent an email on his behalf to Pete demanding Chris receive the majority share of all The Black Crowes' revenue if there was to be a twenty-fifth anniversary tour in 2015. She included an interesting little heads-up before she laid out her terms:

> I think it's only fair to preface the terms by saying we [her, Chris, and some accountant I'd never heard of] all aforementioned agree there will be no negotiating or wiggle room when it comes to the percentages below. Continuing forward with the band any other way is just not something my husband is up for emotionally, physically, and spiritually.

There was only one takeaway: Chris Robinson's emotional, physical, and spiritual health comes with a price tag. Chris Robinson is for sale. Nice to see him finally acknowledge that in black and white.

Her email made it clear that the extra 5 percent from both Rich and me that Chris had demanded, received, and agreed to in perpetuity only 18 months earlier was no longer enough for him. Moving forward, Chris required yet another substantial piece of Rich's share in the band and a full 100 percent of my share.

Adding insult to injury, they would figure out what salary they would offer me, if any, sometime before the start of the tour.

Rich and I gave Pete our immediate answer. "No. We reject your terms."

Our rejection was nonnegotiable, as were their terms. They demanded an answer, and they got one.

Game over.

EPiLOGUE

The Headstone

> No sympathy for the devil; keep that in mind. Buy the ticket,
> take the ride . . . and if it occasionally gets a little heavier than
> what you had in mind, well . . . maybe chalk it up to forced
> consciousness expansion: Tune in, freak out, get beaten.
> —Dr. Hunter S. Thompson, *Fear and Loathing in Las Vegas*

The Black Crowes more than occasionally got heavier than what I had in mind. There was definitely some forced consciousness expansion. And make no mistake—I tuned in, I freaked the fuck out, and I took a beating.

Thanks, Doc.

We should have done the tour in 2015. We should have said thank you to our fans, and to each other. I will always feel that way.

Other than that? I wouldn't change a thing. That's the truth. For one thing, I wouldn't even know where to start. The story of The Black Crowes sits perfectly on a custom set of shelves in my heart and in my mind. We did what we did. But, more importantly, I came out the other end in a really good place.

This is *my* story of The Black Crowes. If Chris, or Rich, or anybody else from the band tells their story, it will be wildly different, of course. From 1987 to 2014, there were a million moments when someone said something they didn't really mean. There were a million moments when someone miscalculated the mood and threw gas on a fire that was just about to extinguish itself. There were a million miscommunications.

And every single one of those moments looked and felt differently to each of us.

The Robinson brothers most likely have countless memories of me saying hurtful things and contributing in large part to the overall dysfunction. I am sure, to them, I did those things many times over. I always tried to maintain a calm demeanor, and it took an awful lot, comparatively, to push me into attack mode. But when that line was crossed, I had a sharp wit and I used it mercilessly. I could be incredibly cutting, especially to those whose vulnerabilities were so clearly waved in my face day after day for years. I never hesitated to push the most sensitive of buttons if I felt the need to escalate a situation. And I was always the tallest and largest man in the room. I used all those things as a necessary means of survival.

I grew up in a house with five older brothers. We were jocks. Trash-talking was a way of life. Sarcasm and condescension were key components, building blocks in how we related to each other. And that all started at the top, with my father. He was a cocky, headstrong former Marine who never hesitated to knock us around if we got out of line. He was big, he was loud, he was strong as a bull, and he scared the shit out of us.

We kept all kinds of family secrets under wraps.

We hid all kinds of trouble behind closed doors.

But outside?

We presented a united front. We were one.

The Gormans stood together.

Kids in my neighborhood fully understood that crossing a member of my family was the easiest way possible to find an unholy hell crashing down upon them. My ability to survive and even thrive in a burning building, and then walk outside with a smile on my face for the outside world turned out to be not only advantageous, but a necessity in the band.

I carried all of that with me into Mr. Crowe's Garden, and then The Black Crowes. I also carried an enormous capacity for love, a strong and unwavering sense of loyalty, and a finely tuned sense of humor. Those traits both served me well and handcuffed me for almost thirty years.

I bought the ticket.

I took the ride.

I am not a victim.

I wasn't wronged.

The Black Crowes often felt like a cross to bear, and The Black Crowes did a number on my central nervous system. But that is not anyone else's fault. I did all of this.

I wanted to be in a band. And I wanted to make great music. In that order. I had to do the first in order to get to the second. And it worked. The music we made will be around forever. It'll always be available anytime someone wants to listen. And, for the most part, I think we made really good music. That really was the whole point. Everything else was secondary.

And the music *still* makes everything worth it.

No matter how intense the internal hatred at any given moment, Chris, Rich, and I could find a connection to each other when playing that simply doesn't exist anywhere else in the world. The Black Crowes are forever unique to me in that regard. And I know it's like that for them as well.

I don't doubt that we have all unconsciously chased that *specific* feeling in other musical projects. And I don't doubt that we have all failed. It's not possible to get it back. Nor is it even desirable. We're not in our twenties anymore. When we started, playing was more primal, more visceral, more immediate, more necessary, and more desperate. I can't feel that way again. I don't want to feel that way again. It's just too much.

There's a reason great bands generally have four or five truly exceptional albums. We burned an awful lot of rocket fuel racing to our creative peak. And we got fried in the process.

But that feeling we shared when everything was right, and working, and *perfect* will always be special to me. I've tried for years to put that feeling into words, but I don't know that I can ever really describe it.

When the gig was great, the next day didn't matter. And not because the fans were standing and clapping and cheering. That was great, and I wanted our fans to be happy. But what I cared about most was the unspoken communication on the stage. No one understood it but us. I would hear a little something in the music that moved me, and I could tell Chris and Rich heard it too, and that it reminded them of the same Big Star song that had flashed in my mind.

More often than not, as the band turned into its greatest self in the mid-'90s, there was no conscious recognition of those moments in real time. It was like we were climbing a wall and our feet knew instinctively where the next toe-hold would be. We *expected* our feet to always go to the right place. During those shows, in those moments, The Black Crowes were truly operating as a single organism, sharing the same body.

As a young band, we didn't hope for good gigs. We hoped for moments. Every band in Atlanta was more consistent than we were, and God knows every other band on the planet was probably better adjusted, but most of them never knew what those moments felt like.

I wouldn't trade those moments for anything.

Eddie Harsch died in November of 2016. I hope he understood the significance of his contributions to The Black Crowes. He raised us up. He was our greatest teacher. The Black Crowes will forever be indebted to him.

It's been over five years since the band last played. At the precipice of our final hurrah, with a chance to finally get it right, our past served yet again as a prelude.

Chris Robinson's greed buried The Black Crowes in a shallow, unmarked grave of no fixed location. He left The Black Crowes to lie dead forever, forgotten alongside countless others who lost their way.

Chris Robinson will ultimately rest forever in such a setting, but The Black Crowes?

No.

Fuck that.

The Black Crowes deserve better.

The Black Crowes deserve, at the very least, a proper resting place.

The Black Crowes, to me, will forever lie alongside a gentle creek, near some worn out train tracks, under the shade of a giant goddamned magnolia tree.

And if nothing else, this book has been my attempt to place a proper headstone at that grave site.

A proud and strong marker to stand forever for anyone interested enough to seek it out.

Here Lies The Black Crowes
A Once Great Band That Parted the Sea
To Find Glory Beyond Their Reach

ACKNOWLEDGMENTS

THANKS

To George Drakoulias, without whom The Black Crowes would never have existed. He gave us direction, hope, and confidence. He opened the door. Forever in your debt, my friend.

To Pete Angelus, without whom any history of The Black Crowes would be a short story. He gave us more than we even knew to hope for. His creativity, vision, and relentlessness never wavered, even long after the same could not be said of the band.

To Karen Durkot, whose indefatigable efforts in service to the promotion and support of The Black Crowes could fill a book of her own. From 1990 until the very end, Karen's formidable shoulders were to the wheel, always going above and beyond. And yet, that pales in comparison to the personal counsel, perspective, humor, and unconditional love she has given me throughout. Love you, sister.

To Clint Steele, for making that phone call.

To our agent Anthony Mattero, and our editor Ben Schafer, for jumping into the deep end and making this book a reality.

To Christine Marra for her steadying oversight of both my writing and my anxiety as deadlines approached.

To the many, many people I haven't named, for fear of leaving someone out, who selflessly and tirelessly shared their respective talents in service to the success of The Black Crowes. Words here couldn't possibly summarize the impact you had, or the appreciation I feel. Thank you for sharing so much of your lives with us.

And finally to my partner Steven Hyden, who guided this odyssey from start to finish with passion, humor, diligence, and patience as I repeatedly found myself lacking in all four. Cheers, my man!

—Steve Gorman

THANKS

I'll never forget the day that Steve Gorman asked me to help him write a book about The Black Crowes. It was May 8, 2015. The *New York Times* reported that Bill Simmons, my boss at Grantland, had just been fired, putting the future of the website (and my job) in doubt.

Steve was the first person to call me. Immediately, he threw me a lifeline. "I want you to do this with me," he said. Even now, I'm not sure if Steve thought I was the most qualified person for the job, or if he simply felt sorry for me. Either way, I'm eternally grateful.

In my friendship with Steve, he's never been one to talk about his past all that much. The most fun part of writing *Hard to Handle* was having an excuse to ask Steve every question I ever wanted to know. I've loved the Black Crowes since I was twelve years old. And Steve was my favorite member. I've always had a thing for drummers who wear suits. I'm now proud to call him my friend.

There were a lot of laughs along the way, though at times I could also see how painful it was for Steve to revisit some of this stuff. I admire and appreciate his candor and courage in telling this story. Thanks again, Steve.

As always, I also have to thank my wife, Valerie, and our two children for their love and support.

—Steven Hyden